When Even the Poets Were Silent

GEORGE POGANY

BRANDRAM

First published in Great Britain in 2011
by Brandram, an imprint of Takeaway (Publishing)

1st edition

Text copyright © George Pogány 2011
Afterword copyright © István Pogány 2011

George Pogány has asserted his right to be identified as the author
of this work

All rights reserved. No part of this publication may be reproduced, stored
in a retrieval system or transmitted in any form or by any means without
the prior written permission of the publisher nor be otherwise circulated
in any form of binding or cover other than that in which it is published and
without a similar condition being imposed on the subsequent purchaser

Takeaway (Publishing), 33 New Street, Kenilworth CV8 2EY

E-mail: books@takeawaypublishing.co.uk

British Library Cataloguing in Publication Data.
A catalogue record for this book is available from the British Library

ISBN 978-0-9563847-5-1

Cover by Shine Design

I lived at a time on this earth
When even the poets were silent
Waiting in the hope, however forlorn
That Isaiah would speak out once more
For who else could utter a fitting curse?

>from the *Sixth Eclogue*,
>Miklós Radnóti, May, 1944
>(trans. I. Pogány)

Contents

vii Foreword

9 Orosháza

45 Persecution

89 Liberation

111 University

135 Almásfüzitő

157 Vegyterv

183 The Thaw

215 Freedom

243 Epilogue

249 Afterword, The Jews of Hungary: From Emancipation to Genocide, by Prof. István Pogány

263 Acknowledgments

Foreword

This is a true story, and I have striven to be as true to the events as is possible after the passing of so many decades. This book is not a work of history, but it is more than just the story of my life. It is also a picture of times, places and people during some of the most momentous events of the twentieth century. During my youth and early adult life, much of the European continent lurched from stability, order and civilised values to persecution, war and genocide before finally veering into Stalinist totalitarianism, and this book is the story of my experiences of those times.

I have adopted the international practice of placing the given name before the family name, although in Hungarian it is the other way round. I have employed the Hungarian words *bácsi* and *néni*, both everyday terms in Hungary, throughout. They are polite modes of address, similar to uncle and aunt, but without suggesting a family connection. In Hungarian, the title *úr* means Mr and *-né* means, 'the wife of'. I have used the title *elvtárs*, 'comrade', and its variations in the chapters on Hungary under Communism. Some of the names have been changed in order to protect the anonymity of certain individuals.

for István, my son

1
Orosháza

MY EARLIEST memory is of lying in bed before going to sleep, listening to my grandmother telling me a story. She would always tell me stories when she visited, old Central European ones, all of them involving wolves, and as a result I was terrified and continually expected to be attacked by them. The fact that in Hungary the only wolves were to be found in Budapest zoo meant nothing to me. As a young boy I shared a bedroom with my elder brother, and if at night I had to make use of the bedpan he had first to get up to convince me that the coast was clear, otherwise I didn't feel safe from the wolves. Only much later did I realise that it wasn't wolves that posed the greatest danger for me.

I was born György Sándor Platschek in January of 1928, but everybody called me Gyuri. My family name, a Slavic one with a rather Germanic spelling, appeared to have travelled from Poland. How had my ancestors reached Poland and from where? We didn't know, yet it didn't seem to matter, for we were Hungarian. The place of my birth, Orosháza, was at the time the largest village in Hungary. Almost anywhere else in the world, a settlement of some 28,000 souls would have been a town, but by some curious, bureaucratic rationale Orosháza was officially categorised as a village until after the war. The whole district of Békés, at the edge of which sat Orosháza, had a reputation for being rebellious, and had long been nicknamed 'Viharsarok'—Hungary's 'stormy corner'. Perhaps it was on account of this that the government paid the area so little attention. Lying in the far south east of Hungary, just fifty kilometres short of Romania, Orosháza's population consisted mainly of poor peasants. The surrounding countryside, the agricultural heartland of Central Europe, was fertile and flat. I didn't see a mountain until I was eighteen years old, or the sea until I was twenty-nine.

The political system in Hungary, especially in the countryside, remained stubbornly feudal. The ruling class, landowners and the top local bureaucrats of the regime, formed a class far removed from the rest of the population. Beneath them was a small middle class of doctors, lawyers, teachers and shopkeepers. Most numerous, though, were farmers scraping a living from the soil and, below these, a mass of landless peasants and day labourers. When the father of a smallholding family died, his land was divided between his sons, which resulted in small, narrow strips of land called 'trouser belts', not suitable for modern production methods and not big enough to support a new family. Eventually the sons had to sell their land and became landless peasants, working either for a larger land owner or as casual labourers. Some tried to take on a loan, but this was a sure way to bankruptcy, because there was never a surplus to pay it back.

We belonged to the middle class. There were four of us in the family: my schoolteacher father, Lajos, whom my mother always called Loli; my housewife mother Eleonora, whom my father in turn called Nóri; my elder brother István, whom we all called Pista, and finally me, Gyuri. I never met either of my grandfathers, who had both died some years before I was born, and only knew my father's mother, Julia, then a frail, old woman with long, white hair rolled up in a bun on the top of her head. It was she whose stories of wolves had haunted me. Wrinkles covered her face and she always dressed in black. She lived with one of my uncles, and my father sent her some money every month.

Orosháza

We were Jewish, but not observant. There were no Orthodox Jews in Orosháza, and not even a shop selling kosher food, though there was a religious slaughterhouse where some housewives brought their poultry to be killed and drained of blood according to Jewish law. Our Jewish community of around five hundred souls observed the Jewish holidays as old traditions, but we were selective at best. None of us had *payot*, those untrimmed sidelocks that marked out the observant, and we covered our heads only in winter or while we were inside the synagogue. Our appearance didn't mark us out as different from the rest of Orosháza's population, who were overwhelmingly Christian—a mixture of Roman Catholics and Protestants—though our Jewishness was well known to them. Some of us kept pigs, ate pork, but still fasted at *Jóm Kippur*. There was an elected committee organising the affairs of the synagogue, of our Jewish cemetery and elementary school, and for looking after the finances, but there was no community life as such, no social get-togethers. At the end of *Rós Hásáná*, the Jewish New Year, it was a tradition amongst the Jews to greet each other with a 'Next year in Jerusalem', but nobody believed it, or had the slightest intention of going there. Hungary was our home. We considered ourselves one hundred percent Hungarian—Jewish Hungarians, not Hungarian Jews. We spoke Hungarian, and scarcely a word of the Yiddish that was common amongst more orthodox communities. For me and my family, being Jewish only meant that we were part of a religious community that called itself, and was called by others, *Zsidók*—Jews.

There were many Jews in Hungary in those days. In the capital, Budapest, in fact, fully a fifth of the population were Jewish. I grew up with no sense of this identity being in any way inferior to other Hungarians. After all, in 1867 the Hungarian parliament had emancipated the nation's Jews, and by the turn of the century Judaism even enjoyed an equal status with Christianity.

My mother was born in the town of Máramarossziget, a celebrated centre of Orthodox and Ultra-Orthodox Jewish life. But Máramarossziget lay in a part of Hungary since lost to Romania under the Treaty of Trianon which in 1920 had left Hungary a mere shadow of itself, some three-quarters of its lands and two-thirds of its population hacked off by the Allied victors in the Great War. My mother's father had been a cobbler, one of many in the town. My father's father, a tailor, had grown up in the Hungarian town of Losonc, which by the time of my birth had, under that same Treaty of Trianon, become the town of Lučenec in Czechoslovakia. My father himself had been born in the western part of Hungary, in the town of Nagyatád. Nagyatád, at least, was still Hungarian. I loved my country, its language and its literature, and I earnestly hoped that one day the territories stolen from Hungary after the Great War would be returned. As a young child I even dreamed of sneaking into the Grand Trianon Palace at Versailles and tearing up the shameful treaty. But while Orosháza's Jews considered themselves to be thoroughly Hungarian, did the rest of the population recognise them as equally so? As a child I never considered this question, but subsequent events answered it for me.

My mother was eleven years younger than my father. Although in later years she became a little overweight, she was a pretty woman with blue eyes and fair hair. She was extremely short sighted and had to wear glasses. She also possessed a lorgnette with a silver handle, which ladies were supposed to use in the opera house or in the theatre although there wasn't anything of that kind in Orosháza. Like the wives of other middle class women in the town my mother didn't have a job, confining her duties to taking care of her family and the house with the aid of a live-in maid.

My parents bought most things on credit. At the start of each month, when my father received his salary, he took out a long, red ledger, where he kept a record of our debts to the various shopkeepers and argued with my mother about who should be paid and how much. The end result was that not all the debt would be paid off, but even so there would be too little cash left over and new purchases went on credit again. I used to hate these arguments about money and as soon as I saw the red ledger I would run out of the room. Still, it taught me to keep within my means, and ever since I have been able to manage my finances.

The major part of my parents' financial problem was the cost of educating my brother István, who attended grammar school in another town because at that time there was none in Orosháza. The local pharmacist's son attended the same school, and his father, a wealthy man, had bought a car and employed a driver for him. To save on the cost of fuel, István was allowed to become a paying passenger.

My parents, especially my mother, tried to keep up in social terms with their much richer friends. They gave expensive dinner parties for Goldman the advocate, Balázs the vet, and Doctor Zelenka. A regular guest at these parties was a corpulent lawyer, a gentile, who had lost one of his legs in the First World War. He had an artificial leg and walked slowly with the aid of two walking sticks. Nevertheless, despite his injury the lawyer remained a jovial man, witty, loud and somewhat vulgar, and he was always the life and soul of the party. His appetite was truly enormous, and he would swallow a whole slice of cake without chewing. A bachelor, it was rumoured that he was sleeping with his housekeeper, a simple peasant woman, but they never appeared together in public. All his friends called him simply 'Papa.' Later I heard that he developed stomach cancer and virtually starved to death.

The meal at these dinner parties always started with a small glass of our homemade *szilvapálinka*—plum brandy—followed by soup, usually chicken or mushroom. The main course was often *ürücomb*, a leg of lamb which was a speciality of my mother, an excellent cook. Most Hungarians didn't eat lamb, but my mother used a lot of garlic and other spices to remove its distinctive smell. It was always much appreciated by all the guests. The meat was served with boiled potatoes or *tarhonya*, the archetypal Hungarian egg pasta, hand-grated to resemble barleycorns, all seasoned with a generous portion of sauce. Vegetables—beans, peas and carrots—were served Hungarian-style, in a roux sauce finished with sour cream. The last course was always a home-baked cake, either *krémes*—a custard-filled puff pastry—or *dobostorta*, a rich sponge with layers of chocolate butter cream, all topped with caramel. The feast ended with *kávé*—coffee. All the dishes were characteristically Hungarian, with no thought for *kóser* dietary laws. As for me, I had to have my simple meal separately, before the party started, and couldn't wait until the next day when I could scrape the remaining morsels of lamb from the *ürücomb*.

My mother played cards for money, particularly rummy, with other housewives from the neighbourhood. Whenever she lost, which happened often, she complained of a migraine and shut herself into a dark room. Even as a child I could always tell when she was planning to head off to play and could visualise the effect of her losing again. I always pleaded with her not to go, but never succeeded. Ever since, I have disliked and still avoid any form of gambling.

My father never gambled for money, but he did have one vice—a small streak of vanity. To all his correspondence he would apply a rubber stamp, conferring on himself the title of 'professor' on the grounds that in Germany all teachers were accorded this status. An intelligent man, he studied Esperanto and started a correspondence in the language with a girl in Australia, but without disclosing his age and the fact that he was married with two children. One day the poor girl sent a photo of herself—she looked to be between twenty and thirty—asking my father to send one of himself in return. My father was already fifty, and instead sent her a postcard of a young motorcycle rider in black leathers, a helmet covering his face. No wonder the girl wanted to visit Hungary, an immense journey back then, but the war put an end to the mischief.

To earn some extra money, during the summer holidays my father took on an extra job. The landlord of the local inn owned a tract of land near to the town on which he grew wheat. It didn't demand much attention from him until harvesting time, when several people were hired to work on the land. He asked my father to go there and supervise the workers, pay their wages at the end of each day and make sure that there was nothing stolen. My father wasn't an expert in harvesting, but the principal requirement was trustworthiness and loyalty, for which he was eminently suitable. There was a small farmhouse with a housekeeper and he would stay there for about three weeks until the harvest had been brought in.

He was a serious stamp collector, too. In those days, stamps purchased to send parcels through the Hungarian Post would not be stuck onto the parcel itself but instead onto an accompanying note to be retained by the post office. Once a year these covering notes, sometimes bearing rarely seen stamps of high denominations, would be sold off by weight. My father would invest in a kilo, and as soon as it arrived we would eagerly search through its contents together looking for the occasional expensive stamp, a five or ten *pengő* bearing the Madonna and child, perhaps. After that we spent a lot of time soaking the stamps off the paper, drying and pressing them between the pages of a book and sorting them. Another of my father's hobbies was reading, but he didn't have the money to buy the books and instead he borrowed them from whomever he could. We also had a radio and he loved to listen to classical music. He was not fond of gypsy music and used to say how pleasant it was to be able to switch the radio off when they started to play. He especially liked to listen to Hilversum, a medium-wave station broadcasting from the Netherlands, though we never dreamed that one day I would be living only eight kilometres from its studios.

My parents' wider families, spread out across Hungary and far beyond, had little impact on my childhood in Orosháza. My father had several brothers and one sister. His elder brother, Kálmán, still lived in the Platscheks' hometown of Nagyatád, a journey of some 250km across the greater part of the country. As a result, I never once met him or any of his family, and they remained for me just names and faces in photographs. Another brother, Zoltán, lived in the capital, Budapest. I met him once after the war, and found him living with his wife in great poverty. A third brother, Dezső, lived in my grandfather's hometown of Losonc. He was handsome, an army officer in Hungary before the First World War, and I still have a picture of him with my father, both of them in uniform. My father had no rank, only a V-shaped flash on his sleeve to indicate that he had had a higher education, a rarity at the time. He wore it with considerable pride.

My father's sister, Emma, was married to the owner of the elegant Hotel Royal in Szeged, a beautiful university city some sixty kilometres' journey across the great southern plains from our home in Orosháza. As a consequence, my parents and I stayed in the Hotel Royal whenever we visited them, which wasn't very often. My aunt Emma had a son, Tibor, who was a successful lawyer. My mother had just two sisters, one of whom had emigrated to Argentina while young and had married there, settling down in Buenos Aires. The other, Adél, had emigrated to New York as a young girl, married, and had two sons. Aside from a few simple but priceless food-parcels which arrived from them after the war, they remained strangers to me and even my mother never again set eyes on them in person. Her aunt, Rezsi *néni*, lived in Budapest with her husband and two daughters. The man of the house, Izsó, was a dealer in Oriental carpets, was wealthy and knowledgeable, and spoke several languages but was short of stature—at least a head shorter than his wife, in fact. Their elder daughter, Rózsi, had married a successful lawyer who became the darling of the whole family and a means to climb Budapest's social ladder. Their younger, Magda, was a beautiful, slim girl who was always immaculately turned out and dressed very tastefully. She was the only member of my mother's family whom I had met before the war, as at one time she had spent a summer holiday with us in Orosháza, hoping to put on some weight. She was a vegetarian, and my mother was supposed to cook for her separately, using vegetable oil instead of pork lard as we always did. My mother, though, cheated, cooking one dish for all but putting some of it in a separate pan to create the impression that it had been prepared specially. Magda fell in love and married Pista, a penniless artist, much against her parents' wishes. He was a charmer, a ladies' man, who even bragged about being a gigolo in his younger days. These were the people I called family.

WHEN EVEN THE POETS WERE SILENT

I was a latecomer to that family, my father already over forty when I was born, and consequently he didn't play with me as other fathers did with their children. Our relationship is probably best described as 'serious'. He only concerned himself with important things, passing on to me a love for logic and the sciences, introducing me to stamp collecting, teaching me to swim, and encouraging me to read literature. I didn't need him to coach me with my studies and he never checked my homework. Above all, he enjoyed a spotless reputation and received limitless credit in every shop he asked for it. I am most grateful to him for teaching me to be as honest as he was, and always to keep my word.

As far as I can remember, my father only ever hit me once. Perhaps he was no harsh disciplinarian, or perhaps I never gave him cause. On that one occasion, though, I was playing with a friend of mine who had some hand-held sparklers, a true luxury item, and I had the bright idea of putting on a firework show. I asked my father to go into the garden and look up into a small opening in the loft. From inside the loft I lit a sparkler and pushed it through the opening. My father almost died for fear of setting fire to our home's wooden roof. I never thought to ask him when I'd grown up, but he might have seen with his own eyes the catastrophic damage a single spark could do. He gave me a good, well-deserved smack as soon as I was down, and I never played with fire again.

On my thirteenth birthday I became an adult according to Jewish tradition and, like any other thirteen-year-old Jewish boy around the world, I had my *bar micva*. I read a passage from the *Tóra* during a service in the synagogue. In richer families a *bar micva* is also an occasion for great celebration, of parties and of giving of presents to the 'man'. I had none of this, just two small gifts: one from my uncle Tibor, the rich lawyer in Szeged, who gave me a copy of *The Eclipse of the Crescent Moon*, a famous Hungarian novel about the heroic defence of the Eger fortress against the invading Ottoman army in 1552. My other gift, Rudyard Kipling's *Jungle Book*, was from Markó *bácsi*, the owner of Orosháza's bookshop. Both books gave me immense pleasure: *The Eclipse of the Crescent Moon* enhanced my nascent patriotism and stirred in me a love of my country and its history, and I read and reread the *Jungle Book*, whose characters became in my imagination as real to me as the people I knew in Orosháza.

One consequence of becoming an adult was that from then on I was also expected to fast on *Jóm Kippur*. To help overcome the hunger, it was customary for children to keep a quince-apple spiked with cloves in our pockets. Smelling the apple from time to time somehow helped to allay the hunger pangs. (I also bought a small jar of ammoniac from the chemist, which served the same purpose rather better.) On my first *Jóm Kippur* I went to the synagogue with my parents, and my father explained that on this day we must forgive everyone who had done us wrong during the year. We didn't have any real enemies, and I strained to find people to forgive. By the time we did, I forgot all about forgiveness.

We Platscheks, while not impoverished, were far from wealthy. My clothes were often repaired with patches, and my only presents came from rich relatives. I had very little pocket money, and was never given a toy or a book by my parents. Once I received a small toy car from Uncle Tibor. It had an extra wheel under its front, set sideways on, which prevented the car from falling off the edge of our dining table. I used to demonstrate it to everybody who came to the house and watched with great delight when they tried to grab the car, expecting it to plummet to the floor. On one other occasion I received from my mother's cousin Magda a German boardgame—*Mensch Ärgere Dich Nicht*—which resembled ludo and which I played with anyone I managed to persuade to join me.

As a child, to compensate for my distinct lack of money I used to breed angora rabbits, which I kept in a hutch in our backyard. I used to shear their long, luxurious fur and sell it to housewives who spun it to make wool for knitting shawls and pullovers. I also took photographs of people from the town, using an enlarger I had built myself from an old camera, working away in the bathroom where I could cover the small window with a towel to make a passable darkroom. This too provided me with some income. I tried, in addition, to breed silkworms, feeding them with the leaves from the mulberry trees in a street nearby. The worms grew and span their cocoons, as expected, but I couldn't find anybody who could tell me how to recover the silk from the cocoons, so this money-earning scheme wasn't a big success. From my accumulated earnings from the angoras and my photography business I was able to buy a second-hand bicycle and an accordion, a heavy, handsome instrument. I never learned to play it properly, but derived great pleasure from just strapping it to my chest. Only after the war, in fact, a number of years after I first bought it, would I play it for others' enjoyment. There was in Orosháza then a Jewish girl of about thirty, a professional dance teacher, who for a very small fee was prepared to teach us young boys and girls to dance, but she had no record player and could only tell us the steps we should use. I wasn't much interested in dancing anyway, so I volunteered to provide the music on the accordion. I had a very limited repertoire, two or three tunes played over and over again. I was amazed to find that people could actually dance to my playing, which to be frank lacked any sense of rhythm.

Orosháza

As a boy, then, I was curious, entrepreneurial, and a little unconventional. I might add precocious, too, for at thirteen I began to read George Bernard Shaw and, fascinated by his aphorisms and eager to come up with my own, started to write down my thoughts in a pocket-sized notebook. I still remember the first sentence: 'My son, if you find this book and read these notes, realise that this was the first year that your father started to think.'

I longed to be witty and, above all, original. I was obsessed with time and destiny, writing elsewhere in that notebook: 'Can there be any other aim in life than to make something that endures?' For me a clock symbolised both time and monotony. I wrote: 'Doesn't this clock realise that it is always following the same route?' I certainly didn't follow the hands of the clock in my own life, a tendency I can trace to my youth. To my regret, the notebook was mislaid somewhere on the way during the war, and my son never had the opportunity of reading it.

Though not particularly strong, I was a reasonably healthy child and there was rarely a reason to call Doctor Hazai. In those days, if I had a fever my mother would wrap me up naked in what we called a *priznic*—a big towel soaked in cold water. For a few minutes it would be impossible not to shiver and shake, my teeth chattering in spasms. After a while I would start sweating, which was the purpose of the exercise. This torture would last a couple of hours, and towards the end of it I usually fell asleep; the effect was a quick reduction of my temperature. But in general, medical practices in rural Hungary in the 1930s were little different from those in the city, and these in turn were much the same as in the cities of Western Europe at the time. More than one thriving pharmaceutical company was based in the capital, Budapest. Even in Orosháza we had ready access to modern pharmaceuticals through no fewer than three pharmacies, and while traditional remedies were still heeded, they were not venerated as somehow magically efficacious. I often had a sore throat, and one day Doctor Hazai suggested that my tonsils be removed. The nearest hospital was in Szeged, but it would have been too expensive to take me there for the operation. Fortunately, the son of one of Orosháza's Jewish shopkeepers happened to be a surgeon at the hospital, and he agreed that when he next visited his parents he would remove my tonsils. On the appointed day, I was seated on a wooden chair in their kitchen. A woman in a white coat, supposedly a nurse, stood behind me holding a kidney bowl under my chin. The surgeon sat himself down upon a wooden chair in front of me, injected my mouth with local anaesthetic, and did the job in less than thirty minutes. As a reward, and to staunch any bleeding, I was given a bowl of ice cream. On another occasion a public health officer came to our Jewish primary school to examine the children. He concentrated on our eyes, using a small instrument with which he turned the upper eyelid inside out. After a painful examination he declared that I was suffering from a serious and contagious eye infection, and I was immediately made to sit alone on a bench at the back of the classroom. The following day my mother took me to the nearby county town of Gyula to be examined by a renowned eye specialist named Doctor Oláh. He had the same instrument but a gentle hand, and diagnosed a simple irritation and prescribed some eyedrops. I was duly returned to my usual bench, and the irritation disappeared within a week.

I received a good education in Orosháza. Between the ages of six and ten (as was normal in Hungary in those days) I attended primary school, next to the synagogue. Though the school was nominally Jewish, our curriculum was scarcely different from any other. We had a brief religious education, just as Orosháza's Christian children had in their schools, but we did not study the *Talmud*. There were four forms, but because of the small number of students all four were accommodated in a single room with just a single teacher, each form occupying one row of desks. We learned to read and write Hungarian and memorised our multiplication tables. We studied the history and geography of Greater Hungary, including the two thirds that had been lost under the Treaty of Trianon after the First World War, some fifteen years before. It was that Jewish school, Hungarian first and foremost, that implanted such a strong feeling of patriotism in me.

At primary school I was good at every academic subject and was well behaved, except for one incident when, during a break, I was playing at soldiers. Lacking a machine gun, I was busy throwing small stones around. Unfortunately, one of these hit a girl in the mouth and broke off a piece of one of her front teeth. I received four strokes of the cane on my open palms as punishment from Mr Hajdú, the headmaster. He was a tall, lean, old man, approaching the age of retirement. Until then the maximum I had ever witnessed was two strokes. Still, I accepted it without a tear. The girl and her parents forgave me and we remained good friends. Mr Hajdú's path was to cross mine again a few years later, in very different circumstances.

My primary education lasted until the age of ten, when I entered Orosháza's new Lutheran secondary school or *Gimnázium*, located just opposite the synagogue. It was a long, single-storey building with eight classrooms, a gym, and a staffroom for the teachers. It had a yard where we had our physical exercises in summer and where we spent our breaks. One class always stayed in the same classroom, while different teachers came to give their lessons. After each year we moved on to a new room, each of which was further from the entrance door. School started at eight in the morning and finished at one in the afternoon. All it lacked was a canteen: instead of queuing up for a cooked meal we took with us a *vajas zsömle*—a simple, buttered bread roll—to eat at breaktime.

I was always top of my class in all the science subjects as well as in Hungarian language and literature. We studied all the usual subjects, besides—history, geography, Latin, German, and later also English. Not surprisingly, given the times he had been born into, our poor English teacher had never been outside Hungary in his life and his pronunciation was shaky. Still, both he and our German master gave me an exceptionally good start when, later, I was to find myself in German- and English-speaking countries.

My favourite subject was chemistry. The chemistry teacher at the *Gimnázium* was a bachelor who lodged with one of the local doctors. The doctor's son was in my class, and we were good friends. One day while visiting his house we set about looking for a book. Entering one darkened room, we found our chemistry teacher lying on a sofa with his landlord's wife, my friend's mother. My friend acted as if it were the most normal thing in the world and even said to me afterwards in a matter of fact style, 'Didn't you know? They are soul mates.' Unfortunately, though, embarrassment on the part of my chemistry teacher ended his friendly attitude to me.

After each school day I had my lunch, then completed any homework I had to do. In my free time I looked after my angora rabbits, feeding them with grass and kitchen waste, worked on my stamp collection, and read. On weekends I went swimming, the only sport I liked. Next to the town's flour mill there was a small lake used as a source of cooling water for the milling process, after which the warm water was returned to the lake. Only once did the water in the lake freeze, because the mill had stopped working, probably for maintenance. People began to use the icy surface for skating, and my father took me there too. I don't know where he managed to procure a pair of buckle-on skates, but I put them on in spite of them being too big for my shoes. My father walked next to me and encouraged me to strike off on my own, but it was an unmitigated disaster. Ever since then I've had a dislike of all sports except swimming, and particularly of those where I can't keep my feet firmly on the ground.

My parents decided that I should learn to play an instrument, and so when I was ten years old they duly bought me a violin from Strausz *bácsi*. Strausz *bácsi* was a rich, corpulent widower with a housekeeper who was almost certainly his mistress and a son who preferred to play the piano. Strausz *bácsi* and his housekeeper came to our house one day with the violin and my parents asked him to play something on it.

'What should I play?' he asked.

'Anything,' they said.

So Strausz *bácsi* took the violin out of its case, put it under his chin, and tightened the bowstrings. He took a big swing, but stopped short of playing a note.

'What should I play?' he asked again, to which my parents' answer was the same. The rigmarole was repeated a few times, after which Strausz *bácsi* put the violin back into its case without a sound. I never did find out why. Perhaps he was worried that his playing was no longer up to scratch.

My music teacher travelled from Szeged once a week, and I entered his class with a number of other young people, including a young Gypsy boy. He was a natural musician and in no time at all was performing complicated classical pieces note-perfect. I though had no innate musical talent, and it took four years for my parents to accept the fact that I would never learn to play the violin, not even as a hobby for my own pleasure, and certainly not for anybody else's pleasure. As for the violin we had bought from the enigmatic Strausz *bácsi*, it was to disappear from our house during the war.

We lived in the centre of Orosháza, close to the Catholic church. Our street was named after Ond, supposedly one of the seven Magyar chieftains who had led the Hungarians into the Carpathian Basin some 1,000 years previously. There was a line of acacias running the length of Ond *utca*, and when they were in blossom their bright yellow flowers gave off a distinctive and beautiful fragrance. Beneath the shade of the acacias, in springtime there grew a carpet of camomile. Ond *utca* had two sharp bends, creating two short and one long sections of roadway. In those days, only the first, short stretch was asphalted. The rest of Ond *utca* was muddy when it rained and generated great clouds of dust when it was dry. Not for nothing was Orosháza nicknamed Porosháza, a pun on the Hungarian word for 'dusty'. And it was for this very reason that there wasn't much traffic in Ond *utca*. A horse-drawn cart laden with peasants occasionally trundled past, sometimes or Doctor Balázs the vet, who lived almost opposite to us, would go to visit a farmer in his old Ford, a rare luxury in those days. Once he took me for a ride while doing the rounds. It was the first time I had ever sat in a motor car.

There was one other user of the road, or to be precise there was a herd of them, white cows with large, brown patches. Every morning a herdsman collected them from around the neighbourhood and led them to pasture just outside the town. In the evening they were brought home, their udders full, ready to be milked. Some ten of them would promenade each evening down Ond *utca*, slow and dignified, as if they had all the time in the world. As they moved their heads, their cowbells gave out a pleasant jingle, each one unique. 'We are coming home,' they signalled to their respective owners, who opened the gate so that they could walk straight in. Each of them recognised their home, and each evening's homecoming was completed without any help from the herdsman. One of the cows belonged to Ravasz the butcher, who lived at the end of our road. We used to buy its milk fresh from his wife. He had a big house with a big backyard, at the bottom of which, next to the cowshed, was a wooden cabin where he smoked meat. Because of the bends in the road, his backyard adjoined ours and was divided off only by a small wooden fence. Their son, Karcsi, was a few years older than I was and whenever we wanted to talk to each other we whistled a simple tune, which called the other to the fence. I put an old bucket upside down and by standing on it we could also see each other. Karcsi had an airgun, and we used to shoot sparrows with it.

Besides Karcsi I had a few other friends, and occasionally we went off cycling together. A boy of my age, Ádám, lodged with the Ravasz family, our neighbours. He was a tall boy, a gentile with blond hair and blue eyes, and his beautiful bike was far nicer than my second-hand one. Ádám wasn't an anti-Semite, yet he was obsessed with German war machines, especially aeroplanes. He used to make paper models of them and knew all their technical specifications.

All of our houses in Ond *utca* were bungalows, separated by fences and painted white or buttermilk yellow. Ours, situated on the long section of roadway, was built from *vályog*—sun-dried bricks of mud and straw—which were traditionally made by Gypsies. The main disadvantage of houses built from *vályog* was that they suffered from rising damp. To solve this problem, my father had replaced the lowest courses with fired housebricks and waterproofed the walls with a layer of bitumen-coated paper. Our roof was covered with traditional wooden shingles, which after many years were in a poor state and had developed several leaks. One of my chores as a child was to position pots and pans in the loft to catch the rain. Our house had four rooms, plus a kitchen and a bathroom, with two windows facing out onto Ond *utca*. One was my parent's bedroom, the other a dining room, nicely furnished with six upholstered chairs around a large polished table, but it was seldom used for meals. These we ate in the kitchen, which was also used for other household duties such as washing, ironing and making the preserves in the autumn. Our free time as a family was spent in the living room. Entrance to our house was from the front garden directly into this room, which had several large windows and which was very light. Our children's bedroom though was austere and dark, with only a tiny window high up near the roof to avoid us looking directly onto our neighbour's property, as was the law in those days.

My parents' bedroom also served to receive important guests. Their double bed was folded up during the day into a settee, with the bedding stored away inside it. The room had a coffee table and four nicely upholstered armchairs, two light grey and two orange-red. There was also a wall unit comprising of a bookshelf containing my father's modest library, a drinks cabinet, and a wardrobe with shelves and hanging cabinets. The room we used every day as a living room housed my father's desk and chair, a table with four wooden chairs, and a large wardrobe, all painted white. Such was our furniture in its entirety.

The only luxury we had was running water, and a bathroom with a bathtub and a flush toilet. Hungarian winters can be bitterly cold, with temperatures of −20°C or worse, and we had wood-burning stoves in each room. For want of money we kept the fire going in one room only, usually in the living room, though because of the numerous windows it was difficult to keep this room warm and so during the coldest days my father would go so far as to climb up and sit on top of the wardrobe to read. As a science teacher, he knew that it was warmer up there.

At the end of the garden we had what was officially a summer kitchen, but it was used throughout the whole year. Next to this was a room for storing our gardening tools. In the summer holidays my brother used it as a hobby room. Like other middle-class Hungarian families we employed a live-in maid who slept on a folding iron bed in the summer kitchen. During the day this narrow bed was stored away. Many peasant girls worked for a spell in this manner, learning skills from their mistresses and saving up for their dowry, which improved their chances of marriage. They received a small monthly salary for which they had to work very hard performing heavy and unpleasant duties, like washing and ironing and, from time to time, killing and preparing chickens for the Sunday meal. Ours would collect the blood and cook it for herself in a saucepan with some chopped onion. I always asked for—and got—some of the freshly cooked blood, even though it unquestionably violated Jewish dietary law.

Our maid had to use the outside toilet, which had been built before we had a proper, indoor bathroom. Our last maid was called Eszter. She was a short, blond woman, already over thirty, ugly, and extremely short sighted. She never owned glasses, maybe because glasses were unaffordable or because they were considered an unnecessary luxury by someone of her background, so she had to view everything so close to her face that it almost touched her nose. Eszter became pregnant. It was all very hush-hush, but I suspected that my elder brother István was the father. Whenever he came home from university in Szeged, Eszter would become strangely excited. This would have been shocking enough, but at the time there was legislation in place prohibiting sexual relations between Jews and gentiles. And because soon after this a new law was passed forbidding Jews like ourselves even to employ gentiles like Eszter, she went back to her family. More than likely my parents had paid her off. Once, after the war, she visited my parents and my mother commented how much her daughter reminded her of me at the same age. It must have been hard for my mother to say goodbye to a child she knew might be her granddaughter, given what had happened in the meantime to István at the hands of the Red Army.

My mother used to buy the firewood which was delivered to our house by a horse-drawn cart just once a year, every autumn. She alone handled the money, since she was better at hard bargaining than my father, who had a more gentle character. It was then his job to go to the market where men gathered hoping for casual work. There were always a dozen or so of these *napszámosok* to be found there, in the traditional black waistcoat, white shirt, black hat, and dark leather boots of the Hungarian peasantry. They would stand in a line, smoking and chatting and spitting on the ground. Everybody in Orosháza knew the place as *köpködő piac*—the 'spitting market'. My father walked along in front of them to select one who looked strong enough, and if the man owned a saw and an axe my father would hire him to cut up the year's firewood, a task which would take a couple of days and leave us with a neat pile against the wall of the summer kitchen. For his lunch the woodcutter would take from his shoulder bag a piece of bread, some cured bacon, and an onion, and I would watch with rapt admiration as he held all three in his enormous left hand and, with his penknife in his right, cut off pieces from each in succession and with the help of his knife deftly put the lot into his mouth.

Most of the other houses on Ond *utca* had no running water, only a well whose water was not suitable for drinking. Several families from the neighbourhood eventually clubbed together to drill an artesian well, whose water was pumped up into a water tower and from there conveyed in pipes to their various homes. We ourselves had a tap in the garden besides, and neighbours used to come by our house with big cans to get drinking water instead of walking to the pump, which was several hundred metres away. The water was quite warm, and tasted strange, but it was declared healthy. To make it more drinkable it had to be cooled, which was a problem during the long, hot Hungarian summer. We had a small icebox and bought ice daily from a vendor who carried slabs of ice, covered with a rag to protect them from the sun, on a horse-drawn cart from street to street. When the icebox was full, I was tasked with taking anything that needing cooling to a neighbour's house, where it would be put in a bucket and lowered into their deep, dark well.

We residents of Ond *utca* were self-sufficient to a much greater degree than is the case these days, growing fruit and vegetables in our small gardens and keeping chickens, ducks, geese, and even the odd pig. The ducks and geese were force-fed to make them abnormally fat, for duck and goose liver were considered a particular delicacy. I must confess that I liked our homemade *foie gras* very much. Normally, and despite our Jewishness, we used pig's lard for everyday cooking, but the fat rendered from a goose was a special delicacy, and we would spread it on our bread for lunch, seasoned with red paprika powder. The feathers of the geese too were invaluable for filling pillows, eiderdowns, and most of all our *dunyha*—an especially thick goose-down quilt. This *dunyha* was thick and warm, and when I climbed under it I felt as though I were sleeping in an oven even on the coldest winter night.

Occasionally, my mother made the dough for our bread, allowing it to rise under a tea towel before I was sent with it to the local baker, who baked it for us in his oven for a small fee. The bread in the Hungary of my childhood was always snow white, round, and with a slash across its top to increase the amount of crust. I loved its smell, freshly baked. It was also customary to prepare *tarhonya* at home. I would watch my mother make the *tarhonya* from flour and eggs, rubbing the mixture against the bottom of a wooden vessel called a *teknő* to produce individual corns no bigger than a grain of rice. Every week my mother baked a simple cake from our home-grown fruit and nuts. In spite of having only a small garden, we had a number of fruit trees, the most precious being a few peach trees. When the peaches were ripe my mother would arrange a few on a tray, decorate them with grape leaves, and give them to me to hawk around Orosháza's shopkeepers for some much-needed extra income. It was never difficult to sell the peaches because the shopkeepers knew that ten minutes previously the fruit had still been attached to the trees. The buyer usually ate a peach on the spot and I could only gaze at him with envy. We ourselves, sad to say, ate only the damaged fruit, or those too small or ugly to sell.

Before the days of pesticides, our apples and pears were often damaged by larvae, and so to avoid this I made small bags from old newspapers and my father fastened these with a wire around each piece of fruit, before the butterflies laid their eggs. In this way the fruit remained healthy, but looked somewhat pale because of the lack of direct sunshine. It was also a lot of work, standing on the top of a rickety ladder, which was not entirely without danger. From these fruit my mother made preserves, putting them into glass jars on top of which she poured a mixture of preserving chemicals that she had bought from the pharmacist. We did the same to preserve our tomato juice. These were important activities, requiring the full attention of my mother and our maid, and a young child like myself had to keep well out of the way.

We had three plum trees, and these produced enough fruit each year for us to eat fresh and also to preserve as jam. Hundreds more would fall to the ground through the work of worms and wind. These we collected in a wooden barrel kept in the garden, allowing the fruit to ferment naturally for a fortnight, just stirring occasionally. My mother used to throw some sugar into the mash to illicitly increase its alcoholic content, and the plums gave off a heady aroma. When the fruit had fermented, we would take the barrel to the state-controlled distillery and, after paying in kind for the work and for the alcohol duty, received some ten litres of *pálinka* plum brandy at about fifty percent alcohol to last throughout the year. On cold winter mornings my father would run out to fetch firewood stored at the back of the garden, but not before he had drunk a small glass of *pálinka*. Most of the rest was consumed while entertaining visitors.

As will have become clear by now, the Platschek family were very much non-observant Jews, and it will be no great surprise to learn that we ate pork just like the gentile population. My parents bought a piglet each spring to raise through the summer and autumn in a sty at the end of the garden. The piglet was a major investment and its health was carefully and anxiously monitored throughout the year.

At times, I was almost jealous of it. When I developed a cough, my mother would simply say 'gargle with salt water!' If that didn't help, she would say 'just sweat it out!' But if ever the pig had a cough, she immediately ran for the vet!

Come winter the pig would weigh over 100 kg, and when the weather was cold enough it was slaughtered. This had to be done in the cold because in those days we had only a small icebox and in the summer heat the meat would have gone bad very quickly. The actual killing was done by a professional butcher, who went from house to house to perform his duties. He usually came early in the morning, when I was still in bed, so I didn't have to witness the death.

After slaughtering the pig, the butcher burnt the hair off the skin and cut the carcass into pieces. The rest of the work was shared by the housewives of Ond *utca*. They each had their own area of expertise and knew what to do without much organisation. My mother was particularly good at preparing the dried sausages. It took a special skill to put in just the right amount of spices—salt, paprika, garlic and allspice—at the start. Another neighbour made the marinade for the ham and the bacon, and a third started cooking the evening meal. Some of the pig's back-fat was preserved as *szalonna*, a particularly fatty kind of smoked bacon with scarcely even a hint of meat, and the rest was rendered into the lard which we used for cooking throughout the year. All the remaining offcuts were cooked in a large pot and turned into *disznósajt*, a kind of brawn made by filling the stomach of the pig with bits and pieces of meat, gristle and fat in the aspic which originated from the bones. I especially liked cooked pig's ear, and would fish out a piece from the pot when nobody was looking.

By the evening most of the work would be done, and we would sit down to the much-awaited *Disznótor*—the Feast of the Dead Pig—starting with a slice of sausage kept back from the previous year, carefully preserved for the occasion. Everybody nodded their heads in approval wishing that what they had just made would turn out to be as good as the last one. The main course would be a dish of *töltöttkáposzta*, a mixture of minced meat and rice wrapped in large cabbage leaves with a pleasingly white dollop of *tejföl*, our distinctively Hungarian sour cream, on top.

After the meal, the butcher was paid and the helpers went home, each carrying a plate of delicacies—*kóstoló*—to consume with their families. When, in turn, one of the neighbours slaughtered a pig my mother would help them and come home with her own plate of *kóstoló*. The day after the Feast of the Dead Pig the meat was taken to Ravasz the butcher to be smoked so that it could be preserved and safely consumed throughout the summer. The sausages had to be kept in a well-ventilated place, so my father would put them into the large tiled oven in the dining room, which was not used in the summer months. He carefully placed the sausages amongst the wood ashes and left the door of the oven ajar for ventilation.

One of our immediate neighbours on Ond *utca* was a childless old couple. Árpád *bácsi*, the husband, was a mechanic, and in the summer he went with a primitive steam-driven threshing machine to Orosháza's landowners who hired his services. During the long winter days I would help them to shell the corn from the cobs, a task familiar to any rural Hungarian. Theirs was a typical peasant home, with a central kitchen, a living-room-cum-bedroom to the right and a *szép szoba* or 'beautiful room' to the left, which was never used for fear of spoiling it. In this was a huge wooden chest painted with geraniums, which housed the best bedding and the wife's dowry of embroidery. The rooms had only the smallest of windows, and the floor was nothing but compacted soil. The whole was heated by a *kemence*, an enormous, round, wood-burning stove made from mud-bricks, built onto which was a bench for people to sit on and lean against the warmth of the stove. In the depths of winter even their domestic animals would come into the kitchen. Árpád *bácsi* and his wife didn't earn enough money to live on, so they used to let a room in their house to a prostitute, a woman of about thirty with long black hair and enormous breasts. As far as I could tell, she only had one regular visitor, a young man of about thirty with an unusual goatee beard, who always dressed in a white suit. In the summer she would sunbathe topless in the garden, and I would peep through the holes in the dilapidated wooden fence whenever I passed by.

On the other side from us lived another childless couple, the Tomas. Tailors by profession, they made a comfortable living. Accordingly their house was also bigger and smarter than ours. Toma *bácsi* made clothing for men, his wife for the women customers. When later I visited my parents with my wife-to-be, she made a dress for her, which she wore at our wedding. Next to the Tomas lived the Maronyáks, a family of chimney sweeps. Seeing a chimney sweep was supposed to bring good luck in Orosháza just as it was elsewhere, so we were always pleased to meet with any one of the Maronyáks. They had a son, József, five or six years older than I was, who instead of becoming a sweep studied art in Szeged. I only met him the once, one morning when he visited his parents. He was in his pyjamas, about to wash himself from a big bowl of hot water. He gave me a piece of paper and a pencil, and asked me to make a drawing of him while he washed. I didn't know where to start, yet when he had dried himself he did the drawing in less than a minute using just a few strokes of the pencil. In time he became one of Orosháza's most famous sons, the winner of one of

Hungary's most prestigious awards for his artistic achievements.

Most people in Orosháza, though, could not lay claim to such exceptional talents. Bazsali *néni*, a poor, elderly widow, owned a dog which she kept in the garden on a long, iron chain attached to a stake. Its only protection from the elements was a small, wooden kennel. The shabby and neglected mongrel used to howl whenever splinters of chicken bone stuck in its throat. Originally white, the dog was forever grey from the dirt, except when it rained and its coat was washed clean. It was supposed to keep the thieves away, and it mattered very little that Bazsali *néni* had nothing worth stealing.

The Orosháza we all lived in was at heart quite a colourless community with very little beauty and no attractions. Dominating the town was a sober-looking Catholic church, but there was also a simple Calvinist church, these two being Hungary's dominant Christian denominations, while in between the two sat a yellow-plastered Lutheran church in late-Baroque style, the most beautiful building in the whole town. A short walk away, our own synagogue was surmounted by two golden, onion-shaped cupolas bearing stars of David.

The main street of Orosháza, just a short step from our home, was named after the national hero who had led Hungary during the ill-fated uprising against Habsburg rule in 1848. On one side of this main street, Kossuth Lajos *utca*, stood the school where my father taught mathematics and physics. There was no industry to speak of in Orosháza, but at one end of Kossuth Lajos *utca*, close by the railway station, there was a flour mill which ground the wheat grown in the surrounding fields. There were two manufactories, one making traditional brooms from sorghum stalks, the other vinegar. The wealthy owner of the broom factory was the much-respected local philanthropist Tafler *bácsi*, the elected leader of Orosháza's Jewish community. Most of Orosháza's shops in fact, many of them owned by Jews, were on one side of Kossuth Lajos *utca*. The most luxurious was owned by the Brünner family and had two large windows, full of samples of their wares, beautifully arranged and brightly lit. The Brünners' emporium sold everything from underwear to umbrellas, and on account of their reputation for excellent quality their customers were drawn from across the entire county. The best shoe shop in Orosháza was owned by the wealthy Schwarz couple, who of their own volition had donated their house, a commodious building with eminently suitable picture-windows, as a home to a humble museum. While women preferred to buy their material in a shop on Kossuth Lajos *utca* and have their dresses made by one of the many local seamstresses, three shops sold ready-made men's clothing. One of these supplied expensive clothes, made to measure from English wool and beautifully tailored. We could only admire the elegant, pinstriped grey bolts in the window, but never ventured inside. The owner, Lefkowics *bácsi*, was one of the best customers for our freshly picked peaches. Beyond Orosháza's marketplace, in one of the side-streets, a second shop provided cheaper clothing for peasants and agricultural labourers. A third, with quality and prices somewhere in between, served middle-class people like ourselves.

Orosháza's bookshop was owned by Markó *bácsi*, who also sold used postage stamps to collectors. I was one of his suppliers. He was a widower, left with his young son, Miki, but Markó *bácsi* possessed a sense of humour which would prove in time to be much appreciated. Down the road, a hardware shop sold everything from nails to cooking pans. Klein *bácsi*, its owner, was a strong, middle-aged man. It never crossed my mind that I would one day try, and fail, to save his life. Kövesi *bácsi* was the owner of a shop selling tableware, plates, cups and glasses, besides complete and beautiful dinner services. He would one day teach me all about business. On one street corner stood one of Orosháza's three pharmacies, where my mother used to send me when she had one of her headaches. As soon as I entered the shop I would be struck by a mixture of exotic smells, strange and pungent. I invariably had to buy ten sachets of migraine powders and waited while the chemist, a middle-aged man with a small moustache and a snow-white coat, prepared them. At the very end of Kossuth Lajos *utca* stood a delicatessen with figs, dates, chocolate bonbons and various other delicacies in its window, though we could never afford to shop there. Just off the main roadway was the grocer where my parents bought most of their provisions, and next to this was a little shop that seemed old-fashioned even in those pre-war days, selling coffee beans, tea leaves, and biscuits. Its owner was an elderly old lady, a tall, thin spinster, who managed her shop the same way as her grandparents had many years before, stubbornly refusing to accept that tastes had changed. She never stocked any new product, and kept her biscuits in large, open paper drums for customers to make their own selection. They soon became soggy and had to be thrown away. The owner of our preferred grocery store wanted to expand, and even offered to buy her out, but she refused.

'What would my customers think of me if I stopped serving them?' she used to ask rhetorically of everyone who came into her shop.

Further on was the Daubner *cukrászda*, a cake shop and confectioners, where occasionally I had enough money to buy a small cornet of ice cream, but I could never afford to sit down on its terrace and eat a portion from a glass bowl. Then one day out of the blue Doctor Klein, a Jewish lawyer, asked me to join him on the terrace. He bought me a large portion of vanilla and chocolate ice cream with whipped cream on top. I could hardly believe my luck, yet when I told my parents they were angry: apparently Doctor Klein, who had founded a rather shady organisation named the Artists' Guild, had a reputation for being a Communist. He was to be the first victim of the coming German occupation.

Daubner, the owner of the cake shop, one day decided to build a new cinema to compete with the old one at the end of Kossuth Lajos *utca*. Schwarz *bácsi*, the owner of the old cinema, hadn't maintained it properly and it had become very neglected, its walls black from cigarette smoke and its wooden stools rickety. He showed mainly American films starring the likes of Mickey Rooney, Judy Garland and Shirley Temple. In contrast, Daubner's new cinema was painted bright blue and red and boasted the latest in acoustic technology. It was much more luxurious, with comfortable seats, and showed modern Hungarian and German films to youths who sat munching on roasted marrow seeds bought from the street vendor who had set up his stall outside.

Kossuth Lajos *utca* ended in a square, in the middle of which stood a bronze statue of Kossuth Lajos himself, his right hand outstretched as if to invite people to join him in his struggle against the Habsburgs. Like Hungarians everywhere, on the anniversary of the 1848 uprising the people of Orosháza would sing a popular patriotic song, which went something like this:

Kossuth Lajos a message sends, running out of men;
If he sends the message again, we all must join him!

I always considered this a stupid song: why did people wait for a second message before joining Kossuth? No wonder the uprising had been lost!

Orosháza

The square was dominated by the large white bulk of Orosháza's only hotel, the Alföld. It had a restaurant, and my parents occasionally visited with their friends to eat the steak for which it was famous and to listen to the Gypsy band which was a permanent fixture. (The bandleader at the Alföld, Náci Purchi, was a colourful and charismatic old man, and when he died it seemed the whole town turned out to witness the long, slow funeral cortège led by his weeping widow. Náci Purchi's coffin, on an elaborate, horse-drawn hearse, was accompanied by the largest ensemble of Gypsy musicians I had ever seen, perhaps fifty in all, playing mournful tunes on their violins.)

Not far away was Orosháza's post office, and beside this the imposing façade of the bank which held the mortgage on our home. It was always immaculately maintained, spotlessly clean, and looked as if it had only recently been painted. In a side road was the shop belonging to Ravasz the butcher, who smoked our pork for us. Ravasz was a strong man and worked alone in the background while his wife Ravaszné in her neat, white apron served the customers. There were various sausages and cuts of meat on trays covering the counter, while parts of the carcasses of pigs and cows hung from hooks at the back of the shop. When I went in to collect what my mother had ordered, Ravaszné always gave me a small slice of spicy *kolbász* sausage.

Upon another side-road, Bakk *bácsi* made and sold leather products. He and his wife forever smelled strongly of leather. They had a small shop, and their handmade wares, from purses to shopping bags, were always hanging outside the entrance. Bakk *bácsi* was a corpulent old man with a remarkably ugly wife but a remarkably beautiful teenage daughter who had the most sparkling eyes I had ever seen. She was the first girl I tried to court. I went to their home one Sunday morning, taking with me a romance I liked very much, *The Golden Man*, by the famous Hungarian novelist Mór Jókai. I read her a section from the book and hoped that she would like it too. Unfortunately she was not interested, but just walked over to the mirror and started combing her hair. I was so disappointed that I didn't want to see her anymore.

The Sternbergs made and sold eiderdowns of the most beautiful brocades and damasks. They owned a machine which fluffed up the down filling by rotating it in a cylinder of warm air. While this was underway, everything and everybody was covered with tiny feathers which escaped from the drum, until the Sternbergs' workshop looked as if it were covered with freshly fallen snow. There was a professional photographer in Orosháza, too, from whom I would buy the photographic paper and chemicals to develop and print the pictures that provided me with a modest income.

Both of my parents smoked, and one of my childhood chores was to go to the local tobacconist to buy ten Memphis cigarettes. The tobacconist was a corpulent lady, always dressed in black, a war widow who had been compensated for the loss of her husband by the granting of a special licence to sell tobacco. I hated the smell of those cigarettes, and never even tried to smoke a single one. I could never drink out of a glass that my mother had used, because of the foul smell of Memphis cigarettes.

As for leisure, Orosháza's swimming pool was located at the edge of town. It had two open-air lidos, one warm, the other for the more serious swimmers, and two indoor pools that were opened during the winter months. There was also a station for a narrow-gauge railway which ferried people the few kilometres back and forth to the shallow Lake Gyopáros. Lake Gyopáros had a public beach with cabins and a shower, and an Olympic-sized swimming pool. During the school holidays I would spend entire days there, one of a team of competitive swimmers, my backstroke fuelled by hunks of salted, buttered bread from the grocer's shop.

Other pastimes too were simple and innocent. Even though we were Jewish, we happily participated in the Hungarian Eastertide custom of *locsolás*, or 'sprinkling', which was meant to be an ancient fertility rite but which was mostly an excuse for a great deal of youthful fun and flirting. On Easter Monday, the day after Palm Sunday in the Christian calendar, all the boys of Orosháza called on the girls and sprinkled their heads with *eau de cologne*. In exchange the boys received either a painted, hard-boiled egg or one made of chocolate. Occasionally we received a chocolate animal, usually an Easter bunny or a lamb. Of course, the biggest rewards went to the earliest callers, which made careful planning of one's calls necessary. For my part, I visited all the Jewish girls in the town, and then some of the Christian girls as well. If their mothers were present, I even poured some of the perfume over them for good measure!

Beside those rare days of festivity, though, nothing much ever happened in Orosháza. There were no murders, no scandals, and any gossip was soon no secret. It sometimes felt to me as though the whole town was dozing, its inhabitants sleepwalking as they went about their daily business. Sleepy Orosháza was an unexceptional community. With its railway station, its flour mill, manufactories and cinema, its teachers, doctors and lawyers, and its thriving shops, it was certainly no barbaric backwater. This only made what was to happen there all the more inexplicable. I had no idea that elsewhere, in Hungary and across Europe, politicians were setting out to punish our Jewish community, my family, and me, for something we hadn't done. I didn't know that my life would change; I had no inkling that we would soon be shaken from our sleep.

2

Persecution

THE OUTBREAK of war in Europe in 1939 did not at first make much difference to life in Orosháza. I was still a child when Hitler's panzers rolled across the Polish frontier—a fat boy, not particularly strong nor sporty, and my flat feet had exempted me from physical education classes. Now, though, all boys were obliged to join a paramilitary youth movement called the *Levente*. In the *Levente*, Jewish adolescents were separated from the gentiles, a foretaste of things to come. Since there was no work for us to do, our time was taken up by physical exercise—mostly running and push-ups—though this was supplemented more and more by straightforward beatings by our 'leader', a big bully of a man about thirty years old, tall, clean shaven, and forever wearing a military cap. One of his front teeth was missing and he hissed as he spoke. Because of my clumsiness, I got more than my fair share of his beatings. Until then I had enjoyed being a student, and had liked going to school. Now everything had changed, and I dreaded it, especially the *Levente*. Beside the beatings and the humiliation, it was the first time I had met a confirmed sadist who obviously enjoyed persecuting us. He didn't even try to hide his pleasure at our suffering, but we were powerless to do anything about it.

One evening my father took me to Kossuth Lajos *utca* to witness a colourful demonstration. A crowd of young men, probably students from the University of Szeged, were brandishing lit torches and shouting '*Lengyel Magyar határt!*' Their wish was for a shared border between Poland and Hungary, an unmistakable demand for the return of the formerly Hungarian lands of Slovakia which lay in between. This, though, was for me the sum total of nationalistic politics. The Regent of the Kingdom of Hungary, Admiral

Miklós Horthy, was trying to steer a difficult course: on the one hand he wanted Nazi Germany's support for the recovery of swathes of the Hungarian territory that had been lost under the Treaty of Trianon, but on the other hand he hoped to retain Hungary's independence from German rule. But if you sup with the devil, Horthy should have realised, you must use a long spoon. His delicate manoeuvring failed, and by the end of June 1941 Hungary had become an ally of Germany and Italy, had declared war on the Soviet Union, and was fighting on the Eastern Front. In Orosháza, my mathematics teacher Mr Bencsik was called up for military service. I last saw him riding a horse at the head of a group of infantry. They were marching to their deaths, although they did not yet know it. As the war progressed, the Hungarian military suffered horrific casualties. Tens of thousands of Hungarian troops were taken prisoner by the Soviets, a not-insignificant proportion of them Jewish men who, barred because of their Jewish identity from joining the fighting forces, had been conscripted into the *Munkaszolgálat*—under equipped, hardpressed labour battalions in which tens of thousands were to die from ill-treatment and starvation.

Just as in other European countries in those days, there was anti-Semitism in Hungary, but we had become accustomed to it. As a child I never questioned or analysed the reasons for anti-Semitism; I simply accepted it as part of my life. In 1920, soon after coming to power as Regent, Admiral Horthy had passed the first of what had since become a battery of laws excluding Jews from public and cultural life and forcing most of us out of white-collar employment. Starting with an act that restricted Jews to being no more than five per cent of university students, by the early years of the war other acts had been passed limiting the number of Jews in fields like journalism, medicine, engineering, acting, law and even commerce. The laws, though not in themselves life-threatening, created a lot of misery and uncertainty. As in Nazi Germany, Jewishness was given a legal definition: a person with two or more Jewish grandparents was considered a Jew, regardless of other factors or even religious non-observance. My family, of course, fell well within the legal definition.

As a response to the growing tide of anti-Semitism, in 1939 a book was published in Budapest under the title *Itéljetek!*, or *Judge Us!*, where 'us' meant the whole of Hungarian Jewry. The book listed famous Jewish-Hungarian scientists, artists and sportsmen, all of whom had contributed to Hungarian culture. It was a long list, full of loyalty and patriotism, and reading it even we Jews were surprised to learn that these people had in fact been Jewish all along. All Jewish Hungarians were proud to read *Itéljetek!*, and copies were handed from one person to the next, but I don't suppose it changed the mind of anyone outside our community. The local population was fed by German black-propaganda films like *Jud Süss*, that portrayed a greedy and unpatriotic Jew. The fact that the Swarcz family had donated their beautiful home to Orosháza to house its small museum made no impression. Gentile Hungary didn't actually *like* Jews; it simply, it turned out, accepted us. Many years later, when I was living in England, someone asked me an interesting question: in the early days of the war, had I believed the Germans would win? I had to admit that I had. Propaganda is a powerful weapon, and we were repeatedly told by the radio, newsreels and newspapers not only about German military successes on the battlefield, but also about their superior weapons, tanks and fighter planes. It wasn't the last time that even I myself succumbed to propaganda and brainwashing, and the fact that so many gentile Hungarians did the same is no surprise to me.

WHEN EVEN THE POETS WERE SILENT

In March 1944, as the war went from bad to worse for the Nazis, Adolf Hitler invited Admiral Horthy to Berlin on an official visit. While he was there, Nazi troops occupied Hungary. They were welcomed by the Hungarian army, by state officials, and by many better-off Hungarians who saw Soviet Communism as the main enemy. As is always the case, the vast majority of ordinary Hungarians had no say in the matter, and could only stand and watch as Panzers occupied their country. In Orosháza we had heard about the persecution of Jews in Germany, and we knew that the occupation was bad news, but never did we imagine quite how much it would affect us during the coming year. And we were amongst the lucky ones.

The Nazi occupation now led to the appointment of a new Prime Minister, Döme Sztójay. Sztójay, an avid supporter of the Nazis, governed Hungary alongside a German named Edmund Veesenmayer, a Brigadeführer in Hitler's SS. In the four and a half years since the German army had first swept across Europe, Hungary's Jewish communities had been left in relative peace, apparently under the protection of a leadership which would shelter them from the worst of Nazism. It had seemed to us Jewish Hungarians that we might escape the fate that was befalling Jews in occupied Europe, and that the Anti-Jewish Laws or conscription into the *Munkaszolgálat* labour battalions were as bad as things would get. That mistaken belief rapidly evaporated, and the Hungarian populace proved as capable as other nations at turning their backs on us. Soon after the Nazi occupation the mass deportation of Jews to death camps began, overseen in person by Adolf Eichmann, who regretted the fact that so many Jews had escaped his 'Final Solution' for so long. Now, even to a child in sleepy Orosháza, the politics of war suddenly became inescapably close.

Persecution

For the first time, we were required to wear a yellow star sewn to our clothes. This alone didn't bother me too much, because everybody in Orosháza knew that I was a Jew anyway. My father went on teaching, even while wearing his yellow star. His fellow teachers and the students accepted the change without remark, and there was no animosity shown to him in the school. Only one of his colleagues, a man of German ancestry, treated him with demonstrable coolness. Otherwise, my father was respected, at least locally. Most of Orosháza's gentile families, who had had children educated by him, were grateful for his encouragement and for helping them get into university, because a university education was not expected of boys in Orosháza. Even our neighbour, Ravasz the butcher, had not initially wanted his son Karcsi to study after secondary school. It had only been my father's persuasion that had allowed Karcsi to become a vet.

Orosháza's Jewish community was obviously unhappy at the new turn of events, but accepted its fate, worrying only about what the next round of legislation might bring. With yellow stars sewn onto our clothing we were now set apart from our gentile neighbours. Most of us stayed at home as much as possible, and ventured out only when absolutely necessary. Rumours circulated about what might come next, and based on their knowledge of Jewish history our elders were expecting pogroms. It would be far worse. Who would have thought that in the end the state itself—my own beloved state of Hungary!—would aid, and indeed engage in, our genocide?

I was sixteen by now, and a student at the *Gimnázium*. There were five Jews in a class of thirty-two, two girls and three boys, including myself. We sat in our usual places, only now wearing a yellow star. The other students didn't bother us especially—at least, no more than usual. The worst humiliation we suffered was from the headmaster, who was also our teacher of Hungarian. He was of peasant stock, and suffered from a bad heart. He used to sit down on the bench opposite us, and lecture us on how we Jews had tried to poison his purer-than-pure Hungarian peasant culture. He would continuously look into our eyes, as though we personally had had something to do with it. He also hated Communism, and explained that the only reason for Marx having the views he had was that he was a Jew.

Soon after the German occupation in March of 1944, my brother István was called up to serve in one of the *Munkaszolgálat* labour battalions attached to the Hungarian armed forces. He had been a brilliant scientist up until then, studying mathematics and physics in Szeged, accepted by the university despite the laws restricting the number of Jewish students. Having sat his last exam and got his diploma, István barely had time to get home with a suitcase of belongings, and the next day he had to go. My mother gave him some food packed in a kerchief and a photograph of the whole family, wrote the addresses of a few of our relatives on a piece of paper, and we all accompanied him to the railway station. István had often left us in the past when bound for Szeged, but this departure was different. My mother wept, and my father's hands were trembling as he embraced István for the last time. My brother stroked my head with affection, we all said our goodbyes, and he left. We three stayed on the platform and waved as long as we could see the train, but still it disappeared around a bend in a cloud of steam.

It was just a few days later that Ágoston *néni*, our widowed neighbour who knew everything that happened in Orosháza, called at our house with the news: 'The Germans are rounding up all the Jewish men.' Ágoston *néni* was a big woman, dressed in black and with a black and white polka dot kerchief over her hair. Her voice was trembling and her eyes were moist, and it was clear that she fully realised the significance of her words. Danger—*real* danger—had arrived, and it wasn't from the wolves who had haunted my childhood imagination.

We lived near the centre of town, but because of Ond *utca*'s two sharp bends we couldn't see out onto the main road. Still, we found ourselves constantly peering out of the window, waiting for the Germans to come. We were in a state of panic, not knowing what to do. Should we close the gate or leave it open? If we closed it and the Germans rang the bell, should we open the door or let them force a way in? We left it open. Should we close the shutters? It would be terrible just to stay in a dark room, waiting, shut away from the world. So we kept the shutters open just enough to be able to peep through them occasionally.

About mid-morning we saw them, two Germans in uniform, briskly marching towards us. They looked like film stars, immaculately dressed in dark leather coats and shining black boots, chatting to each other. At the time I didn't know anything about the SS, but now I assume they were among the SS *Sonderkommando* sent to Hungary with Adolf Eichmann to oversee the deportation of the country's Jews. We were sure they had come for my father and were guessing the number of steps they needed to reach our house. One, two, three… fifteen… twenty…. They must be here by now. We were silent. What was there to say? 'Goodbye father, come back soon'? The three of us stood so close that a feather could not have been squeezed in between us, and we reached out to embrace and protect one another. How long we remained huddled together like that, who knows? We heard the Germans walking past the gate, in front of the house. Were they going to jump in through the window?

No. They crossed the road, walked past two more houses, and called at the house of Doctor Balázs the vet. After a short time they re-emerged, but without Doctor Balázs. Realising that they were coming for him, he had injected himself with morphine. The Germans had watched him lying there, I later learned, foaming at the mouth, and had decided that he would not pull through. (He did, though, and in fact he lived through the war only to be killed along with his entire family by retreating SS troops as it drew to a close.) The Germans walked back, directly past the front of our house, but they didn't stop. They had known exactly where to go, and who to arrest.

That evening, Ágoston *néni* told us that the Germans had rounded up some forty men, the heads of all Orosháza's prominent Jewish families. Among them was Tafler *bácsi*, owner of the broom factory and elected leader of our community. Presumably, the authorities were acting to avoid any organised resistance. The men were not allowed to take anything with them except the clothes they were wearing. No one as yet knew what would happen to them, and only later did we find out.

The reason for the round-up soon became obvious: orders had already been given for all Orosháza's Jews to be moved into a ghetto. The same was happening in every city, town and village across Hungary. There was very little time to prepare for our move. We were told not to take too many things with us because there would be little space. We packed what we thought was absolutely necessary—some bedding, clothes (including thick winter ones), food and a few personal mementoes. We also took my brother István's suitcase, packed by him before he left for the labour battalion and unopened since. My parents didn't have much jewellery, but my father had a golden chain for his pocket watch. He put the chain into a small jar and buried it under

Persecution

a pear tree in our garden. I was made to watch the burial, the third tree from the gate, so that I could find it in case he didn't return. It took time for the full implication of this act of witness to register in my mind. Not everybody accepted with such fatalistic resignation the prospect of life in the ghetto; there was violence, but not against the authorities or the Nazis: a family of three, headed by Doctor Sonnefeld, committed suicide. We all knew about the ghettos of earlier centuries, more or less permanent Jewish living quarters, and we thought that ours would be similar. How wrong we were.

A large wood-processing plant, owned by a Jewish family, had been designated as Orosháza's ghetto. It occupied a considerable area, but had only one proper building which was used as a store and for offices. The building was allocated to the old and the very young, while the rest of us stayed out in the wood yard with a roof over our head, but no walls to shelter us. I wondered how on earth would we survive the winter there. I helped to set up two mattresses for my parents on the ground floor of the main building, but decided not to join them, instead attaching myself to two young boys, apprentice plumbers. They were lean, strong, and dirty from the oil and grease they had to handle. Jenő had no parents, while Jóska had only his poor, old cobbler father. In spite of their hard lives, they were always jolly and looked after me as if I were their brother. I was very impressed with their physical strength and courage and I thought that they could provide me with the skills I needed to survive in this new life.

On a more practical level, it also turned out to be more fun to stay with Jenő and Jóska rather than with my parents. We selected a small space above the store to hang out, and made it comfortable by using some of the wood panels lying around.

My family and I stayed in the ghetto for about a month, and in this very short time I grew up. I had to pull my weight in our small community, and I helped the elderly and the sick. There was no proper organisation, and nobody told me what to do; I had to use my initiative to seek out tasks I could do to help others. My jobs consisted mostly in carrying things from one place to the next, doing some shopping, running errands and the like. In the evenings I would listen to Jenő and Jóska talking about girls, sex and prostitutes, all very new and exciting subjects to a boy who had only recently developed an interest in them. My mother hadn't allowed me much freedom before then, and had forbidden me to associate with certain girls because they came from 'bad families'. Refusals to allow me permission to go out had sometimes left me both angry and desperate, but now, strangely, I felt more free.

One evening, when Jenő and Jóska were talking about their experiences in the local brothel, I asked them half seriously: 'Would they allow a young boy like me to come in?'

'Everybody's welcome, who has money.'

'How much does it cost?'

'Five *pengő*.'

'I've never had so much money in my life,' I concluded with a sigh, but to my surprise Jenő and Jóska gave me five *pengő* with the advice:

'Ask for Gloria, she's the best.' So I did.

I knew of the law forbidding Jewish men from having sexual contact with gentile women, but I reasoned that this couldn't possibly apply to having sex with a prostitute. The door of the ghetto was not closed: we were allowed to come and go so long as we returned before the evening, so with my yellow star on my coat and five *pengő* in my pocket I walked to the brothel on the edge of town. I knew where it was, because I had passed it on my bicycle many times before, but I had never dared to stop. It was a sort of wood-built barracks, surrounded by a high fence, but a girl, probably standing on a ladder, was peeping out inviting in all the men who happened to walk by. Just as I approached, she disappeared, maybe because of my age, or maybe because of the yellow star, but either way she didn't consider me a potential customer.

I summoned up my courage and walked in. When I entered, the same girl guided me into a large room where several others were sitting, talking. The air was thick with cigarette smoke, which almost choked me. The atmosphere was jolly, everybody laughing at something one of them had said, which I hadn't caught. The joke might have been about me. Naturally, I was embarrassed, and didn't know what to do or how to behave. Finally I uttered the name 'Gloria' and a girl stood up. She was indeed a beautiful girl, with dark hair, dark eyes, nice features and a perfect figure, smelling of roses; I think she might have had some Gypsy blood in her. She wore only a dressing gown, decorated with large red and yellow flowers, and she took my hand as she walked over to a room furnished with just a single bed without even enquiring about my age. I was expecting fireworks and church bells, but it was a bit of a disappointment. A maid brought Gloria a bowl of hot water to wash herself. She took my five *pengő* and my virginity, and I returned to my makeshift home in the ghetto. I didn't realise at the time how lucky I was not to have contracted VD.

One day not long after, while I was walking in the woodyard, I met a group of children excitedly looking up into a seemingly empty loft. There was a trapdoor in the ceiling, leading to a small space.

'What are you looking at?' I stopped and asked.

'We think Géza is up there with Kati,' they answered, but their eyes and behaviour were telling much more. 'We don't dare to go up and look,' they added.

I was the oldest among them and I thought it was my duty to solve the mystery, so I climbed up. Géza and Kati, both teenagers, were doing what they weren't supposed to do. I climbed down and, as a gentleman, declared: 'There is no one there, the place is empty.'

The children believed me and walked away. I had mixed feelings: on the one hand I had acted chivalrously, on the other I had lied. How and when Géza and Kati eventually managed to climb down unnoticed I don't know. I met them both the next day and their grateful look was all the thank you I received, and we never talked about the affair again. Mercifully Kati didn't get pregnant, and both survived the war, but they went their separate ways.

It sounds absurd, but I liked living in the ghetto. It was the first time I had been free from parental supervision, and this gave me a feeling at the age of sixteen of being an adult. Seemingly oblivious to the awfulness of our situation, the only thing that bothered me was that I had no idea what was going to happen to my education. I had been in the sixth form at the *Gimnázium*. Would it be possible to continue to attend school from the ghetto? Or would someone like my father take over my formal teaching? But his subjects were mathematics and physics, and he didn't know languages like Latin and English. How could I hope to pass my final exams? I had many questions, but there were no answers. In any case, it would quickly become obvious that the ghetto was only a temporary measure, not a permanent place for us to stay. For the moment, I had to get used to the idea that my formal education was finished, and that my life would from now on be very different.

Orosháza's Jewish ghetto was overseen by the *Csendőrség*, the civil guards of Hungary's Ministry of the Interior, under an officer named János Prokai (he was caught and prosecuted after the war and received a life sentence for the atrocities committed under his command). The usual role of the *Csendőrség* had been to 'keep the peace' outside the cities, particularly amongst unruly social elements, the poorer peasants, gypsies, and landless labourers. They were known to be crueller than the regular police, and they now proved themselves to be willing agents in the Nazis' plans for the Jews. Not for nothing could *Csendőrség* be translated as 'guardians of silence.' They had long been adept at nipping in the bud any expression of discontent directed against the authorities from among the ranks of the poor peasants and day labourers. Until now, these *Csendőrség* had remained a remote threat to us middle-class Jews, my parents never having had anything to do with them, nor they with us.

In the ghetto, the *Csendőrség* issued new pronouncements every day, none of them pleasant. One day, two men in civilian clothes arrived. We were told that they were detectives. One of them was short and well-built, the other tall and thin. They looked a little like Laurel and Hardy, whose films I had seen in the cinema, but there was nothing funny about their behaviour. They collected all our jewellery, sparing only the wedding rings, and started to interview the men about the valuables that were supposedly hidden in their homes and which the *Csendőrség* had been unable to find. It was obvious that the *Csendőrség* were already raiding the homes of the rich. My father suffered a great deal of stress every time the detectives walked by, but in the end he was not called on to be interrogated:

nobody expected to find much of value in the Platscheks' house. Then the beatings started. After the interrogation, some of the men had to be carried out on a stretcher. It was rumoured that the ultimate torture was to push a glass tube into the urethra and then shatter it with a blow. Just the threat was enough to extract a confession. Women were not spared either, and if they were rich they were beaten with a truncheon just like the men. Two women attempted suicide. One survived, but the other, Tafler *néni*, the wife of our community leader Tafler *bácsi*, succeeded. She at least was allowed the dignity of a final resting place in Orosháza's Jewish cemetery.

Then, one day, we heard the news that the whole ghetto was to be moved out of Orosháza, though nobody could tell us where. Did the *Csendőrség* know that the Nazis planned to send us to death camps? Whether they did or not, I am convinced that they didn't care either way, so long as they obeyed their instructions and we were gone.

We could take only what we could carry, so we busily packed a makeshift rucksack for each member of the family, cutting down empty grain-sacks and attaching a strap and a drawstring. Our clothes were neither new nor robust; our shoes especially were of poor quality. Some of the richer families who had more possessions, especially those families whose husbands had been rounded up by the Gestapo, gave us some of their surplus footwear. I was given a pair of beautiful, long, hunting boots of soft, brown leather, which fitted me perfectly. I had never owned such beautiful boots and proudly paraded in them for days. Then someone warned me: 'Do you realise how dangerous it is to wear such desirable items? The fascists might like the boots too, and could make you take them off. Do you fancy walking in your socks? They could kill you for them if you tried to resist.' I decided that the boots were not worth

Persecution

dying for. With a heavy heart I abandoned them and put my old worn-out shoes back on again.

We had at least brought a good supply of our homemade sausage, which was supposed to last until the day the Feast of the Dead Pig came around again. But who now could plan so far ahead as a year? My parents gave sticks of salami to those even poorer than us. Among the beneficiaries were Jenő and Jóska, the two young plumbers. 'I didn't know that your father was a socialist,' said one of them wryly. I hadn't known either.

Shortly before the move, the *Csendőrség* told everyone to surrender any writing utensils they possessed, and all our pens and pencils were collected up. Why this was necessary was never made clear to us, though in retrospect it would have made it that much harder for us to get a message to the outside world of how we were being treated. I loved writing, and the order to give up my pencil was a real shock to me: it was silver-plated and self-propelling, and I treasured it very dearly and decided to hide it in the ghetto's one building, on top of a wooden beam. It was these little things that, in our possession, meant the world, but which, taken for no reason, dehumanised us just a little bit more each time.

The next day we all had to report with the last of our personal belongings to be checked by the *Csendőrség*. Family by family we were summoned by Sergeant Posta, and presently my mother, father and I stood before his desk. He would have looked an insignificant little man had it not been for his uniform and the distinctive plume of black rooster feathers attached to his cap. Now he had absolute power over us, and he made sure everybody was aware of this. He looked up and indicated pettily with his hand to stand further back. All three of us retreated in small steps to the back of the room, like eunuchs before a Chinese emperor.

'Not that far!' barked Sergeant Posta, revelling in his power, and we returned to the middle of the room. Of our interrogation I remember just one tiny aspect, as if burned into my memory: questioned about writing utensils, my father mentioned the unopened suitcase belonging to my brother. What would happen if someone were to open it and find something unlawful, such as a pencil, in it? Sergeant Posta didn't show a great deal of concern: 'The penalty for *this* is twenty-five blows to the sole of the foot,' he declared matter-of-factly, as if to imply that a whole range of punishments covered various other crimes. He didn't even bother to check our belongings, and we were ushered out of the room. I had been brought up to be a law-abiding citizen. I thought Hungary a civilised country. How could they inflict corporal punishment? And all for a pencil, for God's sake?

'Can they do this?' I asked my father when we were outside.

'They can do anything they like,' he answered, still shaking.

After being interviewed by Sergeant Posta nobody was allowed to return to their quarters, but instead we were all forced to sleep under the stars in the woodyard. Fortunately it didn't rain during the night, and the next morning we were told to get ready to move out. Three midwives searched all the women to make sure that they had nothing hidden on their bodies, and then we marched under armed escort, like criminals, to the railway station. Those who were ill or too old to walk were taken on carts. All the Jews from the ghettos that had been set up in the outlying villages made the same journey and now converged on Orosháza. It had been carefully planned. The route took us through a large part of the town, and all along the way people came up to us unbidden, shook our hands, and whispered encouraging words, wishing us well, hoping for our safe return. It was heart warming.... Only that's not what happened. In reality, Orosháza just stared at us from the pavement. Several of the bystanders must have known us personally, or others in our group, but no one, not a single person, came and shook hands with us, or said goodbye, or offered even a few words of encouragement. Were they afraid of the *Csendőrség* who were escorting us? Did they not give a damn either way? Or were they positively glad to be rid of us at last? I have thought about this many times in the decades since, but I still don't know the answer. I do know now that there were good people in Hungary at the time, people who saved Jews, even risked their own lives, but I've not been fortunate enough to meet any of them.

At the railway station our numbers grew to about five hundred, and we prepared to board the wagons waiting for us. Each was in effect just a large, empty box, used to transport either casual farmworkers or else animals. On the doors was stencilled a notice: '40 people or 8 horses.' In our wagon we must have numbered little short of one hundred. Someone had placed a number of galvanised buckets ready in front of each wagon, some for storing water, others still empty, our toilets. János Prokai, the officer in charge of the ghetto and now the deportation, kicked some of them over with his shiny boots.

'There are too many,' he declared. 'Half of them will be enough.' We were left with two buckets full of water, and two empty.

I was physically one of the strongest members of the group now, and with the older men and young boys helped to load all the rucksacks into the wagon, along the side walls. Then we formed an island in the centre, the plan being that the weakest could lean against the walls while the youngest and fittest could sit in the less comfortable centre island. We ourselves had to help everyone get on board, including babies, the elderly and the sick. Then the *Csendőrség* slid the doors to and locked them.

Our wagon had only two small windows with iron bars. The lock on the doors had several positions, and could have been left open just a crack to allow ventilation. No human could have squeezed through that tiny opening, but the *Csendőrség* didn't allow us even that luxury. Soon after that, the engine sounded its whistle and the train started to move. Some of the women wept silently as we left the town where they had been born, and where they had spent their whole lives. They cried for their abandoned homes, their missing relatives, because they didn't know what was waiting for them at the end of the journey. As for myself, though, I didn't cry. I wasn't afraid of the unknown. I looked upon the whole thing as an adventure, sure that we were to be taken to a larger ghetto to work. The thought did not strike me, that we might be facing death. Looking back, I was just a naïve, self-absorbed teenager.

Mercifully, this first journey didn't last too long. After some time, we arrived in Békéscsaba and were moved into the local ghetto. Békéscsaba was a town, larger than Orosháza, and there were many more Jews amongst its population. Even though Békéscsaba was less than 40km distant from Orosháza I had never once been there, though my brother had attended the grammar school in the town. The ghetto there, a single, large building with several spacious rooms, was already crowded, with people sleeping on the floor like sardines in a tin. Again, I didn't stay with my parents but sought out the company of other people my own age. A boy, not much older than myself, was employed to keep order. A member of Hungary's German-speaking Swabian minority, he swaggered around the rooms carrying a stick, dressed in the blue-grey uniform of a German soldier but without any insignia. He relished his role.

Persecution

'*Du Junge*,' he said, pointing his stick at me, scolding me in a mixture of German and Hungarian because I hadn't got up and stood to attention when he walked by. Apparently everybody else, even the women and the elderly, did this. I stood up, but couldn't stop wondering how this had started. Had this upstart demanded this obeisance during his first patrol? I didn't think that probable. More likely, the Jews in the Békéscsaba ghetto were so frightened, so degraded, that they thought it appropriate to honour any authority, no matter how ridiculous it was, and this mere boy had revelled in it.

We only stayed three days in Békéscsaba before an order came through that the Jews from Orosháza had to re-assemble, because we were being moved on. Again, our destination was unknown. There was no registration, and considerable chaos prevailed. We had become completely dispersed amongst the locals, and no one any longer knew where Orosháza's Jews were to be found. As a result, many of them made the decision to keep quiet and to stay on, saving time and, perhaps, their life. As it happened, it turned out to be the other way round.

When all the Jews who had been transferred from Orosháza were ordered back onto the train, we decided to obey: my father might have been just a Jew in the eyes of the authorities, but he was still the same law-abiding civil servant. Back we went to the wagons, under the same conditions, only now we were shuttled around for another day until we were disembarked at the city of Debrecen, the second largest in Hungary, some 100km to the north. We were marched to a brick factory and stayed there under the open sky waiting for the next order. Here, though, we were reunited with the forty men who had been taken by the Germans from their homes in Orosháza a month before. With indescribable joy they rejoined their families: except, of course, those whose families had decided to stay put in Békéscsaba.

The very next day we were herded back into the wagons yet again, passing on the way a policeman in civilian clothing who held out a shoebox and demanded of us all our remaining money and jewellery. This time not even the wedding rings were spared, and dire threats were used against those suspected of hiding anything. Nobody was searched, and we could have taken with us anything we wanted—Boskovich *bácsi* managed to smuggle a little money hidden in his shoes—but we had a great respect for authority and were frightened to our bones. Together, those two traits were a powerful brake on any resistance on our part. In retrospect, the whole thing was probably just a clever piece of private enterprise by one policeman.

This journey proved to be much longer. We were in the wagon for three days and three nights. Looking through the window we could read the names of the stations we passed by. We were going north, toward Poland, but did not know why. Surely they were not taking us to the Russian front to dig trenches? We had not yet heard of the death camps. If we had, I don't know what our reaction might have been, as we would have had nothing to lose by trying to escape, even if we had died in the process. But how could we have escaped? As things were, nobody even tried. Did we reckon on the desirability of having at least one extra day to live, if we just did as we were told? Or was it our slavish character?

We ate what little food we had brought with us, and the drinking water was soon used up. It proved impossible to empty the buckets which were being used as toilets, and so the empty water buckets had to be pressed into service. Eventually, even those people who at first had tried to ignore the call of nature had to ask for the bucket. Husbands tried to shield their wives during the act, but the men were less squeamish. The wagon was so crammed that there was nowhere for the buckets, which had to stay where they were last used. Because nobody had a spare garment to cover them, the result was an indescribably foul smell throughout the whole journey. There were many wagons just like ours in Hungary, and plenty of them had got rather dilapidated with continuous use and without proper repairs. What a pity, I thought, that ours was in such a good condition: a hole or two in the floor might have allowed us to get rid of the stinking stuff and provided some much-needed ventilation. The wagon was so full, in fact, that nobody could take so much as a step in any direction, and the only exercise possible was to stand up on the spot for a while.

In the corner, to my right, sat the Berger family, a young couple with a baby whom the mother had no choice but to breastfeed in front of everybody. Berger *bácsi* had been one of the people rounded up by the Germans and had only the clothes on his back to his name. In normal times they would have changed the baby's nappies, then washed and dried them before re-using them, but these were not normal times. They very quickly ran out of supplies, and tried to leave the baby in his soiled nappy, but this, of course, only made him cry all the more. Opposite me, next to my parents, sat Hazai *néni*, the widow of our GP who had been fortunate enough to pass away just a few months before. Hazai *néni* was a frail old woman, still very depressed over her husband's death, and she said very little but just looked at me with her sad eyes: 'Where are we going to?' she asked me over and over. 'How long will it take us to get there? You are a clever boy Gyuri, you should know.' I tried to comfort her by lying, hoping that in the morning she would not remember what I had said. The only honest answer I could have given her would have been: 'I don't know either, but anywhere will be better than here.'

By night we would inadvertently slump against each other. Sitting in the central island, I could lean backwards onto Lefkovics *bácsi* who was sitting just behind me, so long as he too was leaning back. If his head for a moment dropped forward, my support disappeared. My neighbour to my right, Éva Klein, preferred to lean against me rather than against her own father. Éva was a pretty girl, but still I pushed her away in discomfort. Several people snored. Others, especially the old and the very young, cried intermittently. Weisz *néni*, an elderly woman whose adult children had decided at the last minute to stay in the ghetto in Békéscsaba, took to calling out every five minutes or so in her sleep: 'Mother, help me!' But her mother had died some twenty years previously, and when Weisz *néni* woke up she didn't remember a thing.

Each morning several people, especially the older men, started praying, but because nobody knew Hebrew, they prayed in Hungarian, a babble of words. Secularised for so long, they seemed to make up their prayers as they went along, not asking for a miracle, nor for good fortune, but just to be free again and be able to live in peace. My father included his whole family in his prayer: my mother, our absent István, and me.

'Is God aware of our plight?' I asked him. 'Why does He allow this to happen?' I wasn't particularly religious, but at this time I still believed in God and I was puzzled and confused. My father had to think a long time before answering.

'God sees everything, but we can't always understand the reason for His actions. Maybe He is just too busy to care about us, or maybe He has a special reason for this. When our people left Egypt, their journey was no better either.'

'Weren't the people then leaving slavery for freedom?' I thought to myself, but I didn't force the issue any further.

Persecution

The days were long. Our thoughts drifted to the people who were travelling in the other wagons: were they still with us, or had they been decoupled and shunted on to another route? My father pushed a small mirror through the iron bars of our window and, as far as he could see, they were still with us, but we couldn't communicate with them. In any case, what was there to communicate about? I tried to fill the time by organising rounds of Bar Kochba, a parlour game played by Jewish Hungarians that resembles 'animal, vegetable, mineral'. Our imagination in selecting a subject didn't take us very far, and soon we had exhausted all the people and objects in the wagon. We tried reciting poems we had learned in school, but similarly exhausted all the works we had learned of the famous Hungarian poets—Petőfi, Arany, Ady and the like—and there was no fun in repeating them.

The distance we travelled was not really very great, and in peacetime we should have been able to complete the journey well within a day. But this was wartime, and we were regularly shunted onto sidings where we stayed for long periods of time. Other more important traffic had priority over a few hundred Jews, but in truth it made little difference to us whether we were moving or not.

I can't say for sure what the others were thinking about, but as for me I began to ask myself why this was happening to me. What had I done to deserve it, desperately searching for a relationship between cause and effect, recalling all my sins, like lying to my parents, or being greedy, but none of them made any sense. The whole journey was like a bad dream, but I couldn't wake up. Our minds were concentrated on just one thing—survival—and by the end the only subjects we talked about were God and the *golem*, a mythical figure that legend had it had been created by a chief rabbi of Prague from the clay of the Vltava to protect the city's

Jews from persecution. A *golem* like this was supposed to come and free us from our suffering. I no longer liked this adventure. I'd had enough of it.

But then we noticed that the sun was setting ahead of us rather than to our left, and we realised that we were heading west. We could not fathom this sudden change in direction. Had our roundabout route been determined by the effect of Allied bombing on the railway lines? Was it that workers were needed in the Reich itself to help the German war effort? We reasoned that we were surely being taken somewhere to work, because if they had wanted to kill us they could have done it so easily before we had even started on our journey. We knew nothing of the efforts of foreign diplomats like Raoul Wallenberg or of people like Oskar Schindler, and we knew nothing of any deals being done to save Jewish lives. To judge from the stations we passed through, our train had set out bound inexorably for Auschwitz, a place we had never even heard of; instead, unaware of quite how lucky we had been, we were now heading towards Vienna.

We stopped just after crossing the frontier, presumably to change locomotives and our escort, and soon after that a party of German *Wehrmacht* soldiers opened the doors to our wagon. They stayed slightly ajar from there on. This was pleasant and unexpected.

Summer is hot in Hungary, and in 1944 the heat started early. During the day the temperature inside the wagon was almost unbearable, especially when the train stopped, which was the case most of the time. When we were moving there was a tiny bit of relief from the heat, but this was felt mainly by those near the windows. We were, by now, desperate for water. But then what did we see? Two Austrian women were running up the embankment, now alongside the train, with large water cans in their hands.

They stopped and poured some water into any cups or containers that we had, through the small opening in the doors and through the windows. My father collected some water in his mess tin, and after thanking the lady gave it to me to drink. How did the women know that we were there? Who alerted them? We forgot to ask, and never knew. Such humanity was to us almost unimaginable, something that certainly couldn't have happened in Hungary: the zealously anti-Semitic *Csendőrség* would have chased them away.

There was another surprise to come. On the track next to ours was parked a military convoy—tanks and other heavy equipment. A German soldier was sitting on one of the big guns, and as he took a cigarette from his pocket he threw the rest of the packet into one of the wagons. These three unbidden acts of kindness from people we would not have expected gave us hope.

Not long after this we disembarked at a marshalling yard attached to a village named Strasshof, on the eastern outskirts of Vienna, taking our belongings with us. The dead bodies—there were several by now—were removed.

The men and women were separated and ushered into the large barracks that constituted Strasshof concentration camp. We were made to undress, put our clothes into a bundle, and take a hot shower. After such a long and arduous journey, surrounded by filth and dead bodies, we were relieved to be herded into those shower rooms. It is a comfort to think that the people tricked into the showers in places like Auschwitz might have spent at least some of their last moments in hope. Killing the hope is, perhaps, even worse than death itself.

After the shower we had to find our clothes, which had been disinfected and thrown on the floor of the large anteroom. People had to rummage through the huge pile for their own clothes, but a few old men were incapable of competing with the rest and just sat naked on a bench, my old primary school headmaster Hajdú *bácsi* among them. Just six years previously he had been a strong, upright person, a man with authority, teaching us to become good Hungarian citizens. I could imagine how confused and bitter he must have felt. Now simply even finding his clothes was insurmountable, for he was too frail and could no longer be bothered. In spite of the caning I had once received from him I was grateful for his dedicated teaching, and the least I could do was to help him. He described his clothing to me and I searched the big pile until I found it. He had brought his best suit, the one he wore on special occasions only, dark blue with white pinstripes, and a white shirt and black patent-leather shoes. Perhaps he hadn't wanted to leave them behind, or maybe they were integral to his dignity. I shall never forget his grateful smile, as though he knew that the effort of teaching me had not been in vain, but that was the last time I saw him, and he never returned to Orosháza.

The women went through the same procedure, only with the added humiliation that the staff overseeing the showers were all Polish or Ukrainian men. They were in civilian clothing, and each carried a big stick as a badge of authority. Once the men and women had been reunited, we went through a registration process and were each given a piece of paper with a number. After this we returned to our train, but now we were no more than sixty per wagon, a crowded but bearable number. Even the doors remained open. Could it be that the Germans, in the midst of what was becoming a disastrous war, had more wagons to spare than the Hungarians? Or was it that the Germans were not cruel for the sake of being cruel, while the Hungarians were? We could not decide.

The ensuing journey didn't last long at all, but we then had to continue on foot to a final transit camp in Vienna.

Persecution

It was late and I was exhausted. I don't remember anything about that last forced march, and could swear that towards the end I was quite literally asleep on my feet, probably helped on the way by my father. My only memory is of a German soldier flogging a half-naked young man, who took the punishment without uttering a sound. Who he was and why he was being beaten I don't know. I might even have dreamed it.

It was only years later that I learned the truth about why our train had been diverted. As part of a deal between the Nazis and a Jewish-Hungarian organisation called the Aid and Rescue Committee, five million Swiss francs had been paid to the SS in return for the transfer via Strasshof of Jews from Hungarian ghettos, including Debrecen's, to work in labour camps in Austria. By meekly doing whatever we were told to do, my family and I had escaped being sent to the gas chambers; hundreds of thousands of others, by doing whatever they in turn were told to do, had been murdered.

The day after our arrival in Vienna we were broken up into groups, and for a long time we didn't know what had happened to the others from Orosháza. Later we learned that they had been taken to other, larger camps around the city. After another short march we finally entered the labour camp which was to become our home for the last ten months of the war. No. 4, Hafenzufahrtsstrasse was in the eastern outskirts of the city, right on the southern bank of the Danube near the Stadlauer railway bridge, within sight of the famous Ferris wheel in the Prater amusement park. We found ourselves working for Bauunternehmung Fioravante Spiller und Sohn, a private firm of railway-line builders. We never met Herr Spiller, nor his son: the camp was run by civilian managers and foremen. There were no soldiers guarding us, but we were told that leaving the camp was strictly forbidden.

The camp had two parts. In one, there were some four barracks blocks housing young Ukrainians. Officially they were all volunteers, and free to leave the camp after work. Because they were loud and disorderly, they gave us the impression of being savages, which they were decidedly not. In nominal charge of them was an obviously half-witted Ukrainian, nicknamed Stalin. He went around like a busybody, taking his task very seriously, but the others just laughed at him. In the evenings the boys and girls often formed a choir and sang beautifully. The tunes were strange to us, but we could still feel their sorrow and longing for their distant homeland.

Our part of the camp sat alongside. There was a wire fence between their quarters and ours, and though officially we were not allowed to mix with them it was possible to get into their area by first going through our own main gate and then doubling back through the main gate on their side, and so I decided to try this. Because of their apparent wildness, my parents worried that they might harm me, and didn't want me to go. 'Maybe they hate Jews, just like the Germans,' they said, but this was neither the first nor the last time I took no notice of my parents' warnings.

I went into the Ukrainian barracks not knowing what to expect. I greeted them in German, and they said something in return which I didn't understand. But body language helped, and their smiles put me at ease. They were not very tall, just like us Hungarians, and were all dressed in the same blue-grey shirts and trousers. They were perfectly friendly towards me, but since none of them could speak any other language than Ukrainian, communication was a little sluggish. I was impressed, though, with their knowledge of mathematics and trigonometry, the only subject we could discuss through the language barrier using paper and pencil. After about an hour I returned to my quarters the same way, nobody doing anything to prevent me.

We ourselves had one long barracks block subdivided into four rooms, sufficient for about eighty-five people. The latrine was outside. We had bunk beds, and occupied them so as to keep families together wherever possible, men, women and children all in the same room. The wife of Klein *bácsi*, owner of Orosháza's hardware store, had become an imbecile after the birth of her daughter. Now she continuously muttered to herself during the day and sometimes through the night, as though giving a running commentary on what was going on. She slept with her husband on a lower bunk, while their twenty-year-old daughter Éva bunked with the mistress of the man sleeping above them. I slept alone, above my parents. Next to my bunk slept the widower Markó *bácsi*, owner of Orosháza's bookstore, and his seven-year-old son, Miki. Markó *bácsi* regularly complained that Miki wanted to sleep in the middle of the bed, leaving the two sides to him. Markó *bácsi* had a very pleasant voice, and often burst into singing, but his repertoire was limited to *La Paloma* and *O Sole Mio*. Unfortunately, by night this repertoire was complemented by loud snoring. Markó *bácsi* was also an enthusiastic teller of jokes. I cannot remember now how they ended, because, unlike most jokes, for Markó *bácsi* it was the beginning that mattered. They all started something like this:

'Hitler died and tried to get into heaven....'
'Goering flew his own plane and crashed....'
'Hitler and Mussolini had a fight....'
'Goebbels lost his voice....'

Nobody was interested in the ending: just picturing the beginning gave us such long-lasting pleasure.

Boskovics *bácsi* slept next to the Markós on the lower bunk, continuously complaining about his aching joints, and above him slept young Fekete *bácsi*, a quiet bachelor and a building contractor of appreciable physical strength. Fekete *bácsi* quickly became attached to a young woman named Pollákné, a stunning beauty whose husband had been conscripted into a labour battalion. There was not much romance between them, partly because of the lack of privacy and partly because of our run-down condition, but Pollákné could always rely on the help and protection of Fekete *bácsi*. Their relationship, though, would end in tragedy.

The bunks beyond were occupied by Kövesi *bácsi*, owner of Orosháza's tableware shop, and his wife, while further on slept Vermes *bácsi*, a bank clerk, with his wife and their thirty-year-old spinster daughter. The advocate Doctor Goldman and his wife were good friends of my parents who in better times had often been invited to our dinner parties, and they chose the beds next to theirs. There was also Wallenstein *néni* and her sixteen-year-old son Gyuri, the only other boy my age. Finally, Lefkovics *bácsi*, the owner of the clothes' shop for the rich of Orosháza, was there with his wife and their good-looking twenty-year-old daughter. They had two sons, but both of them had been conscripted into *Munkaszolgálat* labour battalions. The family were the most religious amongst us, and every morning Lefkovics *bácsi* would pray for his sons. Both of them survived the war.

We all chose a leader, Tafler *bácsi*, who had also been elected leader of our Jewish community in Orosháza and who came from one of the most respected local families. His wife had committed suicide in the Orosháza ghetto after being beaten by the *Csendőrség*, and now Tafler *bácsi* was alone. He had to liaise with the Austrians, decide who could be excused work duties, and was responsible for law and order. He was occasionally called upon to mediate between people in conflict: one day, when my mother and Pollákné were walking home side by side, my mother suddenly exclaimed: 'Look, there's a potato on the ground!' But Pollákné was quicker, picked it up, and claimed full ownership of it. Tafler *bácsi* had to be called in to decide who the rightful owner was, and suggested, following the famous precedent from Jewish history, that the potato be cut in half. The potato was solemnly boiled, then divided, and I was the lucky recipient of one half of it.

Fortunately things never reached the state where we would start stealing from each other. Boskovich *bácsi*, who had managed to smuggle a few banknotes past the policeman, bought a small pot of lard from a Hungarian sailor. He kept it under his pillow, yet in spite of this being known to everyone, nobody touched it. Did we have more serious conflicts among us? We ought to have had, crowded together as we were, yet try as I might I can't remember any. If there were conflicts, they didn't make any lasting impression on me and the explanation must be that we all remained humans and didn't become animals. Tafler *bácsi* did his best, though he obviously felt the burden of his responsibilities, and we all obeyed his decisions.

Life in the camp at Hafenzufahrtsstrasse was organised around work. Everyone, except children, the very old and the sick, had to work six days a week. Women were not excused, but neither were they mistreated. Apart from the manual labour, in fact, we received no ill-treatment as we had in Hungary. We could again possess paper and pencil, a great luxury. There was no corporal punishment; in fact there was no punishment at all, and in our free time we could even do as we pleased. True, the whole barracks block stank from our doomed efforts at drying our clothes over our beds, but the main problems were the persistent Allied air raids, the cold of winter, and the lack of decent food.

We were given breakfast and an evening meal in the camp, and ate lunch on the job. After breakfast, one of the foremen would call and collect us. Most of the time we went to work using public transport, but occasionally they took us on a lorry. After the day's work, we had to return home the same way. This was often an arduous task, since during air raids the trams would cease to run and we would be forced to walk miles through a city we hardly knew. We all had to wear our yellow stars, yet we were not subjected to any abuse by the locals. Perhaps they had got used to us, or perhaps they even felt pity.

Work consisted of repairing railway lines damaged by Allied bombing. The work gangs were a proper Tower of Babel: there were German-speaking managers and foremen, two civil engineers—one Greek the other French—doing most of the technical work, and Yugoslav prisoners of war who did the heaviest work of placing the iron rails into position. The Yugoslavs had German military guards but enjoyed a friendly relationship with them, mostly because they regularly received Red Cross parcels containing cigarettes, which they used as bribes. The guards, for their part, consisted of third-rate specimens who were not fit to be sent to the front. Then there were the Ukrainians, and finally us Hungarian-speaking Jews. German, though, was the lingua franca of the camp. I could already speak some German, which I had learned at school, and could converse with the other nationalities. Interested in scientific subjects from an early age, I became especially friendly with the Greek engineer and learned a few Greek expressions from him. The fact that I was familiar with the Greek alphabet from my study of mathematics came in useful. I even learned a little Serbo-Croat from the Yugoslavs, who were delighted by my efforts at their Serbian Cyrillic alphabet, and this proved to be immensely useful during my life after the war when I needed to read Russian scientific manuals.

Very occasionally, we would work in an area where there were Western prisoners of war who must have been captured after D-Day or survived crash-landings, and for the first time I saw a black man. I had seen them before in the cinema, men like Paul Robeson singing *Old Man River*, but never in real life. He was a big, strong man, and as I stared at him, mesmerised, he stared at me in return. Then he smiled at me and simply said 'Hi.' It was the first word I heard a native English speaker utter. For him, this might well have been the first time he had seen somebody wearing a yellow star, and the thought of slavery might have crossed his mind.

Most of the time we worked with shovels; digging, moving ballast, unloading wagons, pushing ballast under the lines, and so on. The work was sometimes heavy, but not unduly so. People complained much less about their personal health than they would have done in good times. My mother, who would suffer from regular migraines at home in Orosháza and retreat into a dark room, never so much as mentioned the word here.

We had one day a week to ourselves. We heated water on the stoves, and women and men washed themselves with as much privacy as was possible. As a result we had no problem with lice, nor did we ever see an outbreak of typhus as others did in the concentration camps. Men took up hobbies like woodcarving, but most of our free time was spent talking about the good old days, the good food we used to eat, and other simple pleasures. We had no access to news, no radio, and no newspapers, not even a fascist one. Rumours reached us only very occasionally:

from Hungarian sailors we heard about D-Day and the second front, which greatly boosted our morale. We often thought about the homes we had had to abandon. Who was staying there now? Who was sleeping in our beds? Were they looking after the property, maintaining it so that we could move back in again when we returned? The biggest question was: shall we ever return? And so the conversation would turn to missing relatives, hoping that they were safe and well and that we would see them again one day.

I often spent long hours talking to Kövesi *bácsi*, the owner of Orosháza's tableware shop, about business, as though he were a teacher passing on the secrets of his success. 'The secret is not to sell expensive,' he would say, 'but to buy cheaply. I once bought a twenty-four-place china dinner service, but because one piece was broken I got a huge discount. I turned it into a perfect twelve-place service which I sold for more than what I paid for the lot. From the rest I was still able to make up a six-place service and another four-place, with a nice profit as a result.

'The other thing important for success,' he continued, 'is trust. You must trust your supplier and the customers must trust you. Without trust a business can't survive.' I found it all very interesting, this window into a world unknown to me. Little did I know that ten years later it would come in very useful indeed in a situation a world removed from a Viennese labour camp.

But most of our time remained dominated by work. One day, working on a bomb-damaged railway line, I noticed that another gang of Jews was clearing the rubble at a neighbouring house which had received a direct hit. Sneaking over, I was surprised to find Klári Herz among them, a girl I knew from Orosháza. Klári's camp was on the other side of Vienna, but I had used public transport alone before and nobody had ever stopped me, and so occasionally on

Persecution

Sundays I would visit her. Klári was three years older than me, slim, with brown hair and big, green eyes. She was a shy, serious girl, and we had a platonic relationship that I at least considered more than just friendship. I would write letters to her, describing my week and my thoughts and feelings, and deliver them by hand. I would watch her face while she read them. On parting she would walk with me to the entrance of their camp where we exchanged a kiss. Perhaps the most important thing for me was that Klári occupied my mind throughout the rest of the week, a distraction from reality. I have no idea how she really felt about me, and I shall never know, for she was killed as the war drew to a close.

There was a shortage of food in the camp, especially nutritious food. Breakfast was a warm, black liquid that they called 'coffee', though what they made it from I didn't dare think: by this stage in the war it was most likely roasted barley, acorns, or dandelions. We were also issued with one hunk of terribly dense *ersatz* bread a day, tasting of the acidic sawdust it was in all likelihood baked from. Whenever we were out working, we received a cooked lunch prepared at some central kitchen and brought to us in a large vat. The food was greasy, but we always managed to wash it down with cold water. (We came to the conclusion amongst ourselves that it was a sort of gelatine, and that it might have been made from the bones of dead Jews just like our bars of soap, whose stamped initials *R.I.F.* were rumoured in the camp to stand for *Rein Jüdisches Fett*—Pure Jewish Fat.) We also had a cooked dish each evening, consisting of some starchy base like potato or barley with tiny scraps of greasy meat. The evening meal was prepared locally in the camp kitchen under the leadership of the cook, a fat, jovial woman who also personally dished up every bowlful.

She was always smiling, and gave the impression of being soft-hearted, but she had a heart of stone. Never ever did she give us an extra drop of food, and she guarded her stock jealously. There was no fresh fruit nor any vegetables to be had, though we were in scarcely a worse position than the Viennese themselves in that particular regard. Because of the lack of vitamins, I developed several boils on my arms and had to bathe them in hot water to get them drained. Food in wartime is worth more than gold. One result of having been deprived in the camp is that now, decades later, I still eat up everything that is placed on my plate and never throw a morsel away.

We survived thanks to the help of others. The best food I got was from the Yugoslav POWs: their rations were much better and larger than ours, and they also regularly received Red Cross parcels containing tinned meat and American cigarettes. You could get a whole loaf of *ersatz* bread for eight German—or six American—cigarettes. The Yugoslavs, in fact, fared better than the German soldiers guarding them, and even gave some of their cigarettes to them. No wonder they were treated so well. On the day they received their Red Cross parcels they didn't even look at their official ration; we could help ourselves to it. I shall never forget the taste of their stuffed cabbage leaves, which reminded me so much of our own Hungarian *töltöttkáposzta*.

Both my parents used to smoke, but they never managed to get any cigarettes from the Yugoslavs. My mother didn't mind giving up, but my father missed it a lot. So every time we had to walk home after an air raid, all three of us would collect the butts of discarded cigarettes from the streets. In winter they were frozen to the ground and we had to scrape them off as best we could. On average it took seven butts and a scrap of waste paper to make one new cigarette. My father's face used to light up as he drew the first puff. What would my father's former students have thought if they could have seen the three of us in our tattered clothes, head bowed, scavenging for cigarette butts? Would they have offered him a cigarette, for old times' sake? My father always wore a torn shoulder bag when we went out to work, and used to promise that if we ever got back home he would nail it onto the living room wall to remind him of something he had never thought possible.

I often wondered why it was that the Red Cross was allowed to send food parcels and cigarettes to prisoners of war, while we civilians didn't receive anything. Was this because the Germans blocked the parcels meant for us, or maybe there was simply nothing for us? One day we did at least receive a visitor, a lady who came in the name of the Red Cross, who said that she could help us in some small ways. The most important thing for us was to search for news about family members, like my brother, from whom we had had no news at all. But I had a practical wish as well. I asked for, and a few weeks later received, some tools to repair shoes. Among them was an iron last, a hammer, a knife and some nails, which came in very useful. I had to cannibalise old shoes for materials, and then worked hard most Sundays to keep our community's feet dry. My only reward was a thank you and a grateful smile.

But the Red Cross proved unable to provide us with extra food, so we supplemented our rations with food gleaned from anywhere we could find it. Our Austrian foreman, Herr Woijcik, lived on a small farm and never went short of food. Whenever he was eating a fried leg of chicken, I would stare at him until he gave me the bone. Then I would endlessly gnaw and suck at it until there was nothing left. We also received little gifts from the locals, mainly while travelling on the trams to and from work. People would not say a word, but would slip a bit of money or some food—a tomato perhaps—into my pocket. Realising that they could get into serious trouble for this, I couldn't even say thank you. All I could do was look at them and hope that my eyes would convey my grateful message. Once we were working near a housing estate in a poor district of Vienna. Suddenly my mother came to me during our lunch break and whispered into my ear: 'Go to number thirty-two and knock at the kitchen door.' I managed to slip away and at number thirty-two found an old couple. I could hardly believe my eyes, for there was a plateful of my favourite *mákos nudli*, fat fingers of pasta smothered with ground poppy seed and sugar, waiting for me. They offered it to me at great risk to themselves. I tried to taste the ingredients separately. The noodles were made of white flour, by itself a great luxury in wartime. But it was the sugar that pleased me most, because I hadn't had any since leaving my home. I would have liked to take my time and eat it slowly, one noodle at a time, but I worried that my absence would be noticed. When my plate was empty, I thanked them by kissing their hands and went back to work in a hurry.

Not everyone was so kind to us. One day returning from work, we had to walk, because the tramline had been bombed. A man with a horse-drawn cart allowed us to climb on. Halfway home, a stranger with a swastika armband started shouting at the driver to throw those bloody Jews off the cart. The driver had to obey, and we walked the rest of the way. This kind of behaviour, though, was memorable for its rarity. So you may well ask why we didn't try to escape. The idea never entered our minds. Maybe it was because our life was bearable, but also because we had no place to go to. Going back to Hungary would have meant jumping from the frying pan back into the fire.

As the weather started to turn cold once more, in the autumn of 1944, we met new problems. We had left the ghetto in the spring, taking some warm clothing with us, but we hadn't been able to carry enough. We especially missed warm gloves now that we had to handle shovels with our bare hands. With no possibility of new clothing, we repaired our old clothes as best we could. Fortunately we had a tailor amongst us, Lőwi *bácsi*, a man who had developed a hump from a lifetime of leaning forwards over his work. He worked alongside us on the labour gangs during the day and helped with the more difficult tailoring in the evenings, complaining all the time that he would much prefer making new suits instead. He missed, he never failed to remind us, his old sewing machine.

Old blankets were fully utilised, but were in short supply. One day I happened across a blanket upon a chair, with nobody around. It must have been abandoned, I thought, and took it back to the barracks with me. Next day the German works manager, a big, ugly man, was raving that someone had stolen his blanket and that he would send all the thieving Jews to the gallows. I admitted my guilt, explaining that I had thought the blanket was not needed, and promised that I would bring it back the very following morning. Still, he wanted to have me hanged, and it took a lot of tears from my mother to save my neck. I am sure he had fully intended to carry out his threat, and was only fortunate that we hadn't already cut his blanket into pieces.

Yet the angry outbursts of bullies like this were as nothing to the air raids. These were the most terrifying experiences of my life, and I lived through some one hundred and fifty of them. The heavy bombers of RAF Bomber Command and the US Army Air Force arrived by the thousands, selecting an area of strategic importance, often an oil refinery, and covering it with a carpet of bombs. Railways were, of course, frequently targeted, and every time we managed to repair a line they were sure to bomb it again within a day or two.

WHEN EVEN THE POETS WERE SILENT

People often say that one can get used to almost everything, but I could never get used to the bombs. They produced a terrifying, whining sound which chilled the blood in my veins. The older men in the camp, those who had been soldiers during the First World War, would say that if you heard the noise the bomb had already fallen somewhere else and you were safe for the moment. I knew from my physics lessons that it took time for the sound to travel, but if the bomb was falling only a few hundred metres away then that time was very short indeed.

Usually we had adequate warning of air raids, and as soon as we heard the sirens we would run to the shelters. Sometimes there was a train waiting to carry us the short distance to the hills just north of the city, to the vineyards of Nussdorf, where we sheltered in wine cellars in reasonable safety. It was a beautiful district of green hills and old houses, peaceful and tranquil, like Canaan. We would first wait outside the cellar, hoping that the planes wouldn't come in our direction. Then we heard them, with their ever louder, ever more intimidating rumble, and then we would see them, like beautiful white birds in orderly formations. The anti-aircraft guns would start to send up shells that would burst in white puffs around them. It was a strange situation to be in: we were in real danger of being killed by those planes, yet they were the vanguard of the only force which could liberate us.

On other occasions, there was no time or no train by which to effect an escape, and we made for one of the local shelters dug into Vienna's sandy soil. These were often nothing more than a long trench, covered with corrugated iron and sand, left open at both ends. Fortunately we never suffered a direct hit, but there were many near misses whose horrific blast waves tore through the open entrances. As a result, I suffered some damage to my hearing, which

I still bear. It was at moments like these that everybody suddenly became equal. It was apparent that most people, men and women, foreigners and Austrians, foremen and workers, Jews and gentiles, were all equally afraid. The Greek engineer always squeezed himself into the centre of the tunnel, while the Frenchman would be squatting as low as possible. Our German foreman would joke and stroll about outside, playing the hero until we could hear the bombs. Then he too came inside, took off his cap, and started to pray. At least we were respected in the shelters. The Austrians never refused us entry, and were distinctly friendlier to us than usual, maybe because they felt a step nearer to Judgment. The bombs certainly didn't distinguish between us.

One of the worst aspects of the air raids was that we had to run to reach the train, terrified of being left behind, out in the open, unprotected against tons of high explosives. My father often urged me to run ahead and leave him and my mother behind, but I never did, and we always made it to the train in the end. Then one day, after the sirens sounded, as we were running up a railway embankment, Klein *bácsi* fell down. His daughter Éva was with him, and she shouted for help. Klein *bácsi* was without any sign of life, but still I tried artificial respiration by moving his arms in and out. He was already dead from a massive heart attack. I just managed to jump on the train before it started to move out, but Éva stayed behind. She survived the air raid, and for a while at least took over the task of caring for her widowed mother.

There was far worse to come. One day in late December of 1944, one month before my seventeenth birthday, while returning from work we realised that our camp had been hit. As fate had it, a larger than usual number of people had stayed back and not gone to work that day. When they heard the sirens they had rushed to the shelter, which had then received a direct hit, killing several women and children. The concrete roof had caved in. People had been sitting on a bench, and their heads had been smashed to pieces. Others, who had been sitting on the other side of the shelter, walked away unscathed.

Bandi Szirt, a seven-year-old boy, felt claustrophobic in the shelter and always chose to remain in his room. It must at first have been an agonising experience for him, but he had grown used to staying there alone. This time, though, his room had been hit by the blast, and the red-hot stove had fallen on his leg. He had passed out from the pain, and once he had been dug from the ruins had been taken to a local hospital. When we arrived back from work, I had to help removing the dead bodies from the shelter. It was a cold winter day, and their brains had frozen to the concrete roof that had killed them. First we had to free them from the rubble, then we pulled them out and gently laid them side by side on the ground. The work was made much worse by the fact that we knew everybody intimately. Next to Goldman *néni* we laid the mother of Éva Klein, who had only just lost her father to a heart attack. Then we took out the body of Weisz *néni*, the elderly woman who had called for her dead mother on the train from Békéscsaba and who had been left in charge of the children while their parents worked. Then there were Boskovich *néni* and two children of six and eight. The younger one was still clutching his teddy bear. Then it was the turn of the stunningly beautiful Pollákné, her shoulders still covered with her shawl of bright red and orange flowers. I wanted to remember her as the radiant young woman she had been, not like this. Who would tell her husband, if ever he came back from the labour battalion, what had happened to his young wife? Finally we had to remove our leader, Tafler *bácsi*. He was a big man and it took a long time to pull him out. He used to say that he wanted to be buried next to his wife in Orosháza, but it wasn't to be.

I had to throw up several times during the work. We tried to keep the relatives from looking at the corpses, but they all went to say goodbye to them for the last time. Nobody talked, but their cries were heartbreaking. The bodies were taken away just as it started to snow. The unusually large, white snowflakes soon covered the place where they had lain and made it look quite peaceful again. Later, all the Jewish men gathered and said the *kádis*, the usual prayer of mourning. All the men, that is, except Fekete *bácsi*, who refused to join us, enraged and disillusioned at the loss of Pollákné. I didn't understand the Hebrew words of the *kádis*, but the solemn atmosphere spoke more than the mere words. For days, none of us could sleep at night for the cries of the people who had lost their loved ones.

Why? We asked again and again. Why did this have to happen? Who was responsible for it? The American airman who had dropped the bomb? Could he not see that it was the site of a forced labour camp? Of course not. His target that day must have been the oil refinery at Vösendorf, a few kilometres south of the camp but near enough to make the difference between life and death when bombing from tens of thousands of feet up. Was it, we wondered, a simple, regrettable mistake, the unconscious movement of a finger on a sensitive trigger? The likelihood is that the bombardier never even knew what carnage he had done. He was rejoicing the fact that he had survived another mission, and we were saying goodbye to our dead. Life in the camp was never the same again. Goldman *bácsi*, who had lost his wife, couldn't stop crying. His scars never healed, and when he returned home he was admitted to a psychiatric hospital. Losing spouses or parents in the destruction of the shelter was bad enough, but it was unbearable for the parents who had lost children.

Only three rooms of the barracks remained habitable, and life became even more crowded than before. A new leader to replace Tafler *bácsi* had to be chosen, but I don't even remember who he was: by now we had got used to the routine, and the role had become less important. No one went to the shelter any more during air raids, and for a very good reason: there was no shelter.

3
Liberation

THROUGHOUT OUR stay in Austria, we knew nothing about the Nazis' infamous death camps. But I still remember a cold, winter's day at the end of January 1945. While working on a railway line, we saw a train moving slowly along. The open wagons were full of people, all dressed in striped uniforms, like prisoners. They covered themselves with blankets, and were packed so tight that they had to stand. They were all shouting one word, which didn't mean anything to us at the time, but which we couldn't forget. It was 'Auschwitz'.

As the war in Europe neared its inevitable end, lots of unusual things happened. Occasionally we would meet Hungarian merchant sailors (the border, of course, lay only 90km downriver from Vienna) who would tell us news of the Russian advance into Hungary. We heard from them that the Red Army was rapidly approaching the Austrian border. Expecting liberation any day, we got bolder and bolder, and even took off our yellow stars while walking outside the camp. One day we heard that there was a barge moored nearby on the Danube, full of Hungarian Jewish men. I thought perhaps my brother István might be among them, and so with Vermes *bácsi*, whose son too had been conscripted into a labour battalion, decided to investigate. We took our yellow stars off the outside of our overcoats, pinned them inside, and approached the ship. It was one of those large commercial barges that operated on the Danube, but instead of coal or gravel it was packed with people. We shouted up to them in Hungarian: 'Is there anyone from Orosháza?' They didn't know.

At this point, one of the guards on the ship saw what was going on and came down the gangplank. We started to run away, but he drew his gun and shouted to us to halt.

It was not difficult for him to realise what we were, and he opened our coats to reveal our yellow stars. 'So, you are Jews, but not wearing the star,' he observed. 'You must have escaped from the ship.' And without waiting for an answer he shoved us up the gangplank and onto the barge.

We only slowly realised the extent of the trouble we were in. We learned from the others that they had been in labour camps in Hungary, and that they were being evacuated to Austria ahead of the approaching Soviet army. The guards were sadists, they said, often drunk, who would shoot into the crowd at random. They had already killed a fifth of the prisoners for fun and thrown their bodies into the Danube. I had managed to survive a year of persecution and now, almost at the final hour, it looked as if I might die. I contemplated jumping into the river and swimming away from the barge, but I thought I might have a better chance at night, if I were still alive by then.

We were squatting speechlessly on the deck, our heads in our hands, not wanting to listen to the men's horror stories any more, when Vermes *bácsi* caught sight of his daughter approaching our moorings with an Austrian policeman. There was a police station near our camp, and she had gone there in desperation when we had failed to return. There was a short and angry exchange of words between the guard and the policeman, who argued that we were the 'property' of Fioravante Spiller und Sohn and were needed for the war effort.

'Come down at once!' the policeman commanded us, and we didn't wait for a more formal invitation. Only when we were on the quayside did it fully dawn on me how much danger I had been in, and I couldn't stop shaking. I suppose I have that policeman to thank for my life. Later, reflecting more calmly on the affair, I would ask myself: 'Who was legally in the right? The policeman or the guard?' It didn't matter: these were the closing days of the war, and there were no rules.

Having heard rumours that the Nazis were transporting some of the Jews further inland, deeper into the Reich, some of us simply decided not to stay in the camp any longer, where we might easily be tracked down. We could already hear the continuous rumble of the heavy guns to the east, and with the foremen having fled there was no more call to work of a morning. The kitchen staff too were gone, the pantry was empty, and there was no food to be had. While the majority remained in the barracks, some of us decided to set up camp in an air-raid shelter a few hundred meters outside our camp and wait there for the Russians. The shelter proved to be deserted, and we spent a whole day there, but by night it grew bitterly cold and we debated what to do next. Somebody suggested that we might try the basement of a nearby block of flats, but others thought that it could be dangerous, perhaps full of German soldiers.

About ten of us decided to take our chances and boldly walked over in bright daylight, hoping that the soldiers, if there were any, didn't belong to the SS. We did indeed meet a few soldiers of the *Wehrmacht*, but they had no weapons on them and in fact were busily trying to get rid of their uniforms as well. Most of the Austrian inhabitants of the flats, mainly just women and children by now, were already living rough in the basement. To our surprise, they seemed happy to accept us, and even gave us some food. Did they do it from a feeling of charity? Or did they think that we might protect them later, after the Russian soldiers arrived, in return for their kindness? No one really knew how the Russian soldiers would behave when they arrived.

We spent two or three more days in the basement of the flats as the fighting went on around us, until at last someone said that the Russians had arrived. The Germans defending the city, it turned out, had finally surrendered the previous day. Soon, a Russian soldier came down to the basement, his revolver drawn, asking where any German soldiers were hiding. We knew very well that there were a few who had taken refuge in the basement just like us, but we didn't want to hand them over. Satisfied, the Russian soldier then got hold of a baby and showered him with affection. '*Nyemyetski propaganda*,' he repeated, as if to underline that the Russians were decent human beings after all, not like the Germans' propaganda described them. Then another came in, saying that the commandant had lost his watch and urgently needed a replacement. My father wanted to give him his pocket watch, but the commandant needed a wristwatch, so I gave him mine. Soon he had collected all the watches he could. Only later did we learn that this was a kind of trophy hunt. Some of the Russians were said to have wristwatches decorating both their arms up to the elbows.

We had already taken off our yellow stars, but only now that the Red Army had arrived did we finally get used to the idea that for us the war was truly over, that we had survived and were free again. We didn't realise at the time quite how lucky we had been: not only had we been sent to Strasshof, but our sojourn in Vienna had spared us from being in Hungary during the short but terrible reign of the fascist Arrow Cross Party which had come to power there in October of 1944. The Arrow Cross had sought out and murdered thousands of Jewish Hungarians and deported tens of thousands more to the Nazi death camps. But most importantly of all, Nazi Germany was beaten. Had the Third Reich won the war, they would have had no more use for us and we too would have ended up in a gas chamber. Winston Churchill's famous speech at the end of the Battle of Britain—'Never in the history of human conflict was so much owed by so many to so few'—applies equally to us as survivors. I am one of the so many, and decades afterwards still feel deeply indebted to the soldiers of the Allied forces, whether British, American or Russian. Later in life, while on a cruise to Hawaii, I watched as a group of US war-veterans was paraded on a podium. I couldn't stop crying, and only with difficulty did I restrain myself from going up and saying thank you to them for saving my life.

Once the Nazis in Vienna had surrendered, there was not much point in waiting around. According to the Russians, it was 'perfectly safe' to go: the Nazis had gone, and would never be coming back. What was 'perfectly safe' for Ivan, however, didn't look safe to us at all. We could still hear gunfire, could see soldiers running about in apparent chaos, and there was no obvious front line. Soviet aircraft were flying overhead, liberally strafing targets with their machine guns. With bullets hitting the ground all about, as far as we could tell the pilots were aiming at us as well.

We left the basement on foot, a small group. In addition to my parents and me there was Goldman *bácsi*, whose wife had died in the air-raid shelter, the Lefkovics family, and Gyuri Wallenstein and his mother. Later we learned that an SS patrol passed by and killed the people who had remained. It is ironic how unpredictable life is. After surviving the first day alternately walking and running in the general direction of the Hungarian border 70km away, taking shelter whenever necessary, we felt reasonably safe. We stopped at a deserted house in the country, where a few chickens were pecking around in a large garden, and soon had company in the form of a young Russian officer, immaculately dressed, whose boots were clean despite his having fought his way across half of Eastern Europe. He was handsome, tall and lean, and blonde hair protruded from under his cap. He approached us with a healthy smile and this immediately put us at ease. He spoke a little German; the rest of the conversation was conducted in body language. As he represented the only authority in the vicinity, we asked his permission to kill a couple of chickens for dinner and he immediately obliged us by shooting three or four with his submachine gun. Later, in the house, he saw a large mirror on the wall. He took his gun and smashed it with the butt. 'They won't need this again,' he explained, and we didn't argue. When we had cooked the chickens, we invited him for dinner, but he declined.

Had we been in Orosháza, we would have had a choice of recipes for our chickens. The most desirable, a Sunday meal, would have been to cut them into pieces, cover them with flour, egg and breadcrumbs, and deep-fry them. Second best would have been to make *paprikás csirke*, simmering hunks of meat on the bone with fried onion and a generous helping of paprika powder. Lacking the vital ingredients in our makeshift home, we couldn't do either. All that was left was to boil the meat in water and pretend that we had a soup. Still, in spite of its shortcomings, it was one of the most memorable meals of our lives.

We had finished eating our first decent meal in months, and were already busy washing ourselves with hot water for the first time in days, when the Russian officer reappeared to see how we were. There was one washbowl, which we were using one after the other in the bathroom. It was the turn of Éva Lefkovics, a pretty girl in her twenties, and her father was guarding the door, which had no lock. This made the Russian officer curious, and he indicated that he wanted to go into the bathroom. Éva's father stood in his way, and for a moment it was a highly charged situation. We could see that the officer was not used to being stopped, and he was not taking this challenge kindly. Lefkovics *bácsi* was joined by his wife, who desperately tried to explain the reason for their stubbornness in a language the Russian could not understand. This seemed to me a bad idea, only likely to inflame the situation. Finally though they succeeded, and the Russian, the perfect gentleman, backed down. Only later did we hear of the countless rapes committed by the Russian rank and file.

Next day, walking inexorably towards the Hungarian frontier, we met yet another Russian soldier. He was coming from the opposite direction, riding on a bicycle. He stopped Gyuri, and with a big, friendly smile pushed the machine into his hands. The handlebar was loose, and the front wheel was buckled, but Gyuri was delirious with his new treasure, cycling forward and backwards until we reached the next village a few miles further. There stood another Russian soldier, who duly took the bike away from him. The first had probably borrowed it from his friend and by this means returned it to its rightful owner.

There was no welcoming committee waiting for us at the frontier. In fact, apart from a deserted barracks and an unmanned gate, there was nothing to indicate that we were back in Hungary. We left Austria with mixed feelings, glad to be rid of the past but uncertain what to expect. Would they welcome us? Apologise, even? Or would they put us straight back into the ghetto? And what would life be like under Soviet occupation? Nobody had the answers, but we had no choice: we were simply going home. My father was worried that Hungary under Russian rule would become a Communist state. Then in one of the villages we passed through we saw a poster on a wall. My father was relieved when he read about a 'Democratic Hungary.' *Demokrácia*, he explained, was much to be preferred to either *fasizmus* or *kommunizmus*. Alas, plain *demokrácia* was soon to be changed to *népi demokrácia* or 'people's democracy', which made all the difference in the world.

Stepping back onto Hungarian soil, I was glad that the three of us had survived the most difficult time in our lives. The feeling of freedom was only slowly sinking in. I began to look forward to seeing my home again. For better or for worse, I felt, my future lay in this country. Magyar was my mother tongue. I was imbued with the culture I had been born into. But while I had once felt safe here, the same was no longer true. I could not forget the suffering, nor the indifference or outright hostility of ordinary Hungarians when we were sent to the ghetto and deported. The cruelty of the authorities, particularly of the *Csendőrség*, was engraved on my mind. Yet at the same time I felt no vengefulness. I knew that I would not and could not hunt down the people who had wronged me. Mostly, I just felt a mixture of hope and sadness as the past year rolled out in my memory like a horror movie.

We kept on walking, resting at nights in abandoned houses, until we came to Győr, a big industrial city where we found that there were still trains running and that there was one bound for Budapest. Our little group divided now into its parts to continue onward to Orosháza, and we said goodbye to each other for the time being. Could we get used to our old lives again? Take responsibility for ourselves instead of having our lives arranged by others? Would time spent in Orosháza heal our wounds and allow us to forget our humiliation? Parting was an emotional affair, the women in tears. Having shared the pain and occasional joy for a year, we had become one big family.

My parents and I climbed up into one of the coaches and found three empty seats, but then gradually more and more people squeezed themselves into the compartment until it was so full that there was almost no air to breath. Even then, it was better than the cattle truck. The majority of the passengers were residents of Budapest, returning home with food they had bought in the countryside. They carried big wicker baskets filled with bread, fatty *szalonna* bacon, eggs, cheese and a few live chickens. The rest were people returning home after the war—refugees like us, volunteers, ex-soldiers in partly discarded uniforms.... There was no conversation, everybody too preoccupied with their own thoughts. The journey was scarcely faster by train than on foot, but it was less strenuous, and after a very long time, most of it spent motionless on the tracks, we arrived in Budapest.

This was the first time I had ever seen my capital city. Even my parents had only been there a couple of times. We made our way across town to the home of my mother's aunt and her family, shocked by the destruction we saw on the way. 'Fortress Budapest' had been vigorously defended by the *Waffen SS* and their Hungarian allies against Soviet and Romanian armies who were eager to demonstrate their power ahead of the Yalta Conference. Some eighty per cent of the city's buildings had been damaged or destroyed, and 38,000 of its civilians were dead.

Our relatives' home had been spared. They lived in a large apartment in Dohány *utca* on the eastern bank of the Danube, at the periphery of Budapest's Jewish ghetto. The men of the family had been called up into *Munkaszolgálat* labour battalions, and the three women had left to find shelter with gentile friends. On the way they had been captured by fascists from the Arrow Cross Party and kept in a detention centre in the most awful conditions. Many detainees had died or gone mad, but they had survived. We found my great aunt Rezsi *néni* and both of her two daughters still alive, but all three husbands were missing and only several years later did just one of them, Pista the artist who was married to my mother's cousin Magda, come back. Towards the end of the war Pista had managed to escape from his brutal labour battalion and cross over to the Russians, who had duly taken him prisoner. But the Russian POW camp had proved just as awful, and Pista had only survived by sketching for his captors likenesses of themselves to send home to wives and sweethearts. In return they had given him enough extra food to stay alive. After the war, told that there were no Jews left in Hungary, he had become a Soviet citizen and joined the Communist Party. Only three years later, after learning that his wife Magda had survived the Holocaust, did Pista finally receive permission to relinquish his citizenship and return home.

As we stood in the doorway of Rezsi *néni*'s apartment, the women expressed their condolences for the death of my brother, István. This is how we heard about his death. I can still see my father slowly sinking to the floor there and then, weeping. I had never seen him cry before. István, it seemed, had survived the war serving in a labour battalion, and had been returning home to Orosháza in civilian clothing when he was captured by the Soviet military and sent to the Soviet Union as a slave labourer. The Russians liked to keep a good stock of prisoners, and regularly took civilians as well as soldiers. If one escaped, they always restored the number by capturing more at random. They supposedly took people on the pretext of working on some or other job but never released them, accepted no excuses, tore up all their documents, and had no preferences as to nationality, race, religion or education. Hundreds of thousands of Hungarians, Jews as well as gentiles, were despatched to the Soviet Union in this way. According to some eyewitness or other, my brother had died from starvation together with countless others. It was a sickening waste of such a talented scientist. For all we knew, by killing him they had killed another Einstein. We never discovered the identity of the eyewitness, who had apparently passed news of István's death to my relatives via a third person. My parents went through a rollercoaster of hope and despair, until eventually hope faded away. They never fully recovered from the loss.

Our relatives told us that there was no war damage in Orosháza, and that our house, though a few items had been looted, was intact. They had already been there, exchanging clothing and other valuables for food. They treated us to buttered bread, which at least brought back many pleasant memories of the time before the war. We didn't want to waste any more time, and obtained papers certifying in Hungarian and Russian that we were Jews returning from deportation. With emergency aid money in our pockets, distributed to us by the local Jewish community to buy railway tickets home, we continued our journey, changing trains in Békéscsaba where we had briefly stayed in the ghetto a year before. As we left the train there, we were stopped on the platform by an armed patrol. They had no proper uniforms, just red armbands with *őrség*—guard—stamped upon them. It was not clear to us who had appointed them, or what they were supposed to be guarding. My father presented our papers to their leader, a young, unshaven man in a mixture of discarded military uniforms, some Hungarian, some Russian, and a pair of dirty boots comically too big for his feet. He carried an enormous First World War vintage rifle as a symbol of his authority. He immediately became suspicious, disappointed perhaps to see Jews returning after he thought Hungary had got rid of them for good. He showed the papers to his colleagues, who kept looking now at them, now at us, until finally agreeing to detain us. In no time they had rounded up a dozen more suspicious-looking individuals, mainly young people travelling without luggage, then marched us at gunpoint to the town hall. It was not the reception we had expected or hoped for. The thought that we were being returned to the Békéscsaba ghetto crossed my mind. Would the young Swabian boy with his stick still be there, asking: '*Du Junge*, where have you been?'

In the town hall we were ushered in front of another official, dressed in civilian clothes, who sat behind a desk. I couldn't stop thinking that he was Sergeant Posta of Orosháza's *Csendőrség* in disguise, but this time without that hat with the black rooster feathers. He put on his glasses after carefully cleaning them with a dirty handkerchief, cast an eye over our papers, and allowed us to go back to the railway station.

'You can go.'

That's all he said. There were no words of apology, never mind any expression of welcome. We walked back to the station and waited an age for our train. Then, after an hour's journey across the relentlessly flat plains, finally we arrived in Orosháza. The conductor called out loudly, announcing the name of the station as he always did, without the least emotion. We recognised the station building as we slowed to a halt, and the red brick of the flourmill beyond. Its chimney was smoking, as if nothing had happened.

'Don't you realise that things have changed?' I was almost shouting at it. 'Everything has changed. We are back, free people with equal rights. Fascism is finished, beaten!' But there was no response. Neither the flourmill nor the rest of Orosháza was interested.

Our house turned out to have been occupied by a stranger, a single man who in all likelihood had come down to the country to escape being drafted into the army. He was a rather dubious character, and must have had connections or managed to bribe some official or other to have got sole possession of our home. He was well dressed, very polite, had a charming smile and showed a lot of sympathy for our plight, but somehow we couldn't trust his sincerity. The very same day we arrived he left with a small suitcase, in a nice pair of shoes which had previously belonged to our relatives in Budapest, and which had been sent to us for safekeeping. We never heard of him again. With a few exceptions, we found most of our possessions untouched. Most had not been worth stealing. I went back to the ghetto in the woodyard, now abandoned, and found my self-propelling pencil where I had left it on the wooden beam. My father dug up his gold chain from under the pear tree, but never did nail his shoulder bag to the living-room wall. People have short memories, and want to forget the unpleasant things of the past. I never found the fine violin my parents had bought from Strausz *bácsi*. My most treasured possession, the accordion bought with money earned breeding angoras, had vanished as well. We quickly learned that the large house next door to ours had been permanently requisitioned by Orosháza's new chief of police. Before the war he had been a bricklayer, but had joined the Communist Party and been appointed to this important post. I complained to him about my accordion, and a few days later (though only once I had presented the police with proof of ownership) it was returned to me without explanation.

'Where was it?' was my first question.

'Be glad you got it back,' the policeman said, 'and don't ask any more questions.'

'And my violin?' I persisted. He got quite annoyed at this.

'Can't you be satisfied with what you've got? I told you not to ask questions.' All this left me with the feeling that it had probably been our new neighbour the chief of police who had taken them from our house.

As soon as they heard of our return, our neighbours came one after the other to greet us. They brought us food—bread, eggs and sausages the like of which we had not seen for a year—and cried with my parents over the death of István. Word spread quickly, and we soon realised just how popular my father really was. There was an almost endless stream of ex-students of his arriving with more food. Where had these good people been when we were taken from the ghetto to the cattle wagons? I couldn't help asking myself.

That first evening, we couldn't find our best bedding, linen or eiderdowns, but managed instead to sleep under the blankets we had brought with us from the camp. It took a full two days before Ágoston *néni*, our neighbour, brought us our 'missing' bedding.

'I only took it for safe keeping,' she explained, somewhat embarrassed, but I was sure she had thought it hers to keep. It had been washed and pressed, and looked unused. Diplomatically, my mother thanked her for looking after it for us.

I had brought a nice, red tartan blanket back with me from Vienna. It had belonged to Goldman *bácsi*, the old family friend who had lost his wife during the air raid. When after Vienna's liberation we had left the basement of the apartment block, he had had it in his hands. After about twenty minutes, though, he had decided that it was too heavy for him and had tossed it over a fence. I thought it was a fine blanket, far better than mine, so I ran back and swapped it. Some weeks after our return, Goldman *bácsi* came to our house and claimed his blanket back, but my parents refused to give it to him. His friendship with my parents didn't continue for long, not because of the blanket but because of his deteriorating mental state. He eventually met a woman, a holocaust survivor, who too was undergoing psychiatric treatment, and he remarried in haste. She was old, and no beauty, but their biggest problem was that

Liberation

she was even more affected by what she had suffered than he was.

Life was not the same in Orosháza. There was no shortage of food, and the market was as busy as ever, but the whole atmosphere had turned sombre. Some of the Jewish shopkeepers who had returned now reopened their shops, but the quality and range of their wares had changed for the worse. Schwarz *bácsi* the shoeshop owner came back, as did the tableware trader Kövesi *bácsi* and the leatherworker Bakk *bácsi*. Markó *bácsi* returned to his bookshop, but the Sternbergs didn't make any more eiderdowns in Orosháza. They emigrated instead to Israel. Many of the town's shops closed or changed hands. The Alföld Hotel stopped serving its famous steaks, and nobody promenaded on Kossuth Lajos *utca* on Sunday mornings anymore, as they had always done as a matter of custom before the war. We didn't hire a new maid, and there were no more dinner parties or card games. It wouldn't have been right.

It was a time to take stock, search for relatives, and tell each other our experiences. A necessary catharsis, you might say. For years afterwards, when two Jewish Hungarians met for the first time, the first question they would ask was 'Where were you?' We heard about the death camps, and gradually came to appreciate just how lucky we had been to end up in a labour camp instead. We were all searching for friends and acquaintances, rejoicing when we found someone returning, and tirelessly waiting for the others until some eyewitness told us the sad news. My father's elder brother, Kálmán, had died, as had his sister Emma's husband and both their sons. Time after time I went to look for Klári, my sweetheart in Vienna, but the people who now lived in her house knew nothing of her and her parents. 'We still haven't heard a thing,' they would say, perhaps hoping that they could remain in their modest family home. Her camp in Vienna had been a lot bigger than ours, with a military commandant. Eventually I heard from the few who had managed to make their way back that the whole labour camp had been evacuated to Mauthausen-Gusen concentration camp in the last days of the war. Many of Orosháza's Jewish families had perished there, including our neighbours, the family of Doctor Balázs the vet. János, husband of the beautiful Pollákné who had died during the air raid, never made it back, saving us the pain of telling him what had happened to his wife. Fekete *bácsi*, suitor of Pollákné until her death, returned, but retreated even further into himself. Only one of the two apprentice plumbers with whom I had lived in the Orosháza ghetto survived, and he immediately emigrated to Israel. In all, a little more than half of the Orosháza Jews returned. Across Hungary, in just one year, more than half a million had been murdered.

Eventually, four of the *Gimnázium*'s five Jewish students turned up in class. Géza Hevesi, whose parents had decided to stay in Békéscsaba, ended up dying with them in Auschwitz. Ági Szekulesz lost both of her parents there, but she herself survived and returned to school, cared for by relatives. Another boy of my age, Jóska Stern, had been in a large camp, and towards the end of the war had been separated from his parents and sent to Mauthausen-Gusen. His parents had come home to Orosháza not knowing what had happened to him. I used to try to comfort them: 'Don't worry, he's a strong, clever boy, and he's sure to survive. It can take a long time to get home, so don't give up hope.' And because Mauthausen-Gusen was liberated by the Americans soon after Jóska arrived there, he did eventually return. The last of our class, Zsuzsa, survived a labour camp in Vienna but was raped by a Russian soldier on her journey home. She caught VD, became pregnant, and had an abortion.

The eastern part of Hungary, Orosháza included, had been liberated from the Nazis in October of 1944, and lessons at the *Gimnázium* had already restarted only a month behind schedule. I had three months to catch up with the non-Jewish pupils, none of whom of course had been forced to leave Orosháza, and complete the year. In the end I managed it, but it was a terrible blow to my self-confidence. It was strange to be back in a classroom again, after everything I had gone through. It was even stranger to be facing the same headmaster who had so resented the Jews, still teaching us Hungarian but no longer blaming us for all the ills of the Hungarian peasantry. I didn't feel like a child anymore, and school had lost its glamour and mystery. Where before I had accepted that I needed permission from both my father and my teacher if I wanted, for example, to go to the cinema, as was the normal practice for boys of my age, I now found it childish. I asked my father to sign a pile of blank permission forms, which he did without saying a word, and I was proud of him. We both understood what had changed.

One major change in my life, just as for so many of my fellow Jews, was a newfound interest in the political aims of Zionism. I joined a Zionist youth organisation, the far-left *Sómér* movement which advocated a single state in Palestine in which both the Jews and the Arabs would co-exist. Having lived through the Holocaust I didn't consider any other solution acceptable and often had arguments, some of them in open meetings, with our rabbi, who advocated a more right-wing solution. Where before the war we had felt ourselves secular Hungarians, we now became much more interested in our Jewish identity and traditions. Orosháza's Jewish youth met each weekend in the yard of the synagogue to sing Zionist songs and dance the *hora*. We sang in Hebrew without knowing the meaning of the words, but it gave us a feeling of freedom and belonging. The ghetto spirit of bowing our head and accepting mistreatment without question or complaint had to stop. We heard about the uprising in the Warsaw ghetto and were determined not to allow the past to repeat itself.

We were young, had all in different ways survived, and we felt more alive than we ever had. I didn't have to look for a girlfriend, for a girl found me. She was beautiful, slim, and with a raging temperament. We spent our free time together, exchanged love letters and a few kisses, but I left her for an older girl and she was heartbroken. Soon after that, like many others, she emigrated to Israel and we lost touch until some sixty years later she telephoned me out of the blue. A grandmother now, she had kept all my letters and sent one of them back to me.

Ardent Zionist that I was, I wanted to go to Israel to work on a *kibuc*, but my mother threatened to commit suicide if I left. She had already had one son taken away from her. My father argued that I could go, but only later, and that I would be of more use to Israel if I had a university education. Finally, I agreed to a compromise. First, I would go to university. Afterwards, with the knowledge and the degree I had gained, I could emigrate to Israel. Of course, things don't always turn out the way a seventeen-year-old boy plans them.

I was more interested in the practical ends of the *Sómér* movement's Zionist agenda than in the political theories of Karl Marx, but it was to be Marxism rather than Zionism that had the greater effect on my life after my return to Orosháza. The political influence of the Soviet Union, whose armies had driven the Nazis out of Hungary at great cost to

Liberation

themselves, remained long, long after the spring of 1945. The Kingdom of Hungary (albeit without a king), under which I had been born, was replaced in February of 1946 with the Second Hungarian Republic under Prime Minister Tildy of the Independent Smallholders' Party, which had won a majority of votes in the national elections of November, 1945. The Soviet-backed Hungarian Communist Party under the leadership of a hardline Stalinist named Rákosi, though it had received only seventeen per cent of the vote, began a campaign of infiltration in the new republic, with the ultimate aim of seizing power. Rákosi's plan, which he aptly dubbed *szalámitaktika*—salami tactics—involved placing Communists in positions of political power such as at the head of the Ministry of the Interior, while dividing and conquering political adversaries in small but ultimately fatal steps. Bit by bit, Rákosi cut thin slices from the salami until, before his enemies knew it, all had been lost. Even though the final declaration of a fully-fledged People's Republic of Hungary was several years away, the Hungarian Communist Party and its Moscow backers were becoming a dominant influence in our daily lives. In Orosháza, the local branch of the Communist Party, taking its cue from Moscow, launched a recruiting campaign aimed at young people. I was invited to a 'discussion' with a Party official, a member of the newly formed secret police. His long, brown leather coat and jackboots left his affiliation no secret.

'Do you want fascism to return to Hungary?' was his first question.

'Of course not!' I was genuinely shocked as the terrors induced by those words flashed through my mind.

'And which party do you think is the best insurance against this happening?'

The choice was limited: I didn't feel any affiliation with the Independent Smallholders' Party, and had to admit that the Hungarian Communist Party was best placed. I told him I was a member of the Zionist *Sómér* movement, but he knew this already and didn't seem to mind. He handed me a membership application form, which I signed. I knew precious little of the theory and even less of the practice of Communism when, at the age of seventeen, I became a paid-up member of the Party.

Because there was no industry to speak of in Orosháza, most Party members were either peasants or intellectuals, and this was equally the case in the youth wing, of which I was a member. Middle-class Party members like myself were not often sincere Communists but more often just opportunists, and most of us were later expelled. The meetings of the youth wing were mainly held in the evening and had very little political content. In fact, it was rarely much more than an excuse to meet the opposite sex, and being seventeen years old this suited me fine. I quickly became attached to a nice girl who was working in a factory, processing chickens for shops in the cities. She was a simple farming girl, pretty, and was devoted to me. For the short time that we were together, in the evenings after the meeting was over, we would walk around the town, embracing and kissing at each corner. I loved going to Party meetings!

In spite of the short time we had before the end of term, all four of us Jewish returnees completed our studies and were allowed to proceed to the last year of *Gimnázium* to study for the university entrance exam in Hungarian, history, Latin, German, maths and physics. In my physics exam I had to explain the principles of television, never imagining that I would ever possess one myself. I passed my exams with flying colours and was accepted on a university course to study for a degree in chemistry. Donning the braided *Bocskai* jacket traditional of Hungarian noblemen, we were

Liberation

paraded over the streets of the town singing *Gaudeamus igitur*, the farewell song of school leavers. I said goodbye to Orosháza. My childhood there had not been a happy one, and I was happy to leave. I was looking forward to living without parental supervision. I had joined, and felt part of, a wider Zionist community, and I saw my future clearly painted in my mind. Caught up by the pioneering spirit of the youthful, vibrant *Sómér* movement, I wanted to study and to go to Israel.

WHEN EVEN THE POETS WERE SILENT

4

University

LESS THAN two years after the war, the situation was still far from normal in Budapest. Many of the damaged houses had not been repaired, and people were living in every corner of every scrap of accommodation, even in what were otherwise almost completely derelict buildings. There was a shortage of fuel, and in many houses luxuries like central heating and lifts were just memories.

After the economic shock of the war, Hungary had suffered the worst hyperinflation in history. The government tried in vain to stop the inflation by introducing the *Adópengő*, a currency backed by a guarantee that its banknotes would be accepted as payment for tax. But the *Adópengő*, too, lost its value. At its worst, in the spring and summer of 1946, just before I arrived in Budapest, another zero was added almost daily to the *pengő*, which accordingly became meaningless. By the end, banknotes with a face value of 100,000,000,000,000,000,000 *pengő* were being issued, but by then people had started referring to the colour of the notes rather than their denomination anyway. Most people, including my father, began receiving their salary on a daily basis. As soon as he arrived home, my mother would go straight to the market and spent his entire salary on whatever she could get. One positive result of this hyperinflation was that my father was able to pay off his mortgage with small change.

In Orosháza, the everyday unit of currency became the hen's egg. Everybody trusted and accepted the hen's egg, even if it was obviously addled: after all, no one wanted to eat them. When I went to the cinema or the swimming pool, I had to take one egg with me and deposit it in a basket at the box office. Eggs could be purchased at the market, though heaven only knows why the peasants exchanged them for useless paper money. Maybe they were impressed by the large number of zeros, maybe they didn't understand or care, or maybe they couldn't alter the habits of many generations. Hyperinflation ended on August 1st, 1946, with the introduction of the Hungarian *forint* at an exchange rate of 400,000,000,000,000,000,000,000,000,000 *pengő* to one new *forint*. Though hyperinflation had been stopped by the introduction of the *forint*, the new banknotes were soon in such short supply that there was no need for any other kind of rationing. No one could afford to buy more than the absolute essentials, and often not even these.

I was accepted at Pázmány Péter University in Budapest, one of Hungary's most prestigious, named after an important Hungarian theologian of the Counter-Reformation. It had always been obvious that I would study a science: my father was a teacher of mathematics and physics and my brother István had studied the very same subjects. I liked experimenting and had a logical mind, the qualities necessary to become a scientist. Of physics and chemistry I found the latter more attractive, more modern, practical and alive with possibilities. What could I do with a physics degree in Hungary apart from become a teacher? Chemistry on the other hand seemed to offer opportunities to work within industry. I was proud to be a university student at last, and hoped that it might be some compensation to my parents for losing their eldest son.

In the Pázmány Péter University of the late 1940s, the chemistry curriculum consisted of organic, inorganic, analytical, colloidal and physical chemistry. I liked physical chemistry most and analytical least, as the latter was like learning a telephone directory by heart and besides, at the time, modern analytical instruments were unavailable so we had to do most things manually using old-fashioned ones.

Pázmány Péter University was located in central Budapest, on the left bank of the Danube just a short walk from my great aunt's apartment where I had learned of István's death not two years before. It comprised of several grand buildings, but they were old and in a very poor state of repair. As for the rest of the capital, intense house-to-house fighting had left large parts of one of Europe's finest cities in ruins, and what had survived was pockmarked with bullet-holes. Budapest's famous panoramas had been marred, the royal castle upon the hill was now in ruins, and the seven beautiful bridges across the Danube had been dynamited. Ugly, emergency pontoons formed the backdrop to the Neo-Gothic splendour of the now shell-scarred Parliament Building. Still, the city was very much alive. Trams and buses were moving, people went about their business, and even the opera house was functioning. There was a spirit of rebuilding, and of hope.

Each faculty building at Pázmány Péter University had its own laboratory, lecture hall and staffrooms, yet there were not even separate toilets for men and women, and what toilets were provided were in a shocking and unhygienic state. The university took on 120 chemistry undergraduates each year. It was a four-year course, but only about half on average finished the course and got their degrees, one of the simple reasons for this high rate of attrition being that there were far too few laboratory workbenches for the advanced classes. There were also very few textbooks in Hungarian to be had, and none of us had mastered any foreign languages, and so we had to attend lectures in person and take notes. What with spending at least thirty hours each week in the laboratory doing experiments, preparing and analysing compounds, measuring their properties, and so forth, there was very little time for anything else outside class. The one great counterbalance to the ugly environment and heavy workload was that our education was provided by the state for free. My father, a lowly civil servant, could not have paid for my university education let alone have provided me with a place of my own in the big city. Fortunately, I managed to secure a place in a rent-free student hostel run by a charity, the American Jewish Joint Distribution Committee. The winter of 1946, when I started my first year, was a severe one in Hungary, and I considered myself lucky to have a roof over my head.

The students' hostel was situated in a pleasant part of the city, next to the picturesque Danube and close to the university. Accommodation did not stretch to breakfast or an evening meal, but to have a simple cooked lunch every day was more than most of us students could hope for in those days. Coming from a relatively small agricultural community to one of the biggest cities in Europe meant making adjustments. For a start, I had never before experienced a real shortage of food. Not even during the war years, when the choice of food was restricted, had we gone hungry in Orosháza. Even in the ghettos and the labour camps I had been exceptionally fortunate never to have starved. Now, for the first time, scarcity was a pressing issue. Because of the cooked lunch we received, we generally went without breakfast, and only had to arrange some kind of a supper. This we did in a number of different ways. Sometimes one of us would receive a parcel from home, and the food would be shared by all. The trouble was that not all of us were as lucky as I, with my parents in the country supplying food regularly. But once a month we got a food parcel from the Danish Red Cross, containing margarine and coffee beans, and for several evenings after the receipt of one of these we lived on bread which we fried in the margarine.

The living accommodation in the hostel occupied the fourth and fifth floors of a large, six-storey house. There were about twenty rooms in all, with two or three students assigned to each depending on its size. The bathroom had no hot water, and neither the lift nor the heating worked. In the middle of that freezing winter, each room was provided with a paraffin heater and enough fuel to keep it going for two hours every day. Because of the cold, we dared not open the windows, and so the fumes stayed in the rooms, which, together with our clothes, forever smelled of paraffin.

I shared a room with Jóska, an art student. He was a shy boy with blonde hair, blue eyes and a face full of childhood smallpox scars, and we got on very well. We were both friendly with our neighbours, who occupied a large, corner room: there was Bandi, a down-to-earth engineering student, Pista, a maths major, and a boy nicknamed Psycho because he studied psychology. As his course progressed, Psycho would practise various psycho-analytical tests, handing out pictures of horrible-looking men and women or meaningless patterns of black spots on white paper and then explaining our psychological tendencies to us guinea pigs. It was all great fun for us, but Psycho always took it very seriously.

We were indeed a disparate group, but apart from our poverty we had one thing in common: a love of classical music. Hungary had no television broadcasts until 1957, and we didn't have the money to buy a radio. But Psycho had a wind-up gramophone and between us we owned two records—Beethoven's Fifth Symphony and the ballet music from Gounod's opera *Faust*. The needle of the gramophone was rather worn, which blotted out the high tones, but we were content to be able to listen to the lower registers alone.

Almost every evening we listened to these records, first one, then the other, then back to the first, and so on until we got tired of winding up the creaking old machine.

One might have thought that a city in ruins in the freezing winter of 1946 would have been no place for romances, but we were in our teenage years, far from home, and had an acute sense of having survived a war that had intended to wipe us out. Bandi the engineer often had some mysterious business which called him away during the evening and kept him out until late at night. He was lucky if he could catch the last tram back, which was about midnight. He was a quiet boy and kept his secret for several months until someone found out that he was, in fact, married. His wife lived with her parents, who knew nothing of the marriage and would never have approved of a student as a son-in-law. Bandi and his wife could not afford to live together, so they had to be content with making love in the parks, as did so many other young couples courting while waiting for a home of their own.

Pista the mathematician had a girlfriend with a reputation for nymphomania, who made great demands on his time and energy. They were not as shy as Bandi and his wife, and regularly borrowed one of the smaller rooms in the hostel for the afternoon. Pista got thinner and thinner as time went on, and used to beg everybody for eggs which he would eat raw in the belief that they would increase his sexual potency. Poor man—he got so nervous about his romantic liaisons that he failed his exams and never graduated.

Officially the girls should have been living on one floor of the hostel and the boys on the other, but there was no supervision and we could rearrange things as the situation demanded. It was quite usual, for instance, for friends to be put up for the night wherever they could if they had missed the last tram home, and such arrangements often meant a boy and a girl sharing a room. Even if nothing passed between them, this was very much frowned upon at the time, but it was hard to think of the social norms that had gone before as being superior to how we as survivors now decided to live our lives. Once, when Jóska was visiting his parents, a girl asked me if she could sleep in his empty bed. Little Arseplug, as she was affectionately but very crudely nicknamed for reasons that weren't clear, had cropped blonde hair, a flat chest, and a boyish look. When she had undressed, without explanation she climbed into my bed instead of Jóska's. Our affair didn't last long: she tried out practically all the boys in the hostel and ended up permanently with Psycho, who fell in love with her, analysing and re-analysing their relationship until he convinced himself that they suited each other admirably well. They got married and could finally afford a rented room of their own.

Living in such cramped conditions, it wasn't always possible to be so discreet. One evening Jóska managed to get one of the resident girls, Sári, to share his bed. Sári was a real beauty, with a cascade of black hair. When she smiled, which she often did, she revealed perfect white teeth. Every boy, myself included, courted her, but in spite of her coquettish behaviour she stubbornly resisted us all. None of us could understand why she finally chose Jóska, given his rather featureless expression and smallpox scars. I wasn't happy about playing gooseberry to their billing and cooing, but as Jóska's room-mate had no choice in the matter, even though it disturbed my sleep. Sári clearly thought that she could stop Jóska before things got too serious, a solution obviously not favoured by Jóska himself, who didn't believe her protestations of virginity. Their resulting courtship consisted of much moaning, sighing, whispering, tossing and turning, all of which would keep me awake into the early hours. I just wished that they would get it over with and be quiet afterwards. Eventually I got up, took my alarm clock, and dressed in my pyjamas went to sleep in Sári's bed in her room on the floor below.

No sooner had I fallen asleep than I was shaken awake by Sári, who was standing in her nightdress. When I refused to get out of bed for a second time, Sári tried to persuade her room-mate Zsuzsi to make room for her, but Zsuzsi too was fed up with Sári's romances.

'*Ki mint veti ágyát, úgy alussza álmát!*' she said: 'You've made your bed, now lie in it!' And she promptly turned her back and went to sleep.

The depth of that winter served to intensify our problems. The two hours we were able to keep the paraffin heater going was hardly enough to de-frost the windows, let alone keep ourselves warm. We decided to combine our fuel rations and keep one room heated for four hours instead of two rooms for two hours each. And because it was impossible to warm up the large, corner room even in four hours, everybody moved into my and Jóska's smaller room. This included not only Pista, Bandi and Psycho but also on occasion Bandi's wife, Anni, a highly intelligent but very short-sighted girl. It was too cold to make love in the park, and she now spent the occasional night with Bandi. We graciously allocated a full single bed to the married couple, while Jóska and I shared a bedstead without a mattress, which had been placed on the floor for Pista and Psycho. There was just sufficient space in the tiny room for the six of us to sleep in a single row from one wall to the other. As winter deepened, with the window continuously closed and the heater producing twice as many fumes the atmosphere became truly foul. We all had dry throats and coughed continually. Eventually by popular vote we decided to keep the window open for thirty minutes each morning, a tightrope act that balanced the icy winds with the need for fresh, healthy air.

While Bandi lived as a married man in our hostel, I myself met my wife-to-be at a Saint Mikulás feast organised by the students during that winter of my first year at the university. For all of us growing up as children, the Mikulás feast had been a time of gifts and sweets, and now as students it was an excuse to have a party. Somebody in the hostel knew a girl, Márta, who played the violin professionally and persuaded her to come and play for us. Márta was overweight, clumsy, and cross-eyed. Raised by her father and a nanny, she had learned precious little about social skills and ladylike behaviour. But Márta had brought her best friend with her. Vera was a little older than me, attractive, cheerful, animated, and smiled a great deal, and I thought it would be nice to try to persuade her to become my girlfriend. The attraction must have been mutual because Vera didn't need much persuasion: it was love at first sight for both of us. I asked Vera to visit me at the hostel, partly to show her off to the others but also to ask her to wash some of my clothes and linen. She agreed, but after the others asked her to do their laundry too she didn't come again.

The weather slowly improved. Having survived one winter in the hostel, most of us had had enough and could not face another. Bandi finished his studies, obtained his diploma, and came out into respectable society with his wife Anni as newlyweds, this time with the approval of her parents. Pista left the university and took a job in a factory a long way from Budapest. He thought this might be a way of escaping from his nymphomaniac girlfriend, but she followed him to his new abode where she persuaded him to raise poultry in the garden to ensure a continuous supply of fresh eggs. Jóska did not feel like following the example of the starving painters of Paris and gave up his art course, opting instead to study Arabic on a scholarship to Egypt, where it was much, much warmer.

Vera Faragó was a native of Budapest, her parents having moved there from the countryside, and her family's story was typical of the hardship faced by so many millions of Hungarians between the wars. Vera's father had been injured in the First World War, a soldier of just seventeen years of age, partly losing the use of his right hand and leg and thereafter only able to earn a living in low-paid jobs. The Faragó family was always poor: Vera, her parents, and her younger brother Bertalan lived in a flat consisting of a single room and a kitchen, sharing a communal toilet on the back staircase. They had no bathroom, and had to heat water on a stove to wash themselves—first the children, then the parents, all in the same water. The only shop which allowed them credit was a dairy, so milk and butter became their staple diet. Dinner consisted of bread and butter followed by watermelon in the summer, toast and tea in winter. Vera went to school in the only clothes she had, which had to be washed and ironed regularly. She had only one pair of shoes. After primary school she went to a vocational college, and graduated wearing the yellow star.

The Faragós were fortunate in receiving a regular, monthly food parcel from the Save the Children Fund addressed to Vera from a Miss Joyce Horstman who lived in Bath, England. The parcel contained the bare essentials only, like flour, sugar and rice, yet made all the difference in the world. But in spite of their financial hardship, the Faragós were a happy family. At weekends they would head out into the Buda hills beyond the city, walking all the way from home to save the meagre tram fare, and Vera naturally grew up with a love of hiking.

Vera and I would talk at length, sharing our experiences of the war. In early 1945, Vera had been called up with several other Jewish girls to work in a labour camp. One day she was marched off to a brick factory, her only pair of shoes held together with string to stop the soles from falling off. In a shoulder bag made by her mother was just a piece of bacon and a raw sugar beet she had found by the roadside. They were not allowed to stop walking, not even for the call of nature. As dusk drew in, however, by hanging back and pretending to tie their shoelaces, she managed to escape together with another girl, got home, and went to sleep. The next morning she was awoken by a group of men from the violently anti-Semitic Arrow Cross Party who were rounding up any Jewish men who had not yet been called up to the labour battalions. The men who came for Vera's father were mere boys, not yet even twenty, in green shirts and sporting submachine guns. Vera's father had just time enough to pick up her discarded shoulder bag. He was marched westwards, and managed to send back a postcard to his wife with the simple message 'Look after the children' upon it. He was never heard of again. His disability, suffered serving Hungary before his captors had even been born, meant that he couldn't walk fast enough, and in all probability he was shot. He had been forty-eight years old.

After her father was taken away, Vera had had to hide out with her mother and Bertalan. The caretaker of their previous apartment block, a gentile, offered them sanctuary in his home while Vera's mother set about obtaining false identity papers. Armed with these, the three of them moved into an empty flat, claiming that they had lived in another town where their home had been destroyed by Allied bombing. They managed to stay there until the end of the war, their Jewishness unsuspected. Only later did they realise quite how lucky they had been to survive in a Budapest ruled in those last months of the war by Arrow Cross Party, whose contribution to the Nazi war effort was to kill all the Jews they could find, some 15,000. They hadn't even bothered to bury their victims, letting many of the bodies simply float away on the Danube. That beautiful river was said to have run red after the execution of Jews on its banks. Their abandoned shoes still line the promenade, cast in iron now as a memorial, some large, some small as if worn by a child, and visitors lay flowers in them.

But even after the Nazis and the Arrow Cross had been defeated there was little relief. The Soviet Red Army began to loot Budapest, deporting thousands of men to Russia and raping women. When Russian soldiers entered their house Vera's mother would make her lie still on the floor, put a blanket over her, and sit on her as if she were a box. Her brother Bertalan was detained by the Soviets, and only escaped from a POW camp because he looked even younger than his sixteen years. Then there was the shortage of food. Like most residents of Budapest, Vera's mother had taken some of her most cherished possessions and gone by train into the country to barter. In the meantime Vera and Bertalan had taken on menial work at the home of an elderly couple in exchange for rations. When life finally returned to normal after the end of the war, the company which had employed her father offered Vera a secretarial job, and she accepted. Later, Vera received a modicum of compensation from the Hungarian government for the persecution she had suffered, and a laughably small sum for the killing of her father. She gave it to charity.

When I met her at the Saint Mikulás feast, Vera was still working as a secretary and was living with her widowed mother and Bertalan. We spent more and more time

University

together, mainly at their home. At night, when it was time for me to return to the hostel, I would leave Vera's apartment to catch the last tram, paying the concierge a small sum to open the door to let me out. Occasionally, and I must confess intentionally, I stayed a little too late and had to spend the night at Vera's. Her mother watched Vera's honour like a hawk, and I had to sleep separately in the living room.

Vera and I got engaged, and I bought two gold rings on the black market. There was no engagement party: we considered it a private affair. Later I took Vera to Orosháza to meet my parents. They gave their consent to our eventual marriage on condition that we wait until I had finished my studies. They should have known me better. I stayed for eighteen months in the student hostel and then, at the ripe old age of twenty and halfway through my second year, I got married. I completely ignored my parents' proviso, and waited until I was twenty only because this was the age at which I no longer needed their consent. Some of Vera's relatives too were concerned about my youth and lack of prospects. They predicted that eventually she would be most unhappy and would bitterly regret her decision to marry me; fortunately, we proved them wrong.

But my parents' concern was not unreasonable: marrying could easily have led to a child, and having a child while studying at university would in all likelihood have meant giving up my studies to find a low-paid job. There was at that time no reliable birth control available in Hungary other than the condom, and condoms were near impossible to buy, probably because the Party wanted to encourage families to have more children and so simply removed all the condoms from the shops. Once, indeed, I had been in a chemist's shop when a young man came in and with great embarrassment showed a letter from his university to the sales assistant.

'I'm a research chemist,' he said, 'conducting experiments on osmosis, for which I need a semi-permeable membrane, and the ideal material would be a condom.' Yet in spite of his letter, which guaranteed that the condom would not be used for anything else but scientific research, still he was refused.

Apart from our birth certificates, and others showing that we were both residents of Budapest, Vera and I also had to have a medical examination to prove that we weren't suffering from any infectious diseases. These formalities complete, official permission was granted to marry, and on the big day we went to the register office taking two witnesses with us. One was a friend from our hiking group, an engineering student named Laci; the other was Márta, the violinist who had been instrumental in bringing us together. We were married by a lady registrar in a civil ceremony, the only form which in Hungary at the time could create a valid marriage. On leaving the room, the usher congratulated first me and then Márta, probably because she had the more expensive-looking dress on.

As was the normal practice for Jews in secular Hungary, the civil wedding was followed by a religious ceremony in the local synagogue, within walking distance of our flat. My observance of even the most rudimentary Jewish customs had by this time waned to such a degree that I wasn't personally interested in a Jewish ceremony, but I agreed at the urging of Vera's mother. To show my youthful disdain for authority and custom, at first I refused to wear a tie and only at the last moment did I put one on. My wife wore a pink dress made by the tailor Toma *bácsi* and his wife, our old neighbours in Orosháza. Clutching a bunch of carnations she looked beautiful, but knowing me, I probably didn't tell her. My mother cried so loudly that a family friend, a doctor, was obliged to lead her outside. At the end of the service I stamped on a glass as tradition required. The reception in my mother-in-law's flat was basic. She herself had baked some humble *pogácsa*, a snack not unlike a savoury English scone. There was no wine for the guests, let alone champagne, but I had concocted liqueurs from ethanol, strong black coffee, vanilla powder, and sugar. The ethanol, otherwise unavailable, I had obtained by forging doctors' prescriptions, inventing fictitious titles, learning the correct style of language to adopt, and always presenting them at different pharmacies. After maturing for a few weeks, those liqueurs were perfectly drinkable.

We received two wedding presents. One, a considerable sum of money from a rich cousin of my wife, was unbeknownst to us handed over to my mother-in-law, who used it to erect a memorial stone for her parents and Vera's late father. The other, from a family friend, paid for a two-day break in a small guesthouse outside Budapest. We went on this honeymoon the day after the wedding, but on our first night as man and wife slept separately so as not to disturb my brother-in-law Bertalan, who was also living in the flat. He and Vera's mother both left early next morning, discreetly giving us time together before catching our bus. On her return, it was said, my mother-in-law took the stained sheet from our bed and proudly showed it to the neighbours.

Our room in the guesthouse smelled of disinfectant, and the bed sagged to such a degree that we almost hit the floor when we lay in it. In the end we laid the mattress on the ground. When we drew the curtains, they fell down. We had no bathroom, and found a chamber pot under our bed. We were young and shy, and had our supper in our room to avoid the other guests. But despite the privations we enjoyed our romantic honeymoon, and then on our return moved into the same cramped, two-room apartment in

Kresz Géza *utca* in which Vera's mother and brother lived. Soon afterwards, Bertalan moved out and married a Jewish girl who like Vera had lost her father during the war.

On the first floor of a four-storey house, with windows looking into a shaded courtyard and a corridor running in front of it, the flat was so dingy that we had to keep the lights on throughout the day. Only one room had a stove, fed with coal carried laboriously up from the basement. The hot water in the bathroom was most unreliable and inconvenient, and instead we washed ourselves in a basin with water heated in the kitchen. The flat provided little comfort and even less privacy. For our first two years of marriage we slept on a settee which opened into a single bed at night. My mother-in-law, who slept in the smaller of the two rooms, had to walk past us if she wanted to use the bathroom.

'Couldn't you at least knock on the door first if you want to come through our room?' I asked her once.

'Why should I knock?' she retorted. 'This is my apartment, isn't it?' She was right, of course, but it didn't help our relationship. No matter how we agreed to arrange matters, I remained an impoverished student sharing a tiny flat with my wife and her mother, in the middle of a city still bearing the deep scars of a war and an economic crisis.

Vera took up a post in the Ministry of Chemical Industry. Every month she handed over her salary to her mother, the head of the family as far as finances were concerned. Rent was negligible, but food was very expensive, and it was not even easy to provide a dinner every day. I continued to eat at the hostel's canteen, and started going there for Sunday lunch as well. At least the food was better than my mother-in-law's, which consisted mainly of pasta with onion sauce or, as a meat substitute, patties of mashed potato and egg, fried in lard.

University

We were unhappy with our home, but there seemed no hope of securing better accommodation until one day there was a knock on our door. One of our neighbours, an old woman, lived in a two-room apartment across the corridor, one room of which she let to a female lodger. Her apartment looked out onto the street, which meant that it was much lighter than ours. The lodger had had a bitter argument with the old woman and had decided to leave. We did not even need to pay rent to 'the old witch', she explained to us, as by law she was only entitled to one room. So Vera and I quickly applied to the local council and, because no other applicants were aware of the empty room, got it to ourselves. 'The old witch' gave in, and our relationship proved amicable. We found our new room heavenly, in spite of the meagre furnishing we were able to bring with us. Only now, as the sunshine streamed into the room, did we realise quite how unhealthy the other flat was. Even its unpleasant, musty smell had become so pervasive that we had grown used to it. Here, though, everything smelled fresh, almost as if we were living in a flower garden.

After staging what amounted to a democratic putsch in the election of 1949, the Hungarian Communist Party swiftly dispatched any remaining opposition. Rákosi, its ruthless leader, quickly established a personal dictatorship over the country along the lines of his Soviet mentor, Stalin. Rákosi was a short, bald man, an atheist who had repudiated his Jewish birth, and who had spent the war years in the Soviet Union.

The Communist Party now began to rid itself of those members who didn't have the right ideological profile, or who came from the wrong social class, or were inactive. They organised meetings where they discussed every existing member in detail, one by one. The leadership read out a summary of their assessment of the individual, and opened the floor for discussion. After everybody had said what they wanted, an 'open' vote decided their fate. If approved, they stayed in the Party. If there were doubts, but not too serious, they might be demoted to a lesser form of membership. The rest were expelled, and had to surrender their membership cards and leave the meeting at once. When my turn came, Péter Gyenes, one of the older students and a committed Communist, made a speech bringing up my Zionist past, in spite of the fact that this had been very well known when the Party had recruited me. By now, though, any form of Zionism was considered incompatible with Communism, and I was expelled. I wasn't exactly happy with my expulsion at the time: I might not have been a flag-waving Communist, but I certainly didn't want to be labelled petty bourgeois. As it turned out, expulsion was the best thing that could have happened to me. There was no other way to leave the Party: you couldn't just decide that you had had enough and wanted to leave, and resigning was not an option.

After the declaration of the People's Republic of Hungary in August of 1949, the economic structure of the country changed dramatically. The Kossuth Coat of Arms on the national flag was replaced by sheaves of wheat and a hammer, below the shining red star of Communism. Factories with more than one hundred workers were nationalised. One morning, simultaneously and without any warning, a representative from the Communist-controlled trade union went into the office of the owner or managing director of every factory or business and ordered him to leave, taking nothing more than his coat. Houses with more than six rooms were confiscated without compensation. (Our home in Orosháza had only four rooms, so we were not yet personally affected.) In a second wave of regulations, small businesses with more than six workers were also nationalised, and the rest, all the way down to the grocer on the corner, were put under pressure to join a cooperative by all sorts of practical restrictions. In the end, only a humble cobbler repairing shoes in a basement was able to remain independent of state control. The result, inevitably, was disinterested employees who didn't care about their work or their customers, and politically motivated managers with minimal qualifications and a job for life who didn't know or care about running businesses efficiently. New ministries were formed to head up major industries such as mining, steel, chemicals and so on. Managers were required to meet the political demands of government central planning, with technical targets motivated by the ideological considerations of the Party leadership, but were forced to rely on their technical staff for day-to-day operations. Because there was a great deal of mistrust between the two, the economy of the country suffered. Only a handful of capitalists could see the writing on the wall and had the courage and the means to escape to the West.

It was in the year or so after my marriage to Vera that these great political shifts took place, and very soon they began to affect every aspect of our lives. Toward the end of my time at Pázmány Péter University (the Communists now replaced the theologian Pázmány's name with that of Loránd Eötvös, inventor of an instrument used to measure the density of rock strata) we were obliged to undergo indoctrination in Marxist theory. We waded through the *History of the Soviet Communist Party*, allegedly written by Stalin himself, along with many other titles such as *Anti-Dühring*, Friedrich Engels' polemical defence of Karl Marx. More interested in Marx's internationalism now than in the Hungarian patriotism which had stirred me as a child, I found the theory good, desirable even. The

Zionist *Sómér* movement I had joined had after all been little short of explicitly Communist. I remained a sympathiser of the Hungarian Communist Party, but no longer an activist. In practical terms this meant participating in a few 'spontaneous' (that is to say, meticulously planned) demonstrations, like carrying the flag on May Day, but that was all. Gradually however I became disillusioned with the Party or, to be precise, with its leadership. The leaders formed a new elite—indeed, a new ruling class, just like the one they claimed to have overturned. Politically suitable individuals from a working class or peasant background secured leading jobs irrespective of their ability, to the inevitable detriment of Hungary as a whole. As the Party used intimidation to underwrite its spurious legitimacy, disappearances engendered a state of permanent fear in the population, typified by a popular saying of the time: we were, we joked, glad to find that the person knocking on the door early in the morning was only the milkman. People could disappear for the most trivial of reasons. When not at the university, by way of example, I spent most of my time in the nearby city library, which was heated and quiet and boasted the most beautiful frescos. One day I watched as an old man in a threadbare suit and red bow tie, after sheepishly looking round, tore a number of pages from a library book. Thinking it unacceptable, I challenged him.

'Please, look at the name of the author. I wrote this book,' he explained, and showed me his ID.

'Then why are you damaging it?' I asked.

'I don't know if you will understand.' He hesitated. 'You see, it's about politics, and on a few points I've changed my mind. I am afraid that if somebody discovers what I once said, I might be prosecuted.'

'Why don't you write a correction?'

University

'That would be even worse,' he said, on the verge of tears. 'It would only draw attention to me. I just want to be left alone.'

So I did.

Vera and I couldn't enjoy our new, sunlit apartment on Kresz Géza *utca* for long, because in 1950 I got my degree and had to begin work. Under Communism we didn't need to apply for a job: a central organisation distributed workers to whatever vacancies there were, a decision in which we had no say. As a graduate chemist, I was appointed to an oil refinery on the banks of the Danube a few hours' journey northwest of Budapest. The refinery at Almásfüzitő had belonged to the Vacuum Oil Company, a predecessor of the US oil company Mobil, but by now it had been nationalised. I would have preferred to stay in Budapest, but couldn't pull the right strings.

I had reached an important milestone, and had to make a decision: now that I had completed my degree, should I emigrate to Israel as I had planned, or give up the idea and stay in Hungary? Different identities—Hungarian, Jew, husband, son, scientist, idealist—each of them important to me in different ways, had been competing for my attention. I had promised my parents I would finish my education before emigrating, but in the four years I had spent at university my life and my outlook had changed. My links with the Zionist movement and its ideas had gradually weakened. The State of Israel had only been independent for two years, and already it had had to fight a bitter war of survival against its Arab neighbours. Many of its policies I found chauvinistic. Meanwhile, time had proved a great healer for me: Hungary under Communist rule had suppressed anti-Semitism, and I had grown used to life there. The language and the customs were all second nature to me, and Vera's family wanted me to stay. Having a university diploma had allowed me entry into a rather privileged class, and I no longer fancied the hard life of a farmer on a *kibuc* in Israel. Though I was no longer the devoted patriot I had been as a child in Orosháza, I was quite sure that the persecution of Jews would not be repeated. So I envisaged staying in Hungary. I didn't consider going anywhere else. It was not just that the border had become physically impassable, choked with barbed wire and landmines, but I knew very little about the wider world, spoke only a little German, and certainly didn't want to live in any country that spoke the same language the Nazis had.

Judaism as a religion and a cultural tradition was not something I cherished any more. Whereas before the war I had fasted when required, and had partaken in religious festivals such as *pészah*, I was no longer a believer but an agnostic. It had been not so much my scientific education as my education in Communism which had led me down that path. I could see the excesses of religion, the unexplainable punishment of the innocent, and thought most religious rules ridiculous and arbitrarily incompatible with other religions. Besides, I was a married man now, looking forward rather optimistically to an interesting career in chemistry and starting a family. I decided this was the right time to make a clean break with the past. I would stay in Hungary, but forge a new life for myself.

My decision made, and my motivations clear in my head, I had actively to try to assimilate. As a first step I changed my family name from the obviously Jewish Platschek to the eminently Hungarian Pogány. It had long been customary amongst Jewish Hungarians to adopt a name which was a direct translation of their original one: so Weisz became Fehér, and Schwarz became Fekete. If the name couldn't be translated, they chose one which started with the same letter: Kohn became Kovács, Frankle became Faragó, and so on. Pogány was short and meant 'pagan', which appealed to me. It would mean a new start as a secular Hungarian, suppressing the Jewish identity which had caused me so much suffering. Yet still I knew that the majority of Hungarians would instinctively sense my Jewishness even without a yellow star and a Jewish surname. The humiliation of my treatment at the hands of my own country had irrevocably marked me out in my own mind as different from the rest of the population. I did not feel that I myself could ever fully integrate into Hungarian society, but I hoped that my children, if I had any, would be more readily accepted. I had already decided to tell them about my life, but not to bring them up as Jews. None of these were easy decisions. I talked them over and over with Vera, but in the end we decided that the chances of the past repeating itself were small, that it would be safe to stay in Hungary, and that my plans were for the best. I attended my last exam, a compulsory one on political studies, with my suitcase beside me, my intention being to catch the train to work at the oil refinery once it was over. The professor, a good Communist but a poor scholar, was not very happy with my performance. He looked at my suitcase.

'I suppose industry needs you, comrade,' he admitted, and entered a 'pass' in my book. I sent a telegram home to my parents telling them the good news, and boarded my train. I was György Pogány, husband of Vera, and soon-to-be head of the process control laboratory at the Almásfüzitő oil refinery.

WHEN EVEN THE POETS WERE SILENT

5
Almásfüzitő

THE END of my time at university and the beginning of my life as an industrial chemist coincided with great social upheavals, as Hungary began to be thoroughly communised. People began habitually to address one another as *elvtárs*—'comrade'. The large farming estates were confiscated and their owners expelled, the land turned into what amounted to state-owned agricultural factories. Smallholders were made to surrender their land to large collective farms on the example of the Russian *kolkhoz*, taking with them all their animals and machinery. Peasants had to work in teams, meeting prescribed production targets and receiving a salary, mainly in kind. With Hungary's agriculture collectivised, food shortages appeared once again. Much of the country's production was exported to the Soviet Union, which had to be 'compensated' for war damages—after all, Hungary had fought alongside Nazi Germany—and we also had to pay for industrialisation. 'We have to secure our future and the future of our children,' they wrote in the state newspaper, *Szabad Nép*. What they didn't write was that we had to toil even harder to offset enormous state inefficiency. The Party was forced to admit to the existence of shortages, but blamed it not on their system but on 'reactionary elements', who were said to be hoarding food. We all knew who these reactionary elements were supposed to be—the *kuláks*, or wealthy peasants. *Szabad Nép* would publish photographs of a sack of flour or potatoes, apparently found by the police in the homes of these *kuláks* after their homes had been searched, and under the picture would be a formulaic caption: 'Our watchful and diligent police searched the house of the *kulák* and found hidden in his pantry a sack full of potatoes. On interrogation he confessed to his crime of trying to create a shortage of food and thereby instigate disturbances.'

The authorities might have been counting on the fact that many city dwellers didn't appreciate that peasants had for countless generations subsisted by storing and eating their own produce. Peasants didn't buy potatoes from the greengrocer: they kept them in their pantry. The *kuláks* would be duly arrested and their potatoes confiscated, but of course the shortages remained. To anybody who had suffered under Nazism, it was readily apparent that the scapegoating was still with us, only now the focus of its target had changed from Jews to *kuláks*.

Food rationing was re-introduced, but in practice we didn't even get what was allowed on the ration cards: 250g of bread a day and 200g of fresh meat and 100g of sausage or such like, a week. Other products—cooking fat, flour, sugar, soap and more—were also rationed, and long queues formed in front of shops that had anything desirable to sell. Whenever people noticed a queue forming they would first join it and only then ask somebody what was on sale. Often the rest of the queue would be unsure, but nobody dared surrender his place to go and find out. It didn't matter anyway, for anything—sugar, sausages, bread, flour, meat, whatever—was equally welcome. Occasionally somebody might try to jump the queue using all sorts of excuses, but every one, except perhaps a pregnant woman or a nursing mother, was forced by the crowd to go to the back of the queue. There were rumours that for a fee you could rent a baby.

The great model for Hungary's agricultural development was the Soviet Union and its guru of 'agronimism', Trofim Lysenko. Lysenko was obsessed with his pseudo-scientific theory of the inheritability of acquired characteristics, an idea that chimed nicely with Communism's doomed plans to create a utopian society. Much effort and money was spent trying to grow sub-tropical crops such as citrus fruits, rice and cotton in Hungary's obviously unsuitable climate, but, of course, none of them thrived. The fundamental problem was that political orthodoxy outweighed objective truth in every sphere. Even before the advent of Communism, my father had begun to give educational talks on popular science in Orosháza's community hall, mainly to local peasant men. Now, under Communism, he mentioned one day during a talk on modern agricultural techniques that the best wheat in the world was produced in Canada, and was promptly rebuked by the local Party Secretary: 'You are surely mistaken, *elvtárs*. As everybody knows, the best wheat is produced in the Soviet Union.' My father didn't argue, but thanked the Comrade Secretary for correcting him.

Even visually, Hungary now changed. Pictures of Communist Party General Secretary Rákosi appeared throughout the country, on buildings, in offices, and on the streets. He was always depicted smiling, whether talking to children, visiting factories or agricultural workers, examining their produce as though he were a real expert.... Statue after statue was erected in praise of the Soviet Red Army and Stalin. A great deal of confusion resulted from renaming the streets after Communist leaders, both past and present, and of all nationalities. No new maps were printed, and so we had to guess where, for example, Rosenberg *utca* was. What was its name before they changed it? Many people couldn't even pronounce some of the foreign names, like that of the Albanian dictator Enver Hoxha. According to one joke, a horse collapsed and died on Enver Hoxha *utca*. The first policeman to arrive, after several unsuccessful attempts to write down the name of the street, asked the owner of the dead animal: 'Would you mind dragging it over to Paprika *utca*?' According to another popular joke of the day, an old man from out of town stopped a passer-by to ask the way to Andrássy *út*.

'Don't use that name!' said the passer-by. 'It's Sztálin *út* now!' So the old man continued on his way until he stopped another passer-by to ask directions to the Chain Bridge.

'Don't use the old name of the bridge!' he answered. 'It's Red Army Bridge now! If you say that once more, you could end up in jail!' The old man, worried by now, carried on to the shore of the Danube, where he was spotted by a Soviet officer who shouted at him.

'Hey, *elvtárs*, what do you think you're doing?'

'Nothing,' replied the old man. 'Just admiring the Volga....'

As the machinery of Communist propaganda became more pervasive and more efficient, gradually every aspect of our worldview fell under its sway. The Hungarian Communist Party unconditionally supported all other Communist countries against all capitalist ones. Money was regularly collected to help the victims of imperialist aggression in places like North Korea, and we all had to contribute. Once I received 100 *forint* as a reward for a small invention which saved the refinery some energy, and I offered it as a contribution to help North Korea's struggle against the South. Whether it ever reached Pyongyang, I can't say. There was nothing I could have bought with it anyway. Non-aligned African and Arab countries were courted, and some African students were given a free education in Hungary. The idea of a Greater Hungary, which had so fired my patriotic zeal as a child, was suppressed: the parts lopped off Hungary after the First World War were now occupied by Romania and Czechoslovakia, who were our friends. But the world beyond the Communist bloc was full of warmongers bent

Almásfüzitő

on destroying us. Such paranoia should have reminded me of my grandmother and her stories of wolves, but we had no information except what the Party told us, and we didn't know any better.

New songs abounded, all composed to encourage production and conformity. One popular theme was work, typified by such lyrics as 'the golden sun shines on the happy harvesters!' The songwriter had clearly never witnessed harvesters toiling in the blazing summer heat. Another common theme was the struggle of the proletariat against reactionary forces: 'The old regime has to die and we shall build a new one!' Songs like these were broadcast almost non-stop on *Kossuth Rádió*, and through loudspeakers by the roadsides and on street corners in every village. We learned the words, and sang them while marching on parades and demonstrations. As the Party tried to replace Hungarian patriotism with the internationalism of Karl Marx, the century-old national anthem *Himnusz*, which began with the patriotic 'O Lord, bless the nation of Hungary!' was replaced by the *Internationale*, which began with the rather bleaker 'Stand up, you damned of the earth!' We were required to sing the *Internationale* at the end of every public meeting, clenching our fists at the last line 'and tomorrow the whole world will become one nation,' when everybody shouted 'Freedom, comrades!'

All media were owned by the state, and all news was centrally edited and tightly controlled. There were two daily newspapers, the Party organ *Szabad Nép*, or *The Free People*, and the trade unions' *Népszava*, *The People's Voice*, plus a handful of weeklies. One of these was the satirical *Lúdas Matyi*, which took its rather odd but eminently suitable title—*Matyi the Goose-Boy*—from a Hungarian folk-tale in which a goose-seller outsmarts his cruel feudal lord. *Lúdas Matyi* had the occasional privilege of criticising official mishaps, though generally only those where a low-ranking individual could be scapegoated. But most of the criticism in the Communist press was directed outward, at 'the enemy'—old capitalists, landowners, Churchill with his cigar, and Yugoslav's ruler Tito, the 'chained dog of the imperialists'. With practice, Hungarians became adept at working out what the official view of an event was going to be before it was even announced. We learned to read between the lines, looking not for what was published but for what had been left out.

To ensure that everybody toed the correct ideological line, the practice of 'self-criticism' was adopted. We had to admit our various mistakes, promise not to repeat them, and hope for forgiveness. After each confession the stage was set for a round of criticism by Party members, and then it was usual practice for the 'culprit' to ask for help from the Party, who could steer them in the right direction. It all brought to mind the Spanish Inquisition. Even General Secretary Rákosi did this, though in his case it was nothing more than a way of excusing a change in policy or justifying a purge of political enemies. 'It was a mistake of mine to trust Comrade X for so long,' he would confess, 'and not to recognise his true colours.' Reading between the lines, of course, Comrade X had fallen foul of Rákosi or Stalin and would soon be no more. If we had no sin to confess, we had to invent one, because self-criticism was expected from everyone, and every now and then had to be done before an assembled meeting or the head of the personnel department.

'Last Tuesday I was three minutes late to work,' I might confess. 'As a leader, I should set a good example to my workers, so I promise to be on time in the future.' Or perhaps: 'I missed the meeting organised to support the struggle of North Korea against the imperialist South because I had a headache. I should have realised how important this meeting was, and should have taken an aspirin and still attended.' People in positions of authority were from time to time required to confess their mistakes—being late with plans, not making use of a waste material, using too much energy, or, for intellectuals such as the writer György Lukács, such basic 'errors' as espousing democracy.

Self-criticism was one of those aspects of life that we couldn't make out a reason for. Did they want to find out something which would otherwise have remained a secret? Was forgiveness automatic if it had been admitted before it was found out by other means, or did they prosecute the guilty even in spite of a confession? These things were far from clear, and for this reason people were very reluctant to confess anything important.

And so it went on. At just the same time that I was realising I had broken the final links with the Jewish traditions of my birth, Communism was becoming a new religion. The Party wanted to organise every aspect of our lives from cradle to grave, even our thoughts. And looking back on it, what is most frightening is that they almost succeeded. Why did the proud Hungarian people tolerate this? Why was there no popular uprising against such a repressive system? After all, very few people had genuinely wanted Hungary to become a Marxist state. The sad truth is that brainwashing works, that humans instinctively take the easiest path through life, and that fear is a powerful tool. We grumbled and complained about shortages, accommodation, and poor living standards, but we were less good at identifying the real source of all our problems and usually blamed individuals rather than the system. Hungary had jumped into Communism straight from fascism with no real experience of democracy, and we couldn't make any useful comparison.

For their part, the secret police force the ÁVH maintained a tight grip on us. Important and well-known dissidents were prosecuted in show trials; ordinary people disappeared, interned or executed without charge. What was worse, we were expected not to inquire what had happened to them or what they were suspected of. If you stuck your nose in, you too fell under suspicion. So we didn't ask questions. We lived from day to day, the best way we could in the circumstances, with one aim—to survive. In spite of all the difficulties, we just made the best of the bad hand we had been dealt. It made us appreciate simple pleasures all the more, like walking in the hills, swimming in the Danube, or reading a good book. Healthcare and education were free, rent was negligible, a job was for life, and it is all too easy to become infantilised and afraid of change. It is human nature to seek happiness under the most unpleasant conditions, as well as to hope that the future will be kinder.

Life in Budapest was hard after the war, and only grew harder under Communism, but things were even worse in the god-forsaken industrial town of Almásfüzitő where I started my professional career. Almásfüzitő pretty much consisting of nothing beyond an oil refinery and, close by, an East German-built plant which processed bauxite—the only raw material Hungary possessed—into aluminium oxide for industry. Almásfüzitő was not a healthy place to be. The oil refinery gave off a foul smell, while the aluminium plant emitted a vast amount of white powder that settled upon everything for miles around. Both had chimneys belching plumes of smoke that acted as a landmark for the town.

Almásfüzitő lay on the southern shore of the Danube, which in northwest Hungary formed the frontier with Czechoslovakia. The foreshore was wooded, and home to a rookery which made a great deal of noise before it settled down for the night. Even though we were both part of the Soviet bloc, no traffic was allowed between the two countries and the nearest bridge, which had been destroyed by the retreating Germans, had not been rebuilt. The nearest town, Komárom, a few kilometres upstream, was now divided in two by the river. There was a railway station in Almásfüzitő, and the main street had a few shops, but there was hardly anything in them worth buying. In Budapest I had grown used to the cultural opportunities a capital city provided; in Almásfüzitő there were none, not even a cinema. The only source of entertainment was a radio which occasionally broadcast classical music in between propaganda and gypsy music. To read, there were copies of *Szabad Nép* and a few books. In comparison to Almásfüzitő, my home town of Orosháza now seemed like a veritable metropolis.

The assistant personnel manager showed me my quarters, a room in a large accommodation block next to the refinery that was home to most of the senior employees. We all had to be available if called upon any time of the day or night, and needed to live in close proximity. My room had an iron bed, a table, two wooden chairs, a wardrobe, a sink and a hotplate.

'You see comrade,' the assistant personnel manager said, 'there is everything here you can possibly need. The Party is taking good care of you.'

From his tone, I could detect a degree of envy. 'What about the bathroom?' I asked. He pointed toward the end of the corridor, to a communal bathroom and toilet. The accommodation was primitive, but at least it provided some privacy. A few weeks later, at her request, my wife was transferred to the refinery, where she began work as a statistician, and so there were two of us living in my little room.

We got a hot meal in the canteen every day, a single course usually consisting of some starchy base like pasta or potatoes, with gravy or some jam or soft cheese, and occasionally an egg. There was no fruit or vegetables, and very little protein. Everything was served on aluminium plates and eaten with aluminium cutlery, cheap, ugly and unappetising. The aluminium coffee spoon had a hole drilled through it, so it couldn't be used for anything else and nobody would be tempted to steal it. There was drinking water from a tap, and an aluminium cup was chained to the tap for those who wanted a drink. We were no thieves, but ordinary people were not trusted by the Party leadership.

Other than that one canteen meal, we sourced our own food as best we could. The Danube, right on our doorstep, provided us now and again with fish. One of my neighbours, a skilled angler, occasionally presented us with a freshwater carp, a rare luxury. A butcher came from the nearest town once a week with part of a cow or pig's carcass to distribute. We queued up in front of his temporary shop with our ration cards, and received a small piece, about 100g per person. If we were lucky, there was meat on it, if not, we got a piece of bone, skin, fat or some other inedible part. Most of the decent meat probably ended up on the black market, and we had to supplement our food by buying on that same black market. I didn't have to travel far: several young peasants worked in the refinery to earn a little extra. Their parents were members of local collective farms, and during the day they helped out by working on the private strip of land the state allowed them to cultivate for themselves. By night, they worked in the refinery. One, an 'analyst', worked for me in the lab. He was about twenty-five years old, thin as a rake, and smelled of garlic. He used to come in for the night shift so tired after a day's work on the land that he regularly fell asleep. He often brought with him a basket of food—eggs, cheese, ham and sausages—to sell. To me it was a cornucopia, and I used to buy whatever I could afford from him. It was rather expensive, and I have no idea what he did with the money. One day, he took a sausage from his basket and handed it to me. It had an unappetising purple colour instead of the usual red, and was soft to the touch, freshly made rather than cured and smoked as would have been normal. I lifted it to my nose; it had a strange smell.

'Horsemeat,' he admitted after some hesitation. Their pig wasn't yet heavy enough to be killed, he said. Hungarians don't eat horsemeat, but perhaps one of the horses on the collective farm had died from overwork. It was a little sweet, in spite of the spices used to camouflage its taste, but it had to do. Vera cooked it for me in a traditional potato stew, but refused to eat any herself.

I had no direct knowledge of industry, but from the propaganda I had been exposed to I had gained the impression that it was the beating heart of Communism. I assumed that everybody was either a Communist or a sympathiser, and at first greeted everyone I met with the clenched-fist salute and a 'Freedom, comrade!'. This was indeed welcomed by Bognár *elvtárs*, the general manager, who before Communism had worked as a joiner. The first time we met he was sitting in the nicely appointed office of the former director of the Vacuum Oil Company, behind a huge mahogany desk on which were a large ashtray, full of cigarette butts, and a statuette of Lenin. Behind him, on the wall, were portraits of Stalin, Rákosi, and Marx.

Bognár *elvtárs* was a zealous Communist, but didn't trust Mr Zakar, the technical director, on whom he nevertheless had to rely for advice on all technical matters. There was no way he would have been able to make the simplest decision on his own, and so he was forever afraid of making a mistake, of falling into a trap set for him by unseen enemies, or of trusting the experts too much. He was under a great deal of stress, and his nervousness was visible to everyone. He couldn't keep his eyes steady for more than a few seconds, he chain-smoked continually, and he spoke in short, disconnected sentences.

'Welcome, comrade,' he greeted me. 'This factory needs you. You studied at university. Great privilege. You can now pay it back. Work hard. Freedom, comrade!'

And so the interview was over. Later I was shown into the office of Mr Zakar the technical director, who looked at me but didn't return my greeting. He was from a devout Roman Catholic family, and one of his brothers had been the private secretary to Cardinal Mindszenty who only the previous year had been sentenced to life imprisonment for opposing the Communist Party. His very appearance commanded a respect that was not due to an apparatchik like Bognár.

'What is glycol?' Mr Zakar asked me out of the blue. 'And what is the structure of citric acid?' For the next half hour he examined my knowledge of organic chemistry. He showed no emotion, and didn't give me any feedback, so I could only hope he was satisfied. It didn't matter in any case, since he couldn't sack me no matter how bad a chemist I was. After that first interview I had little contact with him or, indeed, with any of the rest of the technical staff. There was no teamwork, no co-ordination, and scant communication. Creativity and original thinking gave way to authoritarianism.

I met the chief engineer, who simply replied 'good afternoon' to my 'Freedom, comrade!' Finally the penny dropped: not everyone in the refinery was a Communist; in fact, they were very much in the minority. So the next person I met, a lean young man holding a bunch of papers

Almásfüzitő

under one arm, I greeted with a hearty 'good afternoon!' only to find out that he was the secretary of the refinery's branch of the Communist Party.

The oil refinery in Almásfüzitő refined crude oil into petrol, diesel, paraffin, heating oil, and by-products such as bitumen. A siren loud enough to wake the dead sounded every morning at 5.30am, and at six the day shift started. I found it especially painful, for it reminded me of the air raids during the war. There was just enough time to wash myself in the sink, get dressed, and walk over to the refinery without any breakfast. Samples for analysis arrived at the laboratory every two hours, and each time they arrived I had to report the results of the previous samples that had been brought in. I had to plan every step and every movement in order not to fall behind. My on-the-job training was practical, and started with me learning the ropes by cleaning the used glassware. Eventually, working my way through the various laboratory roles, I took over from the shift foreman and performed his job for four weeks. It was a hard but useful period of training, very much throwing me in at the deep end, after which I became the leader of the production control unit at the refinery's central laboratory.

I enjoyed my work, and in actual fact felt grateful to the state for having helped me to secure such a responsible post, which stretched me and developed my abilities. Still a Party sympathiser, I accepted a job as editor of the refinery's 'wall journal'. Every place of employment had one of these, essentially a pin-board, and every month an appointed worker such as myself would collect what were rather meaningless articles by Party members. They were of little original value, all repeats of popular slogans, Party policies, and encouragements to work harder. If there was extra space on the board, I filled it in with cuttings from *Szabad Nép*.

The laboratory had an overall manager, Konc *úr*, a chemist with vast experience but few 'people skills'. He was always to be seen running about nervously in the same old badly fitting khaki suit, busy with administration. He was a serious man, but on my first day he told me a joke, probably the only one he knew: 'What is the difference between an industrial chemist and a biochemist? The industrial chemist first washes his hands, then pisses. The biochemist first pisses, then washes his hands.' He was quite right.

Working under Konc *úr* was a female chemist doing special assignments for the technical director. She was tall and slim with blond hair, always immaculately dressed under her lab-coat, and she went around in a cloud of perfume so you could always tell when she was about even if you didn't see her. Then there was the technician, a well-built man of at least sixty, unshaven and forever smelling of old sweat. He was always shoddily dressed, and refused to wear a lab-coat. He talked slowly and quietly, scratching his week-old beard, and gave the impression of being a tramp who had wandered in off the streets and been assigned cleaning duties. He seemed to do whatever he liked, and must have suffered terribly from constipation because he regularly consumed liquid paraffin which he himself had just refined, lifting one of the big, white porcelain dishes to his mouth and taking a sip. He claimed that it was the only reliable performance test. There was also a storeman, whose job was to look after the various chemicals and glassware we used, and finally there was me, leading three teams of laboratory assistants working continuously in shifts to ensure the products made in the refinery were within the required specifications. The older members of staff, some of whom had worked as analysts for a good many years, did not at first trust me, a fresh-faced graduate, and for a while they would test my knowledge with apparently innocent questions. I only slowly convinced them of my abilities.

Our stock-in-trade was to measure the flash-point of an oil fraction, to ensure that it didn't ignite at too low a temperature and so make the product too dangerous to use. Another regular job was to test the lightness of the refinery's diesel oil, since the heavy components of the refining process would damage engines.

Both our laboratory equipment and the oil refinery in general were, in scientific terms, ancient. The plant had been bombed by the Americans on two occasions at the end of the war, and five years later some pieces were still missing from one of the distillation columns. This caused a frequent quality problem, but there was neither the means nor the motivation to fix it at source and we had to struggle constantly to meet the specifications. Our sole customer, the state-controlled distribution network, sent a representative to check the quality of our products before each delivery. We would take a sample from the storage tank in his presence and carry out a small-scale distillation in the laboratory before his eyes. On at least one occasion, I knew very well that the batch didn't meet the specifications, but to have had it reprocessed would have meant extra work and, much more importantly, losing any bonus payments for the technical staff.

'Leave it to me,' said the shift foreman. He performed the test for the representative, paying great attention to the thermometer. 'Look!' he said, '125°, 126°, 127°. No more. Well within the specified range!'

The representative had to agree that he was right. What he hadn't noticed was that the foreman had had one hand under the workbench to shut off the heat source at just the right moment. I daren't think how many lorries suffered because their diesel was contaminated with heating oil.

But it was not as though our occasional couldn't-careless attitude toward our output stood in stark contrast to any great feeling of concern toward us from our employer. The state did not seem overly worried, however unhealthy our working environment. We had, for example, to test bitumen samples. By the end of each shift we would have the sticky, black residue all over our hands and arms as well as the lab itself, and would clean ourselves up with benzene. Even in the 1940s, benzene was recognised in the US as a dangerous carcinogen, but in Hungary this either remained undiscovered or was brushed under the carpet. We in Almásfüzitő, at least, were never told.

In Communist Hungary, everybody who had a government job (and this meant practically the whole working population) had twice a year to write an *önéletrajz*—an account of their entire life—which the refinery's personnel department would then compare with all the previous versions. Each *önéletrajz* had to start with our parents, necessary to determine our social standing and so our place within Marxism's schema, followed by the schools we had attended and all previous jobs. Then we had to go into detail on our lives outside work, things like hobbies, friends, politics. We were never given guidelines as to what we should include, and this leeway was one of the biggest challenges we faced. The political authorities at the refinery were not remotely interested in our education or our credentials for doing our jobs, like they would have been in the West, but only in what we did outside work, our spouse, our spouse's family, their political views, and so on in stifling detail. We couldn't merely copy our last *önéletrajz* as this would have aroused suspicion: if they found two

Almásfüzitő

exactly identical versions, they became convinced that we were not sincere, but feeding them a carefully prepared lie. Sometimes we had to write our *önéletrajz* in the personnel manager's office and couldn't make a copy even if we had wanted to. While suspicious of similarity, the personnel department carefully analysed the slightest deviation. The real giveaway, we understood, was not what we added, but what, if anything, we left out, and why? It induced paranoia in everybody, and over time warped our very identities.

The personnel manager attached to the refinery was a simple man, a small one even by Hungarian standards, who would wear a *pufajka*—a quilted military overcoat—well into the summer months. Before Communism he had been a cobbler, and even now still smelled of old boots. He was self-confident, striking me as one of those few honest, convinced Communists one sometimes met. I often wondered if he trusted anybody at all, or whether his job required him to suspect everyone.

'Pogány *elvtárs*,' he asked me one day during an official interview in his office, 'what is your honest opinion of the Soviet Union? Your honest opinion.' He really seemed to believe that, if I had planned to lie, his reiteration of the word would have made me tell the truth. I told him that I had been rescued from the labour camp by Soviet soldiers, but I didn't tell him that my elder brother had been taken prisoner by the Russians and starved to death in one of their POW camps. Later, I wondered what would have happened if I had told him that Stalin *elvtárs* was simply a bloody tyrant. Would he have argued the point with me first, or would he just have called the police?

Another man in the personnel department acted as what today might be termed a security officer. The only difference was that in his eyes the enemy was already within the gates. He was a highly intelligent man, a smooth operator who gave the impression of being everybody's friend. I always felt uneasy in his company. He would call on us in our room after work and start to chat about the difficult times we were having and the mistakes certain political leaders might have made. As a result, we were put in the position of having to defend the regime and its leaders against his insinuations. In other words, he was a stool pigeon of the secret police, hoping to draw us into openly criticising the regime. One day he phoned me at work: 'Return to your apartment right away, I want to ask you something urgently.'

I found this most unusual, but had no choice but to go. I found him accompanied by another man in a long, brown leather coat, just like the Gestapo had worn. His brightly polished boots still smelled of polish. He was obviously from the ÁVH. My first thought was that my time had come. The secret policemen didn't introduce himself, and all the time kept both his hands in his deep pockets. Was he holding a gun there? I wondered. He had a cold, sinister smile, and didn't say a word. The security man did all the talking, and from time to time looked at the other, apparently for approval.

'You have a radio?' he asked me.

'You know I have,' I replied: he had visited us often enough.

'Can you get Voice of America on it?' So that was it: a trick question if ever there was one. If I said no, I would obviously be lying, so I had no choice but to say yes.

'Can you get it for us?' Why on earth was he asking that? Did he want to see how quickly I could find the station? Or did he just want to check whether the broadcasts were jammed? After a short sweep of the dial I found Voice of America, right in the middle of a broadcast coming over loud and clear in Hungarian. What now? Would I even have time to say goodbye to Vera? They looked at each other,

Almásfüzitő

said nothing, and left. Listening to the recently established Radio Free Europe, the BBC World Service or Voice of America was not officially forbidden, but everybody knew full well that it would be extremely dangerous to get caught. We had frequently listened to all of them, and especially the BBC. When night came, neither Vera nor I could sleep a wink, waiting for the ÁVH to ring the doorbell and take us away. But they didn't, and I never discovered the real reason for the visit. Perhaps it had nothing to do with me. Maybe even the ÁVH had to fill in their timesheets with activities real or imaginary, like everybody else. Maybe it was their way of putting the fear of God into us so we didn't dare ever tune in to Western transmissions in the future. It didn't work, and we carried on listening in secret.

Hungary's Communist Party expended a great deal of energy and creativity in inventing slogans, doctrines, and movements. These had several aims: keeping our minds occupied, diverting energies that might otherwise be channelled into anger with the system, subtly introducing some unpleasant new policy, squeezing more work out of us, and so forth. Amongst the many political slogans, one of the most frequently heard was 'The factory is yours! You are working for yourself!' Only a few dedicated Communists really believed any such thing. In fact, every aspect of Hungarian industry—be it working conditions, remuneration, productivity, quality control, management, efficiency, or whatever—changed for the worse after 1949. There was neglect, absenteeism, shirking and pilfering. It was a standing joke that it was dangerous to walk outside a bicycle factory, because at regular intervals bicycle parts would be thrown over the wall. Collected by relatives, in no time a whole new bicycle would be assembled from the stolen parts. The system was flawed.

The oil refinery, like other workplaces, had a trade union, but what was its role in a country where the refinery already belonged to its workers? In practice, the trade union was the mouthpiece of the Party. Far from fighting for our interests, the trade union actively participated in our repression, urging us to do more work or to accept lower pay and poorer conditions for the greater good. I don't know who first had the brilliant idea of collecting pledges for the approaching seventieth birthday of Josef Stalin, but he surely got a medal for it.

As in every other workplace in the country, the union's shop steward appeared one day.

'Pogány *elvtárs*,' he began. 'I am sure *you too* wish to give something to our great teacher, Stalin *elvtárs*, on his seventieth birthday.' His emphasis made it clear that this was something everybody was expected to do. What could I give? I couldn't have got hold of a decent bottle of wine or a box of chocolates even if I'd had the money.

'The workers in the production departments have offered increased production. The maintenance staff have offered to work on their free weekend. Now it's your turn.' We were already analysing all the samples we received in the laboratory. What more could we possibly do?

'You know,' I suggested to the shop steward, 'that we work with glassware, and that some of the pieces are very expensive. Occasionally we do break some of them. I suggest, in the name of our laboratory, that in the coming month we shall reduce our breakage by twenty per cent as a gift for Stalin *elvtárs*.'

We all kept our fingers crossed for a month. It wasn't as if we ever broke anything on purpose, but missing the target would have been considered a sign of sabotage. In the end, we were either fortunate or careful enough to meet the target.

There were many other ways the Party found to keep us pointlessly occupied. One day, the personnel manager approached me.

'Pogány *elvtárs*, are you ready to work and to fight?'

'What a silly question,' I thought. 'I'm already working. Is he dissatisfied with my performance? And fight? Whom should I fight, and why?' He saw my look of surprise and quickly added:

'It's nothing personal, *elvtárs*. Our Party has launched a movement to improve our readiness. It is called 'I am ready for work and to fight!'. You can win medals—bronze, silver or gold. Wouldn't it be nice to have one?'

'How can I improve my readiness?' I asked.

'By improving your fitness, *elvtárs*. There are three kinds of sport—those requiring strength, stamina, or technique. You have to choose one of each group. You can choose running.'

'No, thank you!'

'Jumping.'

'Definitely not!'

'How about swimming?' he suggested in desperation. Now, swimming was my kind of sport, the only one I liked apart from hiking. Back home in Orosháza I had loved those weekends spent out at Lake Gyopáros. There was a lake at the nearby town of Tata, and so that summer we went there on the train and swam. In the end, I got a silver medal, no bad thing in itself. But we all knew deep down that at its heart the 'I am ready for work and to fight!' movement was a cynical ploy, what today we might call 'winning hearts and minds'. It was simply a chance for a large number of people to win a medal. They were mass-produced, made of base metal, with a red star bearing the image of an athlete. The Party hoped that the recipients would be proud of them, and would identify themselves more readily with the regime. And the constant drip-drip effect of such campaigns was that, yes, people did in some way come to feel a certain affection for and reliance upon the Party.

'Pin it to your shirt, *elvtárs*, the next time you are marching with us,' the personnel manager said at the award ceremony. And they organised many such marches.

Life and work in Almásfüzitő went on. On occasional weekends Vera and I might go by train to Tata with its small lake or to the divided town of Komárom on the Danube. There we would stand upon the riverbank staring over at Czechoslovakia; it might as well have been the other side of the world. We read books and listened to our radio. Work started early, and we went to bed early. We only had one holiday, in the summer of 1951, a week in the Mátra mountains of northern Hungary.

On our return, we learned that Vera had been 'drilled'. Being 'drilled' was how we referred to having one's job stolen by somebody with better connections. Vera had no wish to accept the alternative post that was given to her, and straight away started using her own connections to obtain a transfer to Budapest. She soon succeeded and moved to her new job, leaving me behind. It took a few more months and more strings had to be pulled, but eventually I too was transferred to Budapest to work in Vegyterv, the central design office for the Hungarian chemical industry. I never went back to Almásfüzitő.

6
Vegyterv

CUT OFF behind the Iron Curtain and unable to engage meaningfully with the developed economies of the West, Communist Hungary quickly set up organisations to engage in research and design for its domestic industries. I joined one of these, Vegyterv or 'Chemical Planning', just recently established to provide engineering know-how for the reconstruction and development of Hungary's chemical industry. Vegyterv had taken up residence in a huge building which until the advent of Communism had been Budapest's central pawnshop, an enterprise which had since been banned. More than six hundred personnel of all talents were employed—chemists, mechanical and civil engineers, architects, draughtsmen, and administrative staff. From being a medium-sized fish in a small pond in Almásfüzitő, I immediately became a very small fish in a veritable lake. I was assigned to the department dealing with the nitrogen-based industries, plants which produced such chemicals as ammonium nitrate for agricultural fertiliser and nitric acid for explosives.

There was already one such nitrate plant in Hungary, using the Haber-Bosch process to create ammonia, but its capacity would need to increase drastically if the Party's Five-Year Plans were ever to succeed. Using this plant as a model, we concentrated on designing units for providing the feed, which ultimately derived from brown coal, Hungary's predominant fossil fuel. Walking around the plant we would be struck by a variety of odours—pungent ammonia, the rotten-egg stench of hydrogen sulphide, and coal smoke.

We tried our best to keep up to date with developments, and oriented ourselves toward American know-how whenever possible. After the war, the Allies had made a study of Nazi Germany's industries and had published a number of reports describing their secrets in detail. These reports were available to us and we pored over them for technical information. We were also very much interested in the Tennessee Valley Authority's nitrate plants, set up under President Roosevelt's New Deal in the early 1930s. Even though we lagged some two decades behind, we carefully read and analysed all their published information. One of the most useful sources was *Perry's Chemical Engineers' Handbook*. Written in English and published in America, it was rather expensive but invaluable. The library at Vegyterv had a single, old copy of the manual, which all of us designers had regularly to consult. The problem was, how could hundreds of us use the one book, almost on a daily basis? Then I discovered that *Perry's* had been translated into Russian and published in the Soviet Union. Of course, the translation didn't refer to the fact that the original had been written and published in America. Since all books published in Communist countries were subsidised and very cheap, I could easily afford to buy a copy. The only disadvantage was that it was written in Russian, and that is where my knowledge of Serbian Cyrillic from the labour camp in Vienna proved to be a great help. Scientific Russian is not as difficult as Dostoevsky, and after a while I had learnt the nouns for boiling point, vapour pressure, and so forth. It was enough.

The design office at Vegyterv employed some of the best people that Hungary could offer. Our head, Laci Sziget, was an internationally renowned engineer who had invented a furnace to convert brown coal to gas. There was also Sándor Farkas, a project manager who in his previous job had been my wife's boss.

Vegyterv

Sándor Farkas' parents were middle-class Jewish shopkeepers, not rich, but very comfortably off. He was one of those brilliant young men who had luck on their side, a rare but useful combination. Sándor had spent the war years in France, studying chemical engineering at the prestigious *Institut National Polytechnique de Grenoble* and had managed to survive with false papers and by colouring his red hair blonde. He claimed to have worked with the Resistance, and after returning to Hungary had joined the Communist Party. By the age of twenty-five he had a government post leading an important industrial centre.

Sándor was tall and slim, with a row of gold teeth which glinted as he talked. He was very intelligent, a scientist who also appreciated art, and spoke quietly but forcefully, with an air of authority. He had married Klári, a beautiful girl who spoke several languages and wrote articles for a cultural journal. They enjoyed all the perks the Communist system offered them, lived in one of the best parts of Budapest, and had a car with a driver provided by the ministry. Then Klári got ill, and the doctor diagnosed polio. She fought for her life and eventually won the battle, but not without scars. One of her legs became paralysed, and she grew bitter and cynical. In spite of her misfortune, Sándor remained devoted to her. My wife Vera had been his private secretary, a demanding but well-paid job that gave her much satisfaction. We met socially with Sándor and Klári, and sometimes went walking in the hills surrounding the capital.

Then about a year later it seemed that Sándor's luck, too, had run out. Marx's theories predicted that by this stage of the Communist revolution there would be dark reactionary forces fighting against the new order. Who they were was not made clear, but General Secretary Rákosi embarked upon a purge. Sándor was suddenly removed from his prestigious job. The unofficial reason was that he might have been recruited by Western intelligence during his time in France, and could not be trusted. Sándor was interrogated, and a few days later the secret police invited my poor wife Vera to their headquarters in their infamous House of Terror on Andrássy *út*. One did not turn down such an invitation, and then in all probability my own turn would come, guilty by association. It seemed certain that we were to become just two more statistics in the Hungarian gulag.

Vera and I talked at length about what we would say, what tactics we could use. Vera could say that she knew of nothing which would incriminate Sándor, but if in spite of this they still found him guilty they might also prosecute her as an accomplice. Or she could invent something incriminating, but then they would ask why she hadn't reported this before and prosecute her for withholding information. In despair, we decided to stick to the truth as we knew it, and not to say anything incriminating.

They took Vera to a dark room in which, behind a desk, sat the interrogating officer. Vera was seated in front of the desk, a policeman behind her. There was a lamp on the table, and its beam was directed at her, just as you might see in the movies. Halfway through the interrogation, both men walked out of the room and she was left alone for several minutes, during which time she had the feeling they were observing her. The whole interrogation lasted almost an hour, and she was allowed to go home.

We had many sleepless nights waiting for an early morning knock on the door, wondering whether they would take Vera alone or me as well. In the end, without explanation, Vera was demoted to the lowliest clerical job in the office, but she was not arrested. Sándor too considered himself lucky not to have been executed or sent to the gulag like so many others. He lost his job, but managed to obtain work as a part-time lecturer. Later, as with the reorganisation of Hungarian industry they needed more technically trained people, Sándor was rehabilitated and assigned to Vegyterv.

Unlike the topsy-turvy situation at the oil refinery, the design office at Vegyterv was run by qualified technical staff. Some of them might have been Party members, but it was not evident. The personnel department too was less aggressively Communist and had less influence on the day-to-day running. There was, in fact, one young Communist engineer only, who came from a proletarian background and was given the task of organising the younger employees into a group of Party sympathisers, but with scant success. The Party, it seemed, was at least wise enough to realise that too much political interference in Vegyterv was likely to harm its ability to re-energise Hungary's faltering industry. As a consequence, we felt less inhibited to speak candidly about matters that elsewhere might have landed us in trouble.

Pista Kovács, a department head with special responsibility for the use of instruments was a jovial extrovert, continuously looking for an audience with which to share his views of the world. One eminently true observation of his was 'This is going to be an average year—worse than last year, but better than next year.' His favourite subject was the ever-deteriorating economy, and he always complained about his financial position: 'Your standard of living,' he opined, 'is best measured by the smallest amount of money you think about before spending it. Until now I didn't worry about spending less than ten *forint*, but now I carefully consider anything more than one *forint*.'

You couldn't buy much for one *forint*, not even in the buffet, where a pretty girl served strong *eszpresszókávé* and simple sandwiches throughout the day. Though all of us male employees would find any excuse to chat her up, under

Communism we were not supposed to distinguish between men and women at work. The linguistic quirk by which Hungarian uses the same word for 'he' and 'she' might have helped the process along, but in general this was a demand which did not sit well with the traditional attitude of most Hungarian men.

One of the women at Vegyterv was Terike, a mechanical engineer who had taken her final exams while raising twins. She was a very beautiful woman, with blonde hair and piercing blue eyes. I often went with her to the site of the new nitrate plant we were designing. Because of her good looks, several men tried to approach her, but Terike was a loyal wife and never flirted with anybody. Unfortunately her husband, whom I later met in England in the refugee camp, abandoned her and their children. Another female engineer at Vegyterv was Jutka, who in physical terms was Terike's opposite, with long black hair and dark eyes, but as an engineer someone who similarly would not think twice before climbing up a vertical ladder several stories high to examine a leaking valve. Jutke and Terike were a new breed of Hungarian woman. The sexual equality inherent in Marxism had made it easier for capable women, who might previously have taken a 'traditional' job such as a secretary, to contribute to the economy as scientists and engineers.

Our work in the design office centred on two nitrate plants, the outdated one in Pét and a new one we were building in Kazincbarcika. Technical people like myself were painfully aware of the fact that any industrial accident in the new plant which could be traced to a mistake we had made would automatically see us accused of sabotage. The penalty for designing a bridge that later collapsed could be death. It was a matter of somebody, somewhere, being identified, on whom the blame could be pinned, and it would certainly not be a Party member in a position of power. Therefore we and everybody else at the coalface always erred on the side of caution, designing very conservatively. If from *Perry's Chemical Engineers' Handbook* we could see that in the West a safety factor of fifteen per cent would suffice, we in Hungary would use at least triple that. I routinely had to provide data on the volume of materials to be transported in pipelines. As a matter of course, I would increase the design maximum by half as much again before submitting the data to the people who designed the pipes. They in turn would add their fifty per cent safety margin and pass the information to the factory where the pipes were to be made. The factory in turn used their own safety margin of one hundred per cent in making the pipes, which were then so heavy that they needed enormous supporting piles. When the plant was built, it was a grotesque waste of resources, cost the earth, and would have led to bankruptcies in the West, let alone in Hungary.

Another problem that became very clear during my time at Vegyterv was that there was no effective financial analysis. There were budgets, and the budgets did use money as their basic unit, but in the Communist economy money had different values according to what it represented. We had different prices for material produced locally, for material imported from a fellow Communist country, and for material imported from the West. There was a separate budget for each source of materials. For imports I had to use the unrealistic official exchange rate between the *forint* and the US dollar, which made adding up the costs meaningless. In any case, materials available in Hungary or other Communist countries had to be preferred over Western imports, irrespective of price, quality or even suitability. With a separate budget for paying workers, which was not interchangeable with any another budget, it was impossible for industry to switch from manual work to automation. Workers had jobs for life, regardless of whether or not there was actually anything for them to do, and industry was burdened with the salaries of people who performed no function or who had already retired. 'How many people are working here?' ran the old joke, to which the answer was 'about 30 per cent.' The Soviet Union was obsessed with trying to overtake the capitalist economies of the West, but instead fell further and further behind them. Based on the Soviet model, every Hungarian workplace had to have a five-year plan, with goals determined centrally and passed down without consultation. Each year, more would be demanded than in the previous one, regardless of the practical effect. The oil refinery at Almásfüzitő, for example, had been badly bombed during the war, and the resulting scrap metal had been collected and sent to a steelworks as useful raw material for the furnaces. And so, the next year, it received a goal to collect even more scrap metal. 'What should we do?' grumbled the chief engineer. 'Blow up the rest of the plant as well?'

No wonder, then, that Hungary almost collapsed under Communism: we were operating in a bubble which had eventually to burst.

In 1952, during my time at Vegyterv, I was called up for military service. Officially, I should have been drafted into the army at the age of eighteen and served for two years, but as a university student I had been exempt from military service and my call-up papers had not come through even after I had started to work. Now, though, the army caught up with me and I had no choice but to do two months' basic training. It was a bitterly cold spring that year, yet we only had summer clothing to wear and an open-sided tent to sleep in, washing ourselves in cold water from a standpipe. We did not have socks, and had to make do with the traditional but more primitive *kapca*, a piece of cloth folded around each foot. If folded well these were perfectly comfortable, but if badly arranged they would slip down and become like torture on a long march. Army rations, mainly stodge with some fat and a piece of bacon mixed in if we were lucky, were atrocious, as bad as the food in the labour camp during the war. I was sent to the artillery and became a spotter, directing fire, the soldier any sensible foe would try to kill first. Being the only soldier in the platoon with a university education in science, it was left to me to explain to my sergeant the elements of geometry—sine, cosine and tangent—which were used to triangulate 'enemy' positions.

After the disastrous decision to enter the war on the side of Nazi Germany, the new, post-war Hungarian Army was remodelled as an exact copy of the Soviet Red Army. I read a book about the Red Army's defence of the road to Moscow in 1941, which advocated hard training, blind obedience, and summary execution of anybody trying to do less than their duty. Our officers regularly quoted the Red Army's saying: 'Every bucketful you sweat during exercises will save you a drop of blood in battle.'

By tradition, our officers were supposed to make the training harder by pulling stunts like putting grit into our boots before marches. Fortunately they themselves were reservists rather than professional soldiers and didn't take their tasks too seriously. We had a medic in the camp, but it was rumoured that he only had two medicines: for a pain above the belt, aspirin, and for a pain below the belt, castor oil.

We underwent basic training on the Russian *Shpagin* submachine gun, but were only trusted with bullets when guarding the ammunition store, and even then only with two rounds. We were supposed to challenge anybody approaching, but none of our officers had the courage to try us out in case we got trigger-happy. Our guns were regularly inspected, and there were punishments for the tiniest spot of rust, real or imagined. For using too much grease, on the other hand, I was also punished. Our sergeant seemed to come from a peasant family and probably hated intellectuals like me. Still, he was preferable to our thuggish leader in the *Levente* back in school.

The final test was the big route-march, starting during the night with only seconds to get dressed and put all our belongings into our rucksacks. As an enthusiastic member of the Hungarian Ramblers Society I was used to long hikes in the mountains wearing a rucksack, and knew how to pack one so that it didn't chafe. I was well prepared and found the march not too tiring. But we also had a commissar amongst us, Pali, a well-meaning but rather weak city-boy, an accountant by profession. He always unquestioningly followed the Soviet example, defended the Party line, lectured us on patriotism and duty. He practised what he preached, though, and in fact was one of the only selfless Communists I ever came across. As the forced march wore on, he offered to carry things for those who would otherwise have fallen behind. He was in no condition to do so, and was thoroughly exhausted by the time he finished.

At the end of my training I graduated with the two stripes of a *tizedes*, or corporal. They seemed pleased with me, and offered me the possibility of staying on for another two months with the promise of becoming a sergeant, but I declined: there was by now a conceivable threat of war with Yugoslavia, which after declining to obey Stalin, had been ejected from the socialist flock to become our most dangerous enemy. Every time the name Tito was mentioned at a public meeting it would extract a long *boooooo!* from everybody present. While by the end of my training I had almost enjoyed playing soldiers, I had no plans to be part of a real war once more. Besides, Vera was pregnant.

Until now we had been extremely careful to avoid Vera falling pregnant, but in early 1952 we decided that the time was right to start a family. We assumed that it would take several months, during which we could enjoy a more relaxed attitude to marital life. Alas, Vera got pregnant right away. Because women were allowed three months of maternity leave and no more, she kept on working almost until the day she gave birth, to allow her more time with the baby.

Vera's uncle happened to be the administrative manager of a large hospital in Budapest, and he arranged for Vera to see one of the best gynaecologists in the city, a professor who agreed to deliver the baby. To our great joy, our healthy son arrived and after a couple of days we took him home. We named him István, after my elder brother who had been murdered by the Russians. István laughed all day and cried all night, so loudly in fact that he kept the whole apartment block awake. A lady from another flat came out to the corridor one night and shouted at the top of her voice: 'If he's being naughty, smack him! If he's ill, take him to the doctor!'

We did neither. Soon after István's birth, Vera had to go back to work and so we employed a nanny, paying her half Vera's salary. She was the widow of a high-ranking army officer killed during the war. She must have been quite a lady in a different age, but she received no pension and needed a job. We also engaged a paediatrician, and paid him a fee every month. This turned out to be a very worthwhile investment, as one day the worst polio epidemic for years reached the nursery where István spent some of his time, and he too quickly developed a fever.

'You must try to get a dose of a new polio medicine,' advised our paediatrician, but it transpired that whatever drug it was that he had got wind of was not freely available. It so happened, though, that the son of a colleague of Vera's attended the same nursery, and his mother too was worried about the epidemic. Because her husband was a senior functionary in the Communist Party, she had the necessary connections to get hold of the drug and passed a vial to Vera as well. It was administered to István, and he fully recovered.

In spite of the fact that we both had relatively well paid jobs, our standard of living was not high. Our dinner often consisted of nothing more than a couple of *lángos*, thick pancakes of deep-fried dough bought on the street corner. In the winter we bought an apple for István each day, sharing the skin between ourselves. We fed him paprika, Hungary's national spice, rich in vitamin C, while we ate its seeds. Our joint income was higher than the national average, but with our new outgoings we could not afford more than one pepper a day. We certainly had no money for a holiday.

'Why don't you come and spend a week's holiday with us?' suggested Sándor Farkas out of the blue one day. 'We have room in our flat, and the air would do István good.'

To stay in Sándor and Klári's flat in the Buda hills was a real treat for us, and we needed no persuasion to accept their generous offer. By this time István was eight months old, no longer breastfeeding, and had got over the habit of crying all night. He was a cute little boy, always smiling and crawling all over the place. Whether or not his presence made Klári broody, I can't say, but nine months later she gave birth to a daughter, Kati.

What happened next could truly be the subject of a movie. Klári divorced Sándor and married Pali, a younger

Vegyterv

man whom she spoiled like a mother. Her daughter Kati lived with them. Some years later Pali divorced Klári and married his much younger stepdaughter Kati, with whom he eventually had four children. Klári, who had become the mother-in-law of her own ex-husband, remained in their house and looked after her grandchildren. Sándor, meanwhile, who also worked as a part-time lecturer, became involved with one of his students, a much younger girl named Panni, and married her. Panni was almost the opposite of his first wife Klári: she came from a peasant family, didn't speak any foreign languages, and had no idea of etiquette. They had two sons, and her elderly mother lived with them. Sándor stayed on friendly terms with Klári, and whenever he had some official entertaining to do, where foreign guests were involved, he asked her to accompany him as if she were still his wife. Panni never seemed to mind.

While the working environment for Sándor, myself and the others was preferable to Almásfüzitő, the sense of paranoia at the more strategically important Vegyterv was if anything heightened. In the design office, everything had to be kept highly confidential. We had to be alert, and foil the enemy, who, supposedly, was constantly trying to destroy our beautiful socialist system. All our blueprints, papers and data sheets had to be locked away at night in a special strong room, including those few blueprints which we had bought from Western industry in the first place. Of course, it was a futile exercise: nobody in the West wanted to steal designs based on yesteryear's technology, but this sort of brainwashing served to keep us alert and on our toes.

Every morning and every evening, there would form a long queue in front of the window of the strong room where the documents were stored, and we had to wait patiently in line to be served. When we had got what we needed, we had to sign a receipt. The whole process was repeated in reverse every evening, costing us another half an hour. When we had gone home, the security people would open our desks and we would be in a great deal of trouble if they found anything stamped 'confidential'. One day, I hit upon a solution to save time standing in the queue: from then on, I would cut off the title page of documents bearing a 'confidential' stamp and stamp the new top sheet 'out of date'. This way, I could keep the papers I was working on in my desk, as the security people had not an ounce of technical training. The fact that even an out-of-date blueprint might be of use to a real enemy didn't occur to them.

The paranoia ran deep. These were the days long before computers, and everything at Vegyterv was typed with a sheet of carbon paper and a copy filed. If the carbon paper had been used once only, it was quite easy to read the text from it. One of the managers narrowly escaped being accused of spying for the CIA, just because he had thrown carbon papers into his wastebasket instead of sending them to be destroyed. His potentially fatal act was discovered by the security people, who it turned out had been checking all the wastebaskets by night. It didn't even matter what the text was.

Under the system in force at Vegyterv, we had to account for our time by filling in a timesheet, recording what we did by the hour. With no computers, a trusted lady Communist, Olga *elvtársnő* of the personnel department, took upon herself the task of manually checking the output of the technical staff. Olga was a good-looking woman of about forty, whom you could recognise from a distance by her two huge earrings. She always wore a short skirt to show off what she knew were shapely legs, and a brightly coloured blouse with the top three buttons undone. In spite of her coquettish appearance her facial expression was forever sober and her voice officious. I never once saw her smile or heard her laugh. She would come around at the end of each month asking: 'Pogány *elvtárs*, what did you do this month?'

I had to show her all my documents, and all the calculations I had done on my slide rule. With no technical understanding, she couldn't check the quality of any of it, or even tell if it was remotely necessary, but just noted everything down and filled in a big table recording the number of pages I had presented before signing each page. I spent a great deal of time researching in the library, and sometimes there would be nothing to show for this, no paperwork for her to sign off. Would a devoted Communist like Olga understand this, or would she consider it sabotage? In such cases, I took no risks and instead presented her with all the same papers she had signed the previous month, but instead of the originals with her signature I handed over just the carbon copies.

'The originals are no longer with us,' I would say. 'I sent them on to the client.' She found nothing wrong with this explanation and dutifully signed the carbon copies. It was a pointless waste of time.

And so I found it intriguing that while people like Olga rigorously controlled the performance of individuals, the state seemed utterly unconcerned with overall inefficiencies. There was huge overemployment throughout the country. If on the way home from Vegyterv I wanted to buy some aspirin, I had to go to a pharmacy, which had three windows. At the first I said what I wanted and received a paper with the price written upon it. At the second I paid the money and the paper was stamped. At the third window I handed in the paper, which was filed away, and finally received my aspirin. Three workers had been employed to deal with my simple transaction, and more would be needed to deal with the paperwork.

But although we were living in a socialist state with guaranteed employment, there were still mechanisms by which the management tried its best to reward good performance. Our monthly salary was made up on average of a fixed payment amounting to eighty-five per cent, plus a fifteen per cent bonus. The bonus varied by a small margin either way. Every month, each manager had to rate their subordinates. Some workers were rated above average, some below. The departmental head then collected all these ratings and used his own judgment to rate them one against the other depending on whether he considered any given manager too hard or too soft. The fixed proportion of our salary was necessary for survival: it paid for food, transport, and other essentials. With the rest, which we thought of as a bonus even though it came each month, we could buy theatre or opera tickets, or an occasional item of clothing. It was still a pittance. For a shirt or a pair of shoes I had to save for three months, for a dress for my wife six months, and for an overcoat a full two years.

The idea of bonuses grew much more unwieldy when it was applied to entire factories. On what basis do you calculate a bonus for the senior management of a factory? Their individual performance couldn't be measured, and so they received a rather complicated equation from head office on what was expected from the factory as a whole. Points were given for extra production, for savings in raw materials, fuel, and so on. This could create laughable situations. Once, I had to go to the plant at Pét but could not get hold of the head of technology. He was with the chief chemist, chief engineer, and even the director, and they were all indisposed in a meeting. The plant, it transpired, had just received a revised equation from the Ministry of Chemical Industry, and now the entire senior staff were meeting to decide how to operate the plant so as to maximise their bonuses. If it looked like they might receive an extra bonus if only they could increase production of an otherwise useless by-product, this then might be exactly what they would agree to do.

Besides such sleight of hand, there was also a darker aspect to how the government motivated people to do its bidding. One day our departmental head asked all of us to a meeting. To our surprise, a Party official took the chair.

'Welcome, *elvtársak*, to this very important meeting,' he set the tone. 'I'm sure you all want to live in peace, and this means that we have to be able to defend our peace. Our leaders have decided to offer you a direct role in defending our peace by allowing you to purchase Peace Bonds. You can buy these bonds by investing up to ten per cent of your salary. No more than that allowed, because for some of you it would cause hardship.' He gave a sinister smile. 'Of course, the loan—because that is what it is—will be repaid to you in full with interest in no more than twenty-five years. In the meantime, after five years, some interest will be paid out in the form of a lottery, in which every Peace Bond will give you a chance to win large sums of money. How about this, *elvtársak*?'

The first question was obvious, and Pista Kovács asked it: 'Is purchasing these Peace Bonds compulsory?' We already knew the answer.

'Of course it's not compulsory,' the official explained. 'But I expect everybody will buy them voluntarily. Our leaders are expecting this from all of us. You have a whole week to decide.'

I discussed the matter with Vera, who had had exactly the same experience at her place of work. When a person's salary was just enough to survive, a reduction of a tenth meant real hardship, but we could not afford *not* to subscribe. We decided to wait and see what others were doing. The next day, a list appeared on the wall in all places of work with the names of those who had already signed up, and it was updated on a daily basis. The names at the top of the list were those of the Party members, who had no choice but to set a good example. Then the names of the departmental and section heads with the highest salaries were added, followed by a long wait. Then the pressure started. Party leaders in every office and factory across Hungary spent time trying to persuade us, and if necessary pressurise us, to voluntarily buy Peace Bonds. Members of the Party and trade union officials talked to each of us periodically, using a carrot-and-stick approach in which the carrot was rather small and the stick so much larger. I was told bluntly that there was no place for reactionary elements in an important job such as mine. How would I like going back to work in the refinery at Almásfüzitő? There might be a vacancy there for me. In the end we and practically everybody else accepted the inevitable and volunteered to hand our hard-earned wages back to the Communist Party, so that the government could reduce our purchasing power and so manage the economy without resort to rationing. The whole damned process was repeated every year. In spite of assurances, the Peace Bonds were not paid back within the time promised. The last recorded payment was made in 1977, by which time inflation had rendered the sums almost worthless. We had long since entrusted ours to relatives and forgotten about them.

There were very few genuine perks at work, as the most obvious ones—health insurance, child care, free education, pensions—were available to all. The most desirable treat

Vegyterv

was the occasional holiday in one of the resorts around Lake Balaton—the 'Hungarian Sea'—or up in the mountains. These were run by the trade union, and tickets for a week's vacation were handed out as a reward for good work.

There were, however, problems even with these holiday tickets. One was that a ticket was awarded to an individual, not necessarily to a couple, and almost never to a whole family. The other problem was that many Hungarian holiday resorts of the time provided only large, single-sex dormitories, and so even if you managed to get a joint ticket the chances were that you would have to sleep separately from your spouse. Once, Vera and I were presented with a joint ticket to a hotel on Lake Balaton, only to learn that the hotel had only two family rooms, the rest being dormitories. To make sure that we secured one of the family rooms I wrote a letter in the name of our personnel department stating that we were on honeymoon. It was a pure fabrication, but we still looked very young. We sent it to the hotel in advance, and did indeed get a separate room. The hotel we stayed in was good by the standards of Communist Hungary, and offered us full board. Not needing to worry about finding food, we were free all day to use the beach, play table tennis, chess, or paddle out onto Lake Balaton in a kayak, so long as we were on time for the meals.

As a general rule, and following the Soviet model as always, the system selected a few hardworking people and used them as examples to inspire the rest. In the arts, for example, the government introduced rewards for exceptional performance, handing out titles such as 'excellent artist', 'outstanding painter', or 'outstanding sculptor'. Often these amounted to little more than a faithful expression of Communist doctrines in the approved style. In industry, those who exceeded their work targets by more than one hundred per cent were called *élmunkás*—'excellent worker'—and received special privileges, such as holidays in another Communist country. The most sought-after privilege was a flat in a newly built apartment block. They were small and unattractive, had no sound insulation, and almost immediately needed repairs, but were a home for a family.

The first of May, Labour Day, was always a holiday, an occasion to celebrate the rule of the proletariat, and in Budapest a grand parade would be organised. A grandstand was erected on Heroes' Square for our leaders and for representatives of other Communist countries. The parade would start from our various places of work, but with Budapest's public tram system only running until 7am that day I always had to get up at the crack of dawn and make my way across town dressed in my best dark trousers and white shirt, upon which were pinned all the medals I had won. The temperature often reached twenty-five degrees or more.

Vegyterv's personnel department distributed the essential red flags and portraits of Rákosi, Stalin, Marx, Lenin and the rest to carry aloft, and I would try not to 'volunteer' for one. At 9am we would start out, six abreast, to the sound of brass bands from the big factories playing well-known Communist anthems. At first we progressed at a reasonable speed, but as we approached the centre of the city we would be slowed by the sheer press of people. Eventually, after three hours on the road, we arrived at Andrássy út, the iconic boulevard leading to the wide expanse of Heroes' Square with its grand colonnades and its column surmounted by the Archangel Gabriel. There we waved to the dignitaries, who waved back. The loudspeakers broadcast political slogans continuously, interrupted only by more specific announcements relating to the larger organisations who passed the grandstand, each carrying their name on an enormous, braided flag: 'The Party greets the heroic workers of X factory, who exceeded their production norms by fifteen per cent! Long live the struggle of the proletariat!' The leaders would stop waving and start clapping until the factory had passed by.

After we workers of Vegyterv had passed the grandstand and waved to the dignitaries, we would walk a little further in the same, orderly fashion until we reached Városliget, one of the great parks of the capital. Here everybody would deposit the flags and the portraits, which were then taken back to factories and offices across the city in lorries, and we were free to go. By this time I would be stinking from the sweat, and would go to the nearest refreshment tent to buy the largest glass of cool beer they served. The May Day Parade might have been celebrating the proletariat, but refreshments were not included and we had to pay for our own drinks. Budapest's public transport didn't start up again until well after 2pm, I would never be in the mood to walk all the way back home, and so I would sit in the shade in the park with nothing to do. This was what passed as a holiday. The only consolation was to imagine what torture May 1st must have been for the people on the grandstand.

Other dates throughout the year would see celebrations on a smaller scale: the anniversary of 'important' political events, of any real or imaginary successes, and of significant dates in the calendars of other Communist states such as the anniversary of the Russian Revolution on November 7th. These celebrations might be held in the open air, in the ornate surroundings of the Opera House on Andrássy út, or somewhere similarly illustrious, and all the Party dignitaries would be present. Whenever open-air meetings were planned, factories and co-operatives from across the city would send delegates, rounding up as many people as possible by combining the event with a 'spontaneous' demonstration of workers and students to fill the space. Speeches were made, though with experience we could always predict in advance exactly which topics were going to be included: warmongering capitalists, the glorious Red Army, our beloved and wise leader Rákosi, and of course Stalin. Each time one of these was mentioned we would all stand up and start to clap. After a while the applause would become rhythmical—Clap! Clap! Clap! Clap!—to show unity and enthusiasm. Eventually the rhythm would break and the clapping would become disorganised, but continued on and on regardless. Nobody wanted to be the first to stop, and so the clapping would go on for several embarrassing minutes, weaving in and out of rhythm.

Under Communism, naturally, only one political party was permitted, yet elections were nevertheless held, and always on a Sunday when people were available to vote. To avoid unnecessary delay, each and every apartment block had to be present at the nearest polling station at a given time. When the allotted hour approached, the block's fire alarm summoned the tenants down to the inner courtyard where the Party commissar, the political representative of the apartment block, checked off names against a list of occupants. There was no possibility of not voting. At one particular election, my mother-in-law was feeling very unwell and wanted to stay at home, and so the commissar went up to see her. I don't know what conversation passed between them, but a few minutes later she joined us.

'Pogány *elvtárs*,' the commissar addressed me. 'You are the youngest, and must lead us. Which do you want to carry: the Red Flag or the portrait of our leader?'

The paper portrait of Rákosi was stapled to a wooden frame with a long, wooden handle. I chose it because it was lighter than the flag. The commissar distributed the rest of the flags and the portraits and the whole block marched off together to vote. When we arrived at the polling station we each received a voting card which stated that we were voting for the Hungarian Communist Party. We didn't need to do anything other than deposit this card in the ballot box. But at the bottom of the card was a line of small print which read: 'If you are not voting for the Party, put a cross in this circle.'

If we wanted to put a cross in the circle, we either had to do it in front of the electoral officers or else enter a curtained-off booth. In both cases, everybody knew precisely what was happening. The only reason to enter the booth was to vote 'no', and I never witnessed anybody foolish enough to do it. No wonder the outcome was always over 99 per cent in favour of the Communist Party. Even the few 'no' votes, I suspect, were faked, and served both to justify the Party's repression of dissent and to make the election look 'real'.

We did discuss politics, but when we did so openly it was always within a strictly conformist setting. The Friends of *Szabad Nép* was a discussion forum at Vegyterv that met once a week before the start of work. One particular week, the leader of the Vegyterv branch of the Party, a technician who was better at speechifying than working, called upon me for a change: 'Pogány *elvtárs*, could you present us with a summary of the week's news at the next forum?'

And so I collected the week's newspapers and chose a few points I knew would not interest anybody except the branch leader, and maybe not even him. 'Somogyi *elvtárs*,' he began, addressing himself to one man in particular. 'You didn't attend our last forum. Could you explain why?'

Attendance was not compulsory, but it was expected from Party members like Comrade Somogyi, who had to search for an acceptable excuse. His grandmother could only die once.

'Continue, Pogány *elvtárs!*' he gave the floor to me.

I explained that 'the latest policies of the Party have been accepted by the population with great enthusiasm! We are on the road to a bright future! On the international front, the capitalist-imperialist warmongers have suffered a major defeat in Africa!' And so on. A discussion was expected to follow, but it was not easy to get people to talk politics openly, especially not in front of a Party secretary. People just nodded their heads and mumbled bland statements: 'It's been very well summarised.' 'I can't add anything.' 'I've learned a lot from this.'

To compensate for such dreariness, we would sit down as a group during our lunch break at Vegyterv and discuss some or other subject. We were all young people, and with most subjects too politically sensitive to discuss seriously what else could we do but tell jokes and swap anecdotes about sex?

'What time of day do you prefer to do it?' asked Feri Kovács, an architect. Not surprisingly most married people chose late at night, depending on whether or not they had children. One or two preferred the early morning. If someone preferred five to seven in the afternoon, the time between leaving work and arriving home, you knew they were having an affair.

As for jokes, it is amazing how people preserve their sense of humour even under the most difficult of times, perhaps as a safety valve. There were always a few popular jokes doing the rounds.

'A town council was told it had to perform two duties,' went one. 'When it was hot they had to spray the roads with water to keep the dust down, and in the winter they had to clear the roads of snow. Because they were expected to exceed the target set for them, come February the council

Vegyterv

decided that they had reached the target for snow clearance and made a start on watering the roads.'

Other jokes were about the low standard of living: 'Stalin met Eisenhower and asked: 'How much does an American worker earn in a year?'

'About $25,000,' replied Eisenhower.

'And how much does he need to live on?'

'About $20,000.'

'What does he do with the rest?'

'America's a free country—we don't know. How much does a Russian worker earn in a year?'

'About 20,000 *roubles*.'

'And how much does he need to live on?'

'About 25,000 *roubles*.'

'Then where does he get the difference from?'

'Russia's also a free country—we don't know."

Then one day in March of 1953 our peaceful office in Vegyterv became a veritable ant's nest. People were rushing about with excitement.

'Have you heard?' they asked each other. 'Is it true? What do you think will happen now? Who's going to take over?' Stalin had died, and everybody felt that an era had come to an end. Rákosi, the General Secretary of the Hungarian Communist Party, had been a staunch Stalinist, but his mentor was gone. Change was inevitable, but we were far from certain what these changes would bring.

WHEN EVEN THE POETS WERE SILENT

7
The Thaw

AFTER THE death of Stalin, Nikita Khrushchev took over as First Secretary of the Central Committee of the Communist Party of the Soviet Union and, with what came to be known as the 'Khrushchev Thaw', life started very slowly and gradually to improve. The *gulag* was dismantled in Russia as well as in Hungary, and those lucky enough still to be alive came home. One day a new colleague arrived in our department at Vegyterv. Pista *bácsi* had previously been a technical director of the old nitrate plant in Pét, but his membership of the Hungarian Social Democratic Party had seen him interned along with many others after the Communists came to power. He had spent several years in a quarry, breaking up stones with a sledgehammer. They had taken away his glasses so that he was unable either to read or write, the kind of petty behaviour which was familiar to me from my experience of the ghetto. Pista *bácsi* was a big, slow-moving man, courteous, knowledgeable and helpful, and he soon became very popular with everyone. He didn't want to talk about his experience in the *gulag*; we had to drag every word out of him. At first, I assumed that it was simply too painful to Pista *bácsi* to recall the unpleasant memories, but later I realised that he was still very much afraid.

Once, he arrived late in the office looking very agitated, but he assured me that he was all right. I didn't believe him: he was nervous, forever looking at his watch, chain-smoked one cigarette after the other, and jumped every time the door opened.

'When I left home this morning,' he told me at last, 'I noticed a car parked opposite my house, and from its number plate I could tell it belonged to the ÁVH. I was convinced they'd come for me and I tried to sneak away. I thought if they couldn't find me at home they'd be looking for me here, so I've been walking around until I'd collected enough courage to face the music.' The ÁVH hadn't after all come to take him bodily away that day, but they'd long since been the masters of his spirit.

Even after the death of Stalin, all forms of art continued to be heavily subsidised but closely monitored. Art had to be optimistic and represent the working class, the peasants and the Red Army in the endless struggle against reactionaries, defending peace and the dictatorship of the proletariat. Artists using forms other than socialist realism were not subsidised at best, and persecuted at worst, until they conformed. As a result we had to go on enduring paintings and statues depicting nothing but factory workers and peasants smiling and enjoying their work, and soldiers forever engaged in heroic acts. Books remained cheap, but still their publication was permitted purely on the basis of the suitability of their political message. The works of Soviet writers had always been translated, but now the list of approved authors expanded to include people like Ilya Ehrenburg, whose work embodied the 'Khrushchev Thaw', Maxim Gorki, the founder of socialist realism, and the Russian futurist Vladimir Mayakovski. The classical works of such pre-revolution Russian authors as Tolstoy, Chekhov and Dostoevsky, already translated into Hungarian, were reprinted. New and second-hand bookshops opened in abundance, and we could buy books from makeshift stalls all over the city. Occasionally we would get hold of a book which was not available in the shops, an anthology of erotic poems or such like. We would type them out by hand as many times as we could and circulate them amongst our friends. We would simply not have dared to do this just a year or two before.

There were several cinemas in Budapest, and after Stalin's death we visited them more often. *MAFIRT*, the state-run Hungarian Film Industry remained the only body permitted to make feature films, and as well as its politically acceptable light entertainment cinemas went on showing a lot of Soviet propaganda. Hollywood movies and pre-war Hungarian films were still not shown, declared too frivolous (which they were), though they had also been jolly good entertainment. *MAFIRT*'s offerings were not necessarily less frivolous than what had gone before, only instead of a young, handsome aristocrat the hero would be a hard-working Party member or a brave soldier. They were all quite similar, with plots centring on the new system of agricultural production or on attempts by reactionaries to sabotage socialist reconstruction, and predictable locations such as factories, collective farms, or the army. They all had a Communist hero, a beautiful and honest but sadly gullible leading lady, and a villain who courted all the women instead of working. All were equally tedious, with a predictable narrative arc and a happy ending. The villain would invariably be denounced and made to confess his sins, and would promise to work hard in the service of the proletariat in the future. The hero would get a medal for good work and, of course, the girl. Now though, with the onset of the Khrushchev Thaw, directors such as Fábri and Máriássy began tentatively to explore social issues that would have been out of bounds to filmmakers just a couple of years earlier, including hinting at the problems associated with Hungarian Communism.

Then there was the opera. I was still a student at Pázmány Péter University when I first visited the Budapest Opera House, a breathtaking building richly decorated in marble and ormolu. The singers, the scenery, the choir and the orchestra were all world-class, but, though the tickets were pegged at an affordable price, it was hard to get one without paying a bribe. We also regularly went to the theatre, which had a wide repertoire of Hungarian and foreign plays. Most performances were of high quality and, again, cheap.

There was one particular theatre I favoured, which concentrated on political satire. The actors knew exactly how far they could go, and went no further. Laughter is a remedy for all ills in any country where the populace is not free to speak its mind openly, and we would fall about when we heard jokes that employed subtle *double entendre* implying that it was not all milk and honey in Hungary. One even dared to make a joke about Soviet soldiers 'collecting' watches after the war—a practice of which I'd had personal experience, of course—by punning on the fact that in Hungarian we use the same word for 'time' and 'watch'. Given that the Red Army was otherwise portrayed as beyond reproach, it was an enervating and guilty pleasure to be able to laugh at it. Every performance was sold out. One evening, a performer summed up our feeling that the Khrushchev Thaw was only the first glimmer of light in what was surely a very long tunnel: 'With the recent relaxation in political control,' he started, 'everybody can criticise the government. Some people are already saying that, if the trend continues, there'll be no more need for our political satire.' He paused for what seemed like an age, and then continued. 'Still, I don't think things are as bad as all that yet….' The effect was almost unending applause.

Though even after the death of Stalin we still had only one political party in Hungary—another thirty-seven years would pass before the first free elections—we did at least sense a certain degree of relaxation, especially in the economy, which was slowly improving. This led to some guarded optimism, but it went hand in hand with a loosening of morals both in business and in people's private lives. People lived for the day and wanted to enjoy life to the maximum without thinking about the future.

Hungarian women, especially in the cities, began to dress rather provocatively, as they had before the war. Short skirts were back in favour. Often a wife earned more than her husband, which gave her financial independence. Most women went at least once a week to a hairdressing salon, where hairdressers worked in shifts to service all their customers. Manicure, pedicure and beauty salons took off, and women took every opportunity to exhibit their beauty. Divorce was restricted by the simple lack of living accommodation, which kept husbands and wives together under one roof but not necessarily in the same bed. The result was a rather easy-going attitude towards sexual behaviour. Because of the frequent activities organised by the Party after working hours, it was not difficult to find excuses for being late home.

Vera was by now working long hours at the Ministry of Chemical Industry and after work enjoyed a full social life surrounded by male colleagues. When once she was presented with a ticket for a week's holiday in a beautiful mountain resort as a reward for her good work, she went alone, but on her return I kept hearing about a man she had met there and became jealous. The separate lives we were leading were taking their toll on our relationship and we started to have arguments and quarrels that culminated in my having an affair. It started by chance when one day I bumped into Ági, one of the girls who had been living in the same hostel when I'd been a student at Pázmány Péter University.

Ági had spent just a year at the university before getting married, but she had found married life boring and as a solution had taken to trying out new lovers as often as others try out a new shirt. She was a short woman, rather plain looking, who wore glasses, and by now she had a son of about two years old, the same age as mine. On the positive side she was intelligent, well read, loved classical music, and was a conscientious worker as a receptionist for one of the best tailors in Budapest. A clinical nymphomaniac, she had a penchant for making love to different men in different places—the fitting room of the tailor's shop, in the open air, at home in front of her son. When I first visited her flat, her husband was not at home and she asked me bluntly: 'What are you waiting for?'

Her husband Feri, an uninspiring, short and overweight man, was lazy to the bone. He was always at home, babysitting while Ági went out supposedly for French lessons or to the cinema. 'I wish he'd take a lover too,' she would say, 'then I wouldn't feel so bad about being unfaithful to him.'

Be careful what you wish for, for it might come true. Somehow Ági became suspicious that her husband was being more than just friendly with his secretary at the office. This suspicion grew and it started bothering her. What was sauce for the goose was quite unacceptable for the gander. She became irritable, talked about his secretary as 'that little she-devil', and became determined to catch them redhanded.

'Why?' I pleaded with her. 'What will you do when you have your proof? Divorce him?' The question was of course highly relevant to me, as Ági might want to force me to join up with her on a more permanent basis. I had already considered this and decided against it: Ági made a good lover, but a terrible wife. She still held out hopes that I would divorce Vera and marry her instead, but I decided that enough was enough. In desperation she sent Vera a love letter I had stupidly written to her, hoping that Vera would want to leave me. It was agonising for my wife to read my description of making love to another woman, but it achieved quite the opposite effect. We talked matters over, and decided to start afresh.

Many years later we revisited Budapest. Opposite us on the underground sat a middle-aged couple holding hands, obviously very much in love.

'Isn't it nice?' Vera said to me. 'Middle-aged, still in love, and not afraid to show it.' Then at the next stop the women kissed the man and got off. As soon as the doors closed, the man took out his mobile phone.

'Hello darling,' he said. 'I'll be home in ten minutes.'

Nothing had changed....

I am grateful that the advent of Communism didn't mar the daily lives of my parents very much: they were of an older generation, born indeed under the Austro-Hungarian Empire, and had already lived through far too many violent changes. My father's subjects, mathematics and physics, were all but immune from Marxist interpretations. He was not unsympathetic towards Communism, but never joined the Party. Besides continuing to teach after our return to Orosháza, he also grew to become one of the leaders of Orosháza's Jewish community, a successor to Tafler *bácsi*, as it were. To supplement his modest teaching income, he started to work as an accountant for small shopkeepers and tradesmen, bringing the books home to work on them after school. He had no formal qualifications for this, but was intelligent, and soon mastered the subject and the regulatory requirements. Then at last, after completing forty years of service, he retired. The Minister of Religion and Education, Gyula Ortutay, named him in an official dispatch, and expressed his satisfaction at my father's work. It was not much of a reward, but to my father, professional teacher and faithful civil servant that he was, it meant a lot.

He managed to order a copy of the dispatch and almost cried for only the second time in his life, this time from the pleasure of simply seeing his name there.

My mother was ever an uneducated, simple person, who didn't concern herself with the new politics. She performed all her household duties impeccably, without the help of a maid. She kept up her contacts with the other housewives, and occasionally played cards, but no longer for money. My father's health slowly deteriorated, and he started to suffer from angina. Then an X-ray detected a tumour, and the surgeon wanted to operate to see if it was cancerous or not. It was an agonising decision, but my father decided not to take the risk.

My parents had both been delighted with the news of a grandchild, and were grateful that we named him István after their first son. When he was a few months old, my mother visited us to see him, but my father was too ill. Because of the limited space in Kresz Géza *utca*, she slept with me and Vera in the same bed. Under these trying circumstances, she stayed one night only. My father was prescribed a week's rest at Balatonfüred, a resort on Lake Balaton renowned for its treatment of cardiac disease. On the way there, he spent one day with us in Budapest. By this time István was eighteen months old and could stand up in his cot. It was delightful to see how my father enjoyed stroking his little head. I am thankful that he had this chance to see him, because soon afterwards he died at the age of 67 from a heart attack. Smoking, too much animal fat, and the sheer stress of what he had gone through in his life had taken its toll. My mother was awoken one night by a cry of pain. She went to Doctor Zelenka for help, but there was nothing to be done. I received a telephone call early the next morning and took the first train to Orosháza. The funeral took place in the Jewish cemetery and I went there with my mother

The Thaw

in a horse-drawn cab. My father's body was already there, in a simple coffin, according to Jewish tradition. There was no rabbi present: by this time my father was practically an atheist. Soon after the funeral I returned to Budapest, and my mother stayed on alone in our old house in Orosháza.

When István was old enough to travel we took him for a holiday to see his grandmother, who did her best to spoil him. On the surface, life in Orosháza hadn't changed much in the ten years since I had left for university. All the shops I remembered were still open, but every one had been taken over by the state, with their previous owners now employed as managers. The Tomas, our neighbours, were amongst the very few who had been allowed to keep their tailoring business. The market, full of produce grown on the peasant's little private plots, was thriving, but the state-run shops had become dreary. Many of my Jewish friends and acquaintances had left the town, and often also the country. I didn't meet any of my old schoolmates and, to be honest, I had no desire to. I stayed for a couple of days only, for I had to go back to work, but I left István at my mother's house for a couple of weeks. When I collected him, I didn't stay over, but instead hurried back to Budapest to work on a far more important personal project.

Obtaining a home for us—a real home—became my number one objective throughout the coming years. Even after Stalin's death and the start of the long crawl towards greater freedoms, we were only allowed to live in the accommodation approved for us by the *Lakáshivatal*, the 'residence office' of the local town hall. The norm in the 1950s was one room for two people, plus a kitchen and a bathroom, or two rooms if a couple had one or two children. Because of the severe shortage of accommodation after the massive destruction of the war, what had been built as discrete flats were often either divided or let to two families if it was possible to enter through a communally used kitchen or bathroom. After István's birth we were entitled on paper to three rooms: two for Vera, István and myself, and another one for my mother-in-law, but we only had two. Unfortunately for us, being entitled alone was not sufficient, and if we were to have more space I had to find some and, if necessary, pay for it.

One possible option was to have somebody build us a new home. In Hungary's still-devastated cities there was a breed of entrepreneur, mainly architects or builders by profession, who persuaded individuals with enough money to lay claim to the site of a war-damaged house and employ them to renovate it and make it suitable for living once more. An architect colleague of mine offered us to rebuild a partly destroyed house in a very desirable area. We looked at it, but decided that we couldn't afford it. Just as well, because he didn't in the end get building permission.

From my salary, given that we now had a child to raise, it was impossible to save the necessary money either to bribe officials or to pay a hefty sum to someone who might be prepared to exchange accommodation with us, or possibly both. I had to do something drastic about the increasingly fretful situation. I had to find a way to get some extra money, no easy matter in a country where private enterprise was seriously frowned upon.

Many people in Vegyterv, just as in any Hungarian industry, had more than one job. One engineer started a business lending formal outfits to couples wanting to marry. A chemist colleague of mine made money disinfecting homes by killing bugs with cyanide gas he had access to through his laboratory work. His only investment was a bucket and a gas mask, and he worked every weekend. Other people collected money for charitable causes and took a small commission. Communism proved unable to kill the entrepreneurship and creativity in people who were prepared to work hard and take risks in order to improve their lives.

One day, a neighbour of ours, a middle-aged woman whose parents lived in the country, approached me offering a small bottle of lavender oil, pressed from the flowers in her parent's garden, which could be used as perfume. To demonstrate its effectiveness, she invited me to smell her neck, which I couldn't refuse. The oil wasn't refined in any way and its smell was a little harsh, but I bought some from her. I diluted it with ethanol, filtered it through cotton wool, and added a little glycerine to stabilise the odour. Vera was quite happy with it, so I bought more oil paid for with the refined version, which our neighbour too found very good. I repeated the experiment, and hawked the results around Vegyterv.

I started concocting more perfumes, and later hand and face creams, selling them to my colleagues. My customers were mainly men, who would give my perfumes to their wives or mistresses as presents. My products were neither bad nor particularly good, but they were affordable and I was prepared to sell them on credit until payday. This turned out to be an exceptionally important factor in my favour, and soon business was booming. I gave them glamorous names like Chanel and Arpège. The fact that they bore no resemblance to the real thing (which in any case few if any of us had ever smelt!) was unimportant, for in cosmetics the most important thing is not so much the content as the elegant packaging.

My money-making activity was, of course, illegal, and getting hold of everything I needed wasn't easy. I could buy glycerine and lanolin, a basis for face creams, legally; ethanol I got by forging doctors' letters as I'd often done in the past; and I bought perfume essences from an enterprising chemist. Where *he* got them from, I didn't want to know. My main problem was getting hold of the pretty glass containers which are so important when packaging a scent. There were several shops dotted across Budapest for citizens to take empty glass containers of all kinds to be recycled. They would pay the small sum of 10 *fillér* for each item handed in to them. I went one day to such a shop, and when there were no other customers about I admired one of the perfume bottles which the shopkeeper, an elderly woman, had just collected.

'I'd pay you 50 *fillér* for this bottle,' I said, 'and for any others as well, if you keep all the nice ones for me. They must have their undamaged top on.' Naturally, it was illegal for the shopkeeper to sell on anything she had bought, but for a poor woman like her a profit of five hundred per cent was too much to resist. Thereafter she always saved the nicest scent bottles for me and I was assured of a continuous supply. I would go to the shop with an old bottle in my hand, as though waiting to exchange it for my 10 *fillér*, and hang around until I was the only customer before collecting the package she had already prepared for me and handing over her money. I made sure never to keep large quantities of ingredients at my home, so if there were ever suspicions and a search by the authorities I could always claim that what I had was for private use. This meant that I had to work late almost every night to prepare small batches.

I was building up a thriving business, but because of the low prices of the items I made it would have taken far too long to save enough to pay for better accommodation. Then I received help from an unexpected source. During my military service I had met János, a soldier like me, only a little younger and a lot fitter, and sporting a Hitler moustache. János was quiet and patient, and ready to help anybody in need. He too was married with a daughter, and upon our return to Budapest the two of us became good friends. A tailor by profession, after our basic training he was given a job in a workshop where they mended the uniforms of the Soviet troops who, following the 'Khrushchev Thaw', were being withdrawn from occupied Austria. Many of these Russians were smuggling Western goods such as cigarettes, coffee, watches, and ladies' nylon underwear, all of which were a lot cheaper in Austria than in Hungary. János began acting as a middleman, paying for the goods and then passing them on to a network of blackmarket retailers. At his suggestion, I became one of his retailers, selling his goods at Vegyterv in addition to my range of perfumes and cosmetics. Black-marketeering like this was not only illegal but downright dangerous, and could land you with a spell of months or even years in prison. János and I used to meet in public places, where I would take a parcel from him while he took the money from me in an envelope. By Hungarian standards it was a very large sum—a month's salary of 1,800 *forint* at the least—but János never counted it, nor did I ever check the contents of the parcel. I always bore in mind what Kövesi *bácsi* the tableware merchant had taught me in the labour camp, about the importance of buying cheaply and trusting your partner to be successful in business. My turnover and profits skyrocketed.

The most popular items I had in my collection were the ladies' nylons, richly decorated and seductive and unavailable in Hungary. One regular customer of mine was Ildikó Komáromi, a young single girl working as a Vegyterv draftswoman. She had impeccable taste, and dressed modestly in light pastel shades of the latest fashion. She never bought my kitchen-sink perfumes, preferring the famous makes instead, bought on the black market. During the day she worked quietly at her drafting board, was friendly with everyone, but in spite of many suitors had no particular relationship with anyone in the office. In the evenings she used to go to places like the Opera House, where she could meet well-connected men. Some people said that she easily earned the cost of those nylon knickers, which were far from cheap, in one night. Then one day she got married to a successful surgeon, became a perfect, devoted wife, and I lost my best customer.

It was dangerous to keep any quantity of smuggled goods at home, so I would fit them into a parcel, tie a string around this, and hang it down a ventilation shaft. I kept just a small stock in my office, and at night made sure it was locked away in my desk. The only downside to this was that our desks could be, and regularly were, opened up at night by the security officer, who searched them for confidential papers and whatever else he could find. One morning a customs officer visited Vegyterv and started interviewing people. By good fortune I was not the first in line and was warned about the danger. Even better, someone, and a good Communist at that, agreed to hold my stash of goods while the officer searched my desk. He didn't find anything, but it seemed that someone had confessed to having bought something from me. This was sufficient evidence, but without the incriminating goods themselves I was ordered to pay just a small fine.

I had enough willpower not to blow any of the money I earned by illegal activities, instead saving every penny for a new home. There was no possibility of depositing so much money in the bank—it would have aroused too much suspicion—and so I kept it all as cash hidden amongst my old university lecture notes. I got to hear about someone who had the right contacts to bribe officials and get the address of an apartment for me, which I could then claim. He turned out to be a badly dressed old man, overweight,

The Thaw

and utterly corrupt, but he quoted a number of successful deals as references. I paid him a substantial sum, about a month's salary, in advance, but then got no address from him for more than a year. When I complained, he paid some of the money back to me in the form of smuggled cigarettes, but I still lost a lot. One day, when I called at his place, I walked in on him while he was injecting himself. At the time, this was so unusual in Hungary that it never occurred to me that it might be some kind of illegal drug and that my money might have ended up in his arm.

'It's to calm my nerves,' he said without stopping. A few minutes later, the very same customs officer who had fined me for selling smuggled goods came to visit him as an old friend. He was also, it transpired, friendly with the father of the secret policeman assigned to the refinery at Almasfüzitő. The rot had obviously spread deep into the Hungarian body politic even just a couple of years after the thaw. There was nobody to complain to about my loss: I was after all acting illegally.

In the end I was successful in getting decent accommodation for my family. It was an immensely complicated affair, involving several households and venal officials. The net effect was that, in return for a payment from me, a family was prepared to look after a terminally ill old man who lived in a three-room flat with his own family, who wanted to wash their hands of him. His new family set up a bed for him in a tiny space that in very different times had housed the maid. Once the old man had moved out, the rest of his own family were no longer entitled to three rooms and so moved into our two-room flat. Of course, I had to compensate them for the loss of their larger home, and bribe officials to make sure that their empty flat would be allocated to us and not to somebody else. In all, it cost us a year's salary.

WHEN EVEN THE POETS WERE SILENT

As soon as we had moved home, I stopped all my illegal activities. Our new flat was still in central Budapest, in Zichy Jenő *utca*, just a kilometre away from our previous home, on the first floor of an old building. Our windows faced onto the street, but because the street was very narrow our rooms were not much lighter than those in our first flat. But now at least we had one bedroom for my mother-in-law, one properly sized bedroom for ourselves, and a shared living room in between the two.

We had brought with us sufficient furniture for two rooms only, and so I decided to get an extra settee for the living room. This proved to be far easier said than done. I found a second-hand furniture shop a fair distance away, and saw a suitable settee in the window. It was big, with light-green upholstery extending to the ground, covering legs that ran on little castors. It wasn't expensive, and I snapped it up. The shop, however, didn't deliver, and suggested that I put in a request to the state-owned lorry service. This, though, would have cost more than the settee, so I asked Feri, an athletic colleague of mine, to help me take it home.

It proved to be far heavier than it had looked in the shop window. First we tried lifting it up and carrying it, but had to stop and rest every fifty steps. So we put it down and tried pushing it along on its castors. The pavement, though, was in a terrible state, all cobblestones and potholes, and eventually the castors broke off. We struggled on as best we could, when it started to rain. It proved to be a real downpour, and as the water soaked into the settee it grew heavier by the minute. We too by now were soaking wet, but this was the least of our worries.

'What do we do now?' Feri asked, obviously sorry that he had volunteered for the job in the first place. The only sensible thing was to abandon the settee by the side of the road and hope that we would be able to pick it up again later.

The Thaw

We should have known better, and by the next morning it had disappeared. Budapest was full of people far poorer than us, who would have looked upon an abandoned settee, albeit a sopping wet one, as a godsend. Even without the settee, though, we found our new home pure heaven.

Vera, István and I enjoyed the little pleasures that life in Budapest had to offer following the end of Stalinism. People who had access to the hard currencies of the West could now buy luxury and imported goods in designated shops (not that we ourselves had any hard currency, possession of which was not permitted for ordinary citizens). Rationing had finally ended in early 1952 with an announcement by Rákosi and, although the rise in food prices had far outstripped the increase in everybody's salaries, as a treat we could even afford to eat in a restaurant now and then. The menus would consist of simple Hungarian stews like *gulyás* and *paprikás*, well prepared and tasty. In the warm weather of summer, restaurants would open their terraces and people would eat *al fresco*. Our favourite was located in a large, well-kept garden amongst the landscaped parks of Margaret Island in the middle of the Danube. The island had two swimming pools, an open-air theatre, and a famous water tower which played a tune on the hour. In those days, Hungarians were required to work Saturday mornings, but on Sundays Margaret Island was always full of people promenading, families with children playing football or just picnicking on the lawn. Occasionally Vera and I might travel the 100km by train to a resort on Lake Balaton, which became very crowded in the season. We had Vera's mother to thank for babysitting—and thoroughly spoiling!—little István on these occasions while we found some time to ourselves.

By far the cheapest, and therefore most popular, entertainment was walking. Vera and I belonged to a ramblers' club and would walk in the low hills just north of Budapest in the company of others, mainly students and their partners. At the summit of most hills there was a simple hut with primitive accommodation, where one could buy hot soup and a snack.

The possibilities for travelling much further in our leisure time than could be managed by means of Budapest's public transport system were restrained by several factors. We did not, of course, own a car. In fact, I only ever met one person in those days who owned a private car, and he was a mechanical engineer who spent most of his time and money to keep his dilapidated Fiat on the road. For business travel we had the use of company cars with drivers, but none of us working in a place like Vegyterv ever thought about learning to drive. Flying was possible for people who needed to get somewhere for business or politics, and I was considered important enough to fly on Hungary's fleet of DC-3s. The DC-3 took off and landed on grass, flew rather low, and the ride was often bumpy, but this was made up for by the breathtaking views the trip provided. I often flew from Budapest to the industrial city of Miskolc in the northeast, from where I would be taken by chauffeured car to our new nitrate plant.

Private travel within Hungary's borders was allowed, but spending a night in any location other than one's hometown meant having to register with the local police within twenty-four hours. This required the purchase for a few *fillér* of a form at a post office, which then had to be completed and stamped at the police station. It was always quite an effort to find both a post office and a police station in an unfamiliar town and to catch them when they were both open. Private travel to other countries, even other

Communist ones, was impossible. The official reason for restricting international travel was the unavailability of foreign currency; the real reason was to keep us ignorant of what was going on elsewhere. A few people other than high-ranking Party members—people involved in sport and the arts—were permitted to travel to the West, but they had to go alone. The Party was so afraid of defections that they did not allow families to travel together: parents had to leave their children at home, and if they ever wanted to see them again they had to return. I myself did get a passport, once, when I was sent to the neighbouring Romanian People's Republic on a business trip. It was valid for just that single journey and only into another Communist state.

The biggest improvement to our quality of life at this time came not from some ideological shift in the far-away Kremlin but from buying a second-hand kayak. We stored it at Szúnyog *sziget*—Mosquito Island—which in the 1950s was a popular resort on the Danube just a few kilometres north of Budapest city centre. The law demanded that at least one person in any kind of boat, including our kayak, must have a sort of maritime 'driving licence'. To obtain this I first had to prove I could swim 400 metres non-stop in a swimming pool, this being roughly the width of the Danube. After that I had to pass a theoretical exam, followed immediately by a practical one using my own kayak out on the river—starting off, stopping, turning about and so on.

After passing my kayaking test, our next problem was to get a cabin on Mosquito Island so that we could spend a night there and make a weekend of our river trips. There were already a number of cabins in a row, each just big enough to sleep two people, but they were all on permanent leases and their tenants were unwilling to part with them.

'Do you want a cabin?' asked the resort's caretaker, a crafty old man who did everything in his power to earn a little extra money: the city's boat owners were better paid than the average worker and, if anyone, could afford to give him generous tips. 'If you do, I can make one for you at the end of the row. There's just enough space for one more in the corner.'

He was not a professional joiner and the cabin was a very primitive affair, built from salvaged planks of wood, with just a single bed, a straw-filled mattress, and a couple of nails in the wall to serve as hooks. There was no running water, but he had managed to hang an electric light from the ceiling. There was no switch: we had to turn the bulb in and out of its socket. When it was finished, I had to go to the resort's residence office to apply to hire a cabin.

'None available,' said the official without even looking at the records.

'There is now,' I corrected him, and pointed out the location of our cabin on his plan, which he duly corrected. It became state-owned property, and we became its first tenants on condition that we pay the yearly rent. We considered ourselves very lucky, and were grateful to that enterprising caretaker.

All through the summer we would take out our kayak every Saturday after work and paddle north upriver. There was an empty barn, and there would always be several young boat owners who stopped and spent the night there. Our kayak was big enough for two adults and a child, and occasionally we took István with us, who loved the water. On weekends there were always plenty of small vessels on the Danube, mainly rowing boats which travelled faster than our kayak but had to keep farther away from the shallows by the shore. In our kayak we could hug the bank, which meant less resistance from the current, while a foot-operated rudder, an unusual feature in a kayak, allowed us perfect control.

On the following Sunday morning we would go swimming in the Danube, then in the afternoon pack our few provisions up, head for the midstream, and slowly travel down with the current, back to our cabin, undisturbed in those days by commercial shipping. Sunday night would be spent on Mosquito Island, and early the next morning we would return to work.

The Danube, Europe's second-longest river, was fast but peaceful, and perfectly safe for our kayak, but it could become treacherous in stormy weather. The Meteorological Institute would fire a cannon to warn sailors of an approaching storm, which could arise from nowhere. The law required that, on hearing the cannon, vessels had to find moorings until the storm had passed. One afternoon, when we were returning home and already on the outskirts of Budapest, we heard the warning shot ring out. Fortunately we saw a landing stage nearby where we could tie up and paddled there at great speed. We had just managed to get out before the storm hit, when two huge men came running towards us, shouting at us to get back into our kayak and leave at once.

'There's a storm coming,' we protested. 'Can't we just stay here until it's over? We have a young child with us.'

'You can't land here,' they insisted. 'This is private land.'

'*Private* land?' I retorted. 'Under Communism? What nonsense!' But the men became even more threatening and we had no option but to climb back into the kayak and paddle away.

The storm was by now fully upon us, the wind blowing from the south, the very direction in which we were heading, and whipping up the waves. We were not very far from home, but on the wrong side of the Danube, and we decided to try to cross the river and make for Mosquito Island. It was an immense effort to paddle against the wind and we took on a lot of water. I was scared, fully aware of how precarious the situation was, but had to behave as if everything were under control so as not to frighten little István, who thought that the whole journey was a great adventure. By the time we reached the shore the kayak was almost full and we were sitting in water. The landing stage where we had not been allowed to sit out the storm was a resort reserved for the high functionaries of the Communist Party. Private land indeed! George Orwell's *Animal Farm* had already become reality, and scarcely a few years after the Communists had come to power. Everybody was equal, but already some were more equal than others. It was a minor epiphany. That the Hungarian Communist Party had considered the privacy of its functionaries over and above the safety of my wife and child planted within me the seed of a conviction that there was no future for us in Hungary.

I am convinced that the Hungarian Uprising of October 1956 was a largely spontaneous outburst by a people oppressed. The Communist Party had not polled one eighth of the votes cast in the 1945 election, but with its salami-slicing tactics had inveigled its way to power by 1949. A mutual assistance treaty had allowed the Red Army to remain on Hungarian soil, giving the Soviet Union the final say in how Hungary was run. The Soviets had demanded the lion's share of Hungary's agricultural output, and war reparations of $300 million were strangling the economy. Rákosi's paranoid Stalinism had seen many thousands arrested, tortured and shipped off to camps by the hated ÁVH. Rural collectives and the nationalisation of industry had led to shortages and privation. The Peace Bonds had left us bitter. We wanted freedom of information, freedom of choice, of movement, and above all freedom from political oppression. The first signs of a thaw which had occurred after the death of Stalin made us hungry for more and more. I don't truly think most people wanted necessarily to get rid of socialism altogether, consciously opting for capitalism in its place; they just wanted to reform the system, to make it more humane. They also dearly wanted Hungary to become an independent sovereign state once more, free from Soviet domination. When things began little by little to change, events gained their own momentum. It was like Rákosi's salami-slicing tactics all over again, but in reverse. I loved the excitement of the thaw, looked forward to changes which brought something new and always pleasant every day. I longed for freedom, although I didn't know quite what I would do with it.

One popular weekly paper, the *Irodalmi Újság* or *Literary Gazette*, the journal of the Free Union of Hungarian Writers, played an important role in the period leading up to the Uprising. Available only in a small print run, there was always a long queue of people waiting for it each week at the newspaper stands. After scouring it, we would hand it on until eventually it obtained a massive readership. Expressing their increasing dissatisfaction with the status quo, well-known writers and poets used the *Gazette* to advocate a rebalancing of the very one-sided relationship between Hungary and the USSR and a thorough overhaul of a Party which had promised a socialist utopia but which had delivered corruption and economic failure.

In the summer of 1956, after violent demonstrations against Communist rule in Poland, Hungary's highly unpopular ruler Rákosi was indeed removed by the Soviet Politburo, only to be replaced by another hardliner named Ernő Gerő. On October 23rd, a date now celebrated as Hungary's National Day, a student demonstration in

Budapest turned violent when the ÁVH opened fire on a crowd outside the radio building. The crowd, joined by soldiers who sided with the protesters, turned on the ÁVH. The next day, Soviet tanks were on the streets amongst chaotic fighting. Ernő Gerő fled to the Soviet Union, and Imre Nagy, a well-known moderate and the popular choice of the student demonstrators, became the head of a new government. As the protestors felt the tide turning in their favour, there were lethal reprisals against the ÁVH and the Soviets, and the governmental structures and visible symbols of Hungarian Communism began to be dismantled. By the end of the month, the Red Army had fallen back from Budapest to regroup. For the moment at least, Hungary was free. Across the country now, people broke into Party offices and personnel departments to hunt for their personal files. When the files for my family in Orosháza were broken into and read we discovered that our major crime was receiving parcels from my aunt Adél in New York containing coffee, cocoa and nylon stockings.

Tragically, Imre Nagy's National Government held office for less than a fortnight before the Politburo in Moscow decided to crush the uprising by force. In hindsight, Nagy's hints that Hungary might withdraw from the Warsaw Pact seem to have forced the Soviets' hand: at a dangerous juncture in the Cold War, Moscow could not possibly allow one of its satellites to leave the fold, while the US could not risk an open conflict with the USSR by intervening militarily in support of Nagy. On November 4th the Red Army rolled into Budapest for the second time in just over a decade, only this time as conquerors rather than as the liberators they proclaimed themselves to be.

The fighting was very one-sided now, the Russians opening fire with tank rounds at anything that moved. Buildings were destroyed, and many more damaged. Fortunately our own Zichy Jenő *utca* was so narrow that the tank commanders didn't dare to enter, wary of Molotov cocktails, and so our home was spared. In less than a week, though, the uprising had been put down. More than two thousand Hungarians had been killed.

I inadvertently missed all of this, the most pivotal episode in the history of modern Hungary. On October 20th, three days before the student demonstrations turned violent, I had departed with our old friend Sándor Farkas and a few other colleagues from Vegyterv on a trip to Romania, where we had designed a pilot plant to make chemicals from natural gas. We had been staying in Bucharest, in one of Romania's only good hotels, the Athénée Palace. We had found life in Romania even more backward than in Hungary, and had been surprised to be treated almost like Western Europeans. People had approached us on the street wanting to buy everything we had, from our cameras to our raincoats. By contrast, the only thing we had found worth bringing back was black pepper, scarce yet much in demand in Hungary but available in abundance in Romania.

After we had been in Romania for a few days, word rapidly reached us at the chemical plant that there was fighting and shooting in Budapest. I didn't understand: who was shooting whom, and why? Finally we assembled a picture of what was happening. Each and every one of us Hungarians wanted to return: our families were in Budapest, and we wanted to be part of the uprising. Every day we were told by the Romanian Ministry of Foreign Affairs that we needed an exit visa in order to leave, and that they would give us our exit visas in due course. They were biding their time, it seemed: had the uprising succeeded, Hungary might, like Tito's Yugoslavia before it, have left the Communist fold, and Hungary would have become

Romania's enemy. The Romanian authorities had no desire to allow a group of experienced chemical engineers to leave its territory and rejoin the enemy.

I don't remember a thing about the chemical plant we were supposed to be overseeing, but only that my whole being was filled with fear at the thought that I would not be able to see my family again. I managed to telephone Vera one evening and suggested that she should flee the country and travel with István to Vienna by train. According to some information that had reached us in Bucharest, this would have been a simple matter, a risk-free opportunity during the first few days of the uprising, when the border with Austria was thrown open and refugees spilled across into the West. I told her I would manage somehow to get to Vienna via Yugoslavia and that we could meet there. Vera, though, was far from confident about fleeing to Austria without me, a good deal scared at what might go wrong, and István had a painful ear infection. She said she would wait for me at home rather than risk one or other of us failing to make it to safety.

I discussed our predicament with my colleagues in the Athénée Palace, and all but one agreed that we should all leave Bucharest as soon as possible. If we couldn't return to Hungary directly, at least we should try to get to Yugoslavia, or preferably even Austria. There were rumours that the Yugoslavs were allowing displaced Hungarians transit to Austria, but details were sketchy. There was just one conscientious Communist among our delegation, who said that we should stay in Romania and finish the job.

'*Maul halten und weiter dienen!*' he insisted, quoting the old slogan popular under the Austro-Hungarian Empire: 'Shut your mouth and do your duty!'

Sándor Farkas, though, held quite the opposite view. 'Okay, Communism didn't seem to work,' I started the ball rolling one evening, 'but what about socialism? Assuming of course that we're talking about *real* socialism, not the sort we had in Hungary.'

'That won't work either,' said Sándor. He was always a bit authoritarian, almost pig-headed, convinced that he was always right. 'It runs contrary to human nature. People are selfish and want to get the best deal for themselves and for their family. They won't share wealth and privilege of their own free will.'

'What if everybody were to benefit from the whole being worth more than the sum of its parts?' I reasoned.

'It might work for a while,' he conceded, 'but only until one person tries to cheat and take a bigger share for himself. That would undermine trust, and the whole system would collapse. You must have seen how quickly an orderly queue can disintegrate if just one person tries to barge in ahead of others? Everybody else in the queue either resents him or starts to jockey for their own little advantage.'

'How can an old Communist like you, Sándor, hold views like *that*?' I asked in astonishment.

'Don't you see, Gyuri? I'm the best proof of what I just said....'

On November 3rd we were surprised to receive exit visas from the Romanians, who in hindsight must have been informed by the Soviets of what was about to happen. I took a taxi to the Gara de Nord and, finding that there were still no direct trains between Romania and Hungary, eventually got a ticket for the night train to Belgrade, the capital of Yugoslavia. The fact that I should have had a seat reservation as well as a ticket didn't matter, for this was Romania: I gave a royal tip to the conductor and he took care of me.

With the Romanian *lei* I had on me, which in Yugoslavia would be worthless, I bought a second-hand camera, thinking I might smuggle it across the border without declaring it and then sell it in Belgrade. To my delight it perfectly fitted the toilet-paper box in the carriage's WC. After crossing into Yugoslavia I went to recover the camera I'd planned to smuggle, but it had been stolen. What had Sándor said, about everybody trying to cheat, and to take a bigger share for himself? Stealing a little here and there from the state was commonplace under Communism, but stealing from your fellow man was as unacceptable as ever, and I felt very hard done by.

When the train stopped, I heard Hungarian voices from outside the window. This was no surprise: what were in 1956 the northern territories of Yugoslavia had until the Treaty of Trianon in 1920 been part of the Austro-Hungarian Empire, and a large proportion of the population in that border region remained ethnically Hungarian.

'*Hallottak valami újat Magyarországról?*' I asked anxiously: 'Any news from Hungary?'

Yes, there was news, but it was the worst I could have expected: the Soviets had attacked Budapest just a few hours earlier. Imre Nagy had made a radio appeal to the West for help, but in vain, and he and a number of other revolutionary leaders and their families had sought refuge in the Yugoslav Embassy. I arrived in Belgrade later that same day, but found that I was in no better position to continue my journey to Budapest than I had been in Romania. Hungary was cut off from the rest of the world. With a small crowd of Hungarian state employees, all of us unwilling refugees now, I was put up in a cheap hotel and given enough money to survive by the Hungarian commercial office in Belgrade, where we spent every day waiting for news from the north. Telephone connections with Hungary were down, and we had no way of discovering what had happened to our families, who we knew were trapped in a city at war.

Eventually, after what seemed like an age since our arrival in Belgrade but which must have been less than a week, the telephone at the commercial office rang, and the Hungarian official in charge demanded silence. 'It's Budapest!' he shouted in an excited voice. I didn't wait a moment longer, but ran to the central telephone exchange and handed over the number of my home.

'There are no lines to Budapest,' the operator said without trying.

'There are now,' I corrected her, and within a few minutes I was talking to the wife of my brother-in-law. Bertalan and his wife had been living in a flat overlooking a prominent square where a lot of fighting had taken place, and for their safety they had moved into ours in Zichy Jenő *utca*. A colleague and friend of mine from Vegyterv, a bachelor named Péter Schiffer, had taken it upon himself to look after Vera. During the fighting he had come around checking if everything was all right, bringing food for her and for our son.

The short-lived resistance to the Red Army was brutally crushed, and on November 14th the situation over the border was quiet enough for us all to board a bus to Budapest with papers in both Hungarian and Russian stating who we were, just in case we arrived back during the night-time curfew to be confronted by a Soviet patrol. I had on me the black pepper I had bought in Romania, a few tins of sardines (a luxury not to be found in Hungary), a toy for István and some handmade silver jewellery for Vera. The journey home was uneventful, and our return after such a cataclysm an anticlimax.

I needed time to find my bearings. The uprising was over, but there was still a Workers' Council representing the ordinary citizens, actively negotiating with the new, Soviet-backed government. In the design office at Vegyterv, nobody was working, just drinking coffee and talking, weighing up the political situation and guessing at the future. People were divided: the optimists still held out hopes for a Western intervention, or for a compromise between the government and the Workers' Council; the pessimists predicted a return to the years of Stalinist terror. The atmosphere was sombre. There were no laughs, and no jokes. This was too serious for political satire. The streets of Budapest were deserted, cold and dark, as if some terrible plague were stalking the city.

Toward the end of November, the revolutionary leader Imre Nagy left the Yugoslav Embassy under a safe-passage agreement, only to be arrested by the Soviets and spirited away to Romania. Charged with treason, he was later tried, hanged in secret, and buried facedown in an unmarked grave. Then we heard on the radio that the new regime had abolished the Workers' Council and had ordered the arrest of its leaders. This was what finally made up my mind. With the outlawing of that last shred of hope, there seemed to be absolutely nothing to look forward to. I felt sure that every one of the humble improvements we had seen since the end of Stalinism would now be reversed, and that Communist rule would switch back to repression. I had no intention of being part of it. Most of all, I didn't want my son to grow up in a society like that. Anything would be better. The only choice was to leave the country.

We tuned in to Radio Free Europe, which was broadcasting non-stop in Hungarian, urging people to leave. There were messages from refugees who had made it across the border to Austria and were now bound for the United States and other destinations. They described in vivid detail the financial assistance they had received, and the great welcome they had been given by the locals. I must honestly say that this in itself didn't influence my decision to leave. For a start I didn't trust everything they said, and in any case I was not particularly motivated by financial gain. Neither was I particularly afraid of being arrested for involvement with the uprising, as so many thousands were, because I had demonstrably not been in Hungary during the fighting. I had simply had enough of Communism and wanted a better life for my wife and child.

We Hungarians were relatively lucky in that Austria, whose eastern regions had until the previous year been occupied by the Russian Army, had been officially declared a politically neutral democratic state. As a side effect of the recent political thaw, the mines and the barbed wire had been removed along the frontier. There were rumours that the new regime was already busy replacing them, but, with 366km of forests and fields to cover, the task could not be completed overnight. There was a short window of opportunity that we might regret not taking for the rest of our lives.

WHEN EVEN THE POETS WERE SILENT

8
Freedom

TO UNDERSTAND why we left Hungary you would have to understand—no, you would have to *feel*—the hopelessness of our situation in the winter of 1956. At the age of seventeen, a Jewish boy returning from Nazi persecution, I had joined the Communist Party, only to be expelled at the age of twenty. It is true that I was never an active member, but even after my expulsion I remained a sympathiser. Communism was the only ideology that made me feel confident of not being persecuted again. But then as the years passed any sympathy I felt to Communism wore away, and I became more and more critical of the excesses of the Party, the development of a new ruling class, the simple but overwhelming difference between theory and practice. By reading the thoughts of dissident Hungarian intellectuals in the *Literary Gazette*, and by listening to the broadcasts of the BBC World Service and Radio Free Europe, an alternative was slowly forming in my mind—*demokrácia*, the same word I had seen on a poster upon a wall when I had crossed back into Hungary in 1945.

Following the footsteps of some 200,000 fellow Hungarians who had already crossed the frontier, Vera and I took the decision to flee with four-year-old István. We were amongst the last to go. Those who had left in the fortnight between the student demonstrations and the Red Army's reoccupation of Budapest were mostly opportunists, quickly taking advantage of the possibility of leaving. Amongst those who left after the tanks arrived were many who had taken up arms against the regime, who now had either to escape or face persecution or death. Others had left because they had been faced with a simple question: 'My best friend has left, my neighbour too, and my colleague, so what am I still doing here?' Then there were people like us, who had had enough of Communism and wanted a better life for their children. Irrespective of the different reasons why people left, the exodus was a great loss to Hungary, for amongst those who left were many well-trained people with a spirit of adventure, a gift of entrepreneurship, unafraid of change. In all, four per cent of the population crossed the borders, most of them to Austria but some to Tito's Yugoslavia, and in some towns in Western Hungary more than one in ten fled. Most had already left by November, but I had been unavoidably detained in Bucharest and we had still not left by mid-December, by which time the 'improvement' in border security had made leaving even more difficult. I thought it positively amusing, that in 1944 the Hungarian state had thrown me out of the country and been unconcerned whether I lived or died, while now it was trying its utmost to keep me in.

During the days leading up to our departure people discussed the flight in general terms in the design office at Vegyterv. Some were dead against leaving Hungary and advocated loyalty and patriotism. Those of us thinking of leaving said nothing, just kept our thoughts to ourselves. And, of course, most people did in the end stay put, whether from genuine patriotism, or more often apprehensiveness, or simply inertia and fear of the unknown. 'I heard that the frontier's mined again,' they would say, or 'Yesterday a family of five was shot by the Russian border guards,' or 'I heard that Austria's had enough and is sending refugees back.' They were all based on rumour, and you can't argue with rumour: you either believe it or you don't. It didn't deter me. I was convinced that they were repeating doubts to justify their inaction, and more to themselves than to others. Some of those who did leave didn't initially even plan to stay long abroad, and thought that they would soon come back, after the dust had settled and life in Hungary had returned to normal. I was not one of these. I left Hungary knowing that I would never return, that I would have no choice but to integrate and to build a new life for my family in a new country. I was prepared to burn my bridges behind me.

'I hope you realise,' I warned Vera, 'that escaping won't be easy, and that it involves a fair amount of risk besides. If we're caught I'll be sent to jail, I'll lose my job, and we'll be marked for life. Even if we make it into Austria it will be painful, but for István's sake we have to do it. This is his chance to grow up in a new country, to assimilate, to become like the majority and not have to put up with persecution like we have.'

Because of the real possibility of getting captured, we took no valuables with us—no foreign currency (not that we had any), no documents, no address books, no camera (to avoid accusations of spying), just a change of underwear and some sandwiches. We wore walking boots and old clothing, so as not to spoil our best clothes should we have to abort our plans and return to our old life. I reasoned that, if we were caught, it would be best have nothing on us that indicated any plan to make a new life in the West. We would at least be able to spin a story about looking for a distant relative who lived in the 'forbidden zone' that in recent days had been set up along the Austrian frontier. While the security forces probably wouldn't have believed us, there might have been enough uncertainty in their minds to allow Vera and István to return home to Budapest, though I would probably have had to spend time in jail.

It was not an easy decision to leave our worldly goods behind, but I presumed that, if we were successful in our escape, we would eventually be able to replace the material things. What was irreplaceable, though, were the memorabilia, the letters and the photos. I told myself I would not need my chemistry diploma: it wouldn't be accepted in the West anyway, and I'd be lucky to get a job as a lab assistant.

We both left widowed mothers in Hungary. We telephoned to tell my mother in Orosháza of our decision to leave: there was no hope of a proper discussion at such a remove. My mother-in-law gave us her full support, and was concerned only because Vera would be separated from her brother Bertalan. On her instigation, Bertalan and his now-pregnant wife followed on a week later. We could tell very few people about our plan, simply because in Hungary's unsettled state we could not trust nobody except closest family. Besides, on a practical level, there was no guarantee that we would be successful, and we didn't want to give up our jobs in case we had simply to return quietly home.

One Friday evening, when Vera arrived home from work, I told her that we ought to leave the very next morning.

'We can't!' she protested.

'Why not?' I asked.

'Because I've just bought a goose in the market! We've enough to eat for a whole week! How can we go now?'

I managed to persuade her that the future of our son was more important than the goose, and on the morning of Saturday, December 15th, 1956, we boarded an early train bound for Vienna, our tickets valid as far as Mosonmagyaróvár, the last town before the restricted border zone. Bertalan came with us to the station to say goodbye. Genuinely unsure whether we would ever see each other again, we tried very hard to hide our tears in case they gave us away.

The train was still standing at the platform, and we could so easily have disembarked and got to work without even being late. No one would have known what we had been planning, and we could have picked up our lives where we had left off. But we stayed, and finally the station-master came out of his office holding up his green flag. The conductor blew his whistle, and the wheels started to turn in a cloud of steam. There was no way back now.

Our six-seat compartment was already occupied by two ladies and a uniformed railway official of about my age. He took the day's edition of *Szabad Nép* from his coat pocket and began to read. The two ladies, probably mother and daughter, were impeccably dressed, had Austrian passports, and were returning to Austria, but could speak Hungarian. They had probably emigrated before the war, I surmised. The older lady started talking to István, and with an encouraging smile asked him his name.

'Pisti,' he replied, giving her his pet name.

'And how old are you, Pisti?'

'Four.'

'And where are you going to?

'To visit my grandmother,' was his reply, since this is what we had told him.

'And where does your grandmother live?'

'In Orosháza.'

Everyone in the compartment, except István, knew that the train was heading in exactly the opposite direction. Nobody said a word, but just looked at each other in embarrassment. The lady stopped smiling. The railwayman went on reading his paper as if he hadn't heard. We had scarcely left Budapest, and already our cover was blown. I could only hope that nobody would give us up to the authorities. The two ladies were unlikely to, but what about the railwayman? He might have been a conscientious Communist who would make it his duty to stop us, or he might simply have been afraid of becoming an auxiliary to our crime. After all, he was reading *Szabad Nép*. I considered getting off at the next station and trying our luck later, on a different train. I went out into the corridor to get some air, and to my horror the railwayman followed me.

'Look here,' he said, 'I know very well where you're going.' He winked to make sure I understood the situation before he continued. 'You might as well know that I want to go the same way. Let's exchange plans—perhaps we can learn from each other.'

My plan was to leave the train at Mosonmagyaróvár and spend the day hiding before crossing over during the night into the forbidden zone. I planned to hide again during the next day and then, the following night, simply walk over the border to Austria. Looking back, it wasn't a very viable plan, especially not with a child of four in tow. I had no clear picture of where we could hide, either before or inside the forbidden zone, nor what we could eat or drink, or where we could sleep, but I was optimistic and determined. The railwayman however was unimpressed by my half-baked plan, and he had inside information.

'I have a better one,' he said. 'You see, the security forces aren't yet sufficiently organised to be at each and every station waiting for each and every train. I know for sure that if they're waiting at Levél, the first station inside the forbidden zone, the signalmen will deliberately stop the train outside the station so that people can get off and make a run for it. But if the train enters the station without stopping, it means the security forces aren't there.'

Levél was inside the closed border zone, one stop after Mosonmagyaróvár but still one stop before Hegyeshalom, which lay just three kilometres short of the frontier. Getting off at Levél would fully halve the distance to the border and reduce the likelihood of us being detained. Our tickets were for Mosonmagyaróvár only, but it was very unlikely that they would be checked. I decided to adopt the railwayman's plan, and to team up with him. As the neat station at Mosonmagyaróvár disappeared behind us we kept our fingers crossed. Where would the train stop? Would we have enough time to get off and run away if the signals turned red before Levél? You can imagine our joy when the train pulled up inside the station of Levél without stopping, and our horror when we saw that the platform was full of soldiers. We were not sure if they were regulars or members of the ÁVH, but it didn't matter much either way. One officer was checking each and every passenger's documents at the exit from the station, and a lorry was waiting to collect all those who were travelling without the right papers. It was clearly too late to jump off the train on the wrong side and make a run for it without being noticed. Then, without a word, the railwayman put on his cap, walked briskly to the other end of the platform, and entered the signalmen's hut as if he had come on official business. We else could we do but follow him? It was dark inside, and there was insufficient room for so many people. We ended up squatting under a small window, concealed from outside but at the mercy of the two signalmen already working there. One of them, a young man of about twenty, was rather hostile and wanted us to leave. The security forces had discovered their practice of stopping the train before the station and had warned them not to do it again. They were under suspicion, he thought, continuously watched. The other signalman though was much older and friendlier, and he pleaded with the younger man to be patient for the sake of the child. Listening in to their argument, which was to decide our fate, it was as if we were paralysed.

After several long minutes, the soldiers left the station with their haul of prisoners, leaving us where we were. I was convinced that some of them had seen us slinking into the signalmen's hut, but were either too lazy or too unmotivated—or perhaps too sympathetic—to take any action.

'My house is near the railway line, about four hundred metres further on,' said the older signalman. 'You can stay there until dark.'

So we walked there in silence, shaken, glad that we had at least escaped being caught right at the outset of our journey. His house was an attractive building that stood on its own in a sizeable garden, all provided for him by the state railway. A number of chickens, ducks and turkeys were pecking away in a courtyard. He invited us into his kitchen, a dark room with a small window and a wood-burning stove like the one in my parent's house in Orosháza. There was a table, covered with a tablecloth decorated with yellow flowers, and four wooden chairs around it. The woman of the house was middle aged, dressed in black with a red-chequered apron over her bulging stomach. The whole place smelled of a mixture of garlic and a huge but friendly Alsatian dog.

'You'll have to wait here,' the signalman explained. 'The frontier's guarded by Russian soldiers, and they wait until the last train has passed before combing the fields and rounding up any escapees as they head for Austria. That way they can catch everybody, including anyone who's jumped from the train.'

That's all we need, I thought: the Russians would not be gentle with escapees after the killing of hundreds of their comrades in Budapest during the uprising. And we couldn't even talk to them in Russian to plead our case. With the Red Army at the frontier, the only language was that of the gun.

'The Russian soldiers returning from their sweep of the frontier will pass by our house,' he went on. 'After that you can leave, and you shouldn't have to worry anymore, though you might still run into a night-time patrol.'

Despite his reassurances, I was still concerned about finding our way into Austria. This was, after all, unfamiliar territory to us, and the border was unmarked. I asked whether somebody could be found who might take us at least part of the way. I had half of my last pay packet with me and would gladly have given it to a guide with local knowledge. The signalman went into town to make enquiries, but returned with bad news.

'You've left it too late,' he said. 'The situation's getting dangerous. The number of patrols has increased, and nobody's willing to risk the journey. Our honest advice? Give up and go back home.'

'Are there any mines laid?' I asked.

'I don't know. Nobody knows what they're up to.'

Mines or not, we were aware there would be dangers and had already decided to take our chances. Would I have started out if I had known the true risk? Maybe not, but fortunately I didn't know, and by now it was too late. I told him we would be going alone, if that's what it took. Seeing that we would not be dissuaded, he explained the lie of the land to us.

'Start by walking parallel to the main railway line, but not too close to it. The last station, Hegyeshalom, is a stone's throw from the frontier and full of soldiers. Don't get too close. Use the lights of the station to guide you—you can see them a long way off. Everything has already been harvested, so you'll find the fields are ploughed and empty. The ground will be easy to walk over. You'll have to cross a branch line at one point, but it's easy, there's no embankment.'

The farmland that straddles the Austro-Hungarian border is quite flat, and from the signalman's cottage it was a walk of just seven kilometres to the frontier. If we'd been hiking in daylight, as we'd so loved to do in the hills near Budapest, we would have made short work of the distance and the terrain, but this was no leisurely hike. I was still worried.

'Won't we meet any more serious obstacles than a railway line?' I asked.

'Beyond the branch line you'll come across a gravel quarry and have to decide which way to skirt it. If you go to the right, you might get dangerously close to Hegyeshalom station; if you go to the left, you'll be in danger of running into a military barracks.'

Hobson's choice, I thought, and started to doubt my optimistic assumption of our chances of getting through. Soon after the last train came and left, just as the signalman had said, we heard the sound of Russian soldiers passing the house. To our horror, they stopped and knocked on the door. Anyone could see that we were not part of the family, and the Russians would surely not ask permission to come in. Hiding would only put our hosts in even greater danger. I automatically reached for István, as if already hoping for pity. The signalman's wife opened the front door, and to our great relief the soldiers had no intention of searching the house but only asked for some water to drink.

'Wait here,' she said. 'We have a rather vicious dog inside.' The otherwise friendly dog barked right on cue. The woman took a can of water out to them, and after quenching their thirst the Russians left with their unfortunate prisoners. 'They caught at least twenty tonight,' said the wife after they had gone.

Eventually it was time for us to go. Afraid that István would cry on the way, I gave him a sleeping tablet. Wary of accidentally overdosing such a small child, I gave him too little, and as a result he remained half-awake, dozy but thankfully quiet for much of the time. We thanked the signalman and his wife and left. It was only now that we realised there were several others who had not been invited into the house, but who had been hiding outside in the courtyard. The railwayman from the previous day was amongst them. We were a group of eight adults, then, and a boy of about twelve. It was the dead of night in the middle of winter, yet the lad didn't have anything besides his shabby summer clothing. Instead of a winter coat, he had only a dark blue shawl to wrap around his shoulders and his head. His mother, he said, had been dead three years, and the woman his father had married did not like him. They would be only too happy, he said, to know that he had left for good. We tried to discourage him, but he was determined to come with us and always followed us at a short distance. I can only hope he was well looked after in Austria.

The group, containing several strong, young men, was the saving of us, for all the men took turns carrying István. Now was not the time for friendly conversation and formal introductions. We all had our pasts, and our reasons for escaping, but we all had a common goal. Everybody travelled light, saying little. For no particular reason, the group seemed instinctively to adopt me as its leader, though I had no more practical experience of the landscape than anybody else. It was a cold night, with a ground mist rising, and I could only hope that we were walking in the right direction. Because the frontier was not a straight line, but zigzagged rather in unpredictable doglegs, one worry was that we might leave Hungary only to cross back in again. When we arrived at the quarry, I decided to go around to the left of it, taking our chances of keeping clear of the barracks.

Then we bumped straight into a night watchman. At first we didn't even realise that he wasn't a soldier waiting to arrest us and send us back to Budapest. We just stood in front of him, mesmerised, like rabbits caught in headlights.

'What do you think you're doing?' he asked in an unfriendly voice. There was no use denying it, so we told him. 'I know *that*,' he said, sounding a little friendlier. 'But why on *this* road?'

'Why not?' I retorted.

'Because a patrol's just started off on this road—*that's* why.'

We simply thanked him, and he watched as we changed tack and headed to the right, towards Hegyeshalom. But we hadn't got far when a volley of flares shot up, lighting a large area like day, including the very place where we had just been. We all dropped to the ground and kept as low and as quiet as possible. I had great trouble keeping little István, who was still half-awake, from crying. We heard shouting from the road we had just left, across the quarry. There was shooting. The patrols were not after us, it seemed, but another group who must have taken the wrong road.

After the commotion had died down, we continued on our way guided by the lights of Hegyeshalom. I became bolder, and ventured nearer, until we could hear the clanking of the railway carriages being shunted and the shouting of workmen. There were no military commands to be heard. An image of Icarus flashed unbidden into my mind: I was hoping we were not flying too close to the sun. We pressed on, the main railway line away to our right as the signalman had said, until only by looking back over my shoulder could I make out the station lights in the distance. We walked on, until through the darkness we made out a number of hay bales. What were these doing here, in the middle of nowhere in December? I had grown up in the country, and it was not usual for Hungarian farmers to leave bales out in the fields like this. Then the realisation dawned upon me that the bales could only have been brought there deliberately, to allow refugees some rest. We must have arrived in Austria! So tired that we could scarcely walk much further, we sat down on the hay and ate what little food we had with us. After a while, we saw moving lights and the outlines of people, and heard voices, one of them Hungarian. Was this a Hungarian patrol, then, the bales of hay brought here to catch people trying to escape? So we hadn't made it into Austria after all? We were paralysed by fear, speechless, just watching the figures approaching, helpless. They'd known exactly where to find us. As they got nearer, I saw that only one of them was wearing a uniform. He got closer, and his dim form resolved itself into an Austrian policeman, followed by an American journalist, and finally a Hungarian interpreter chatting to another refugee.

The policeman asked us to hand over any weapons, but none in our group had any. Through the interpreter, the journalist eagerly asked for the latest news from Hungary. The refugee happened to be one of the group who had run into the patrol and been shot at. He was the only one who had managed to escape. His wife and young son had been captured. We realised how lucky we had been and listened with sympathy to his story, but said nothing. What is there to say in such a situation?

Because of my sleeping son, the American journalist offered us a lift in his car to the refugee camp that had been set up by the Red Cross in the nearest village, Nickelsdorf, while the others in our party had to walk the few kilometres there under their own steam.

In Nickelsdorf, a Danish student took down our personal details. The children who had made it over the border that night were given a drink of hot chocolate, the adults a cup of chicken noodle soup. The camp was a transit camp, and had to be cleared each day and made ready for the next flood of refugees arriving the following night. The Red Cross never knew how many would be coming, but no refugee was ever refused entry. The camp consisted of a large room, a sort of clubhouse, used by the locals as a place of entertainment in better times. The floor was covered with straw. Everybody was given a blanket and had to find a spot to sleep. Children and their mothers, Vera and István included, were taken to the village school where they could sleep on army-issue beds, on straw-filled mattresses. We were separated, and told to be at the village church at four the following afternoon to be taken to a permanent refugee camp. Under different circumstances, at another place and time, we might not have obeyed the request to separate. We felt so vulnerable, in a foreign country together for the first time, with no money, no papers, and knowing nobody. We talked, and decided that we hadn't risked the hazardous journey just to behave as if we were still living under Communism. These people were here to help us. We had to trust them, and so we did.

I took a blanket and selected a spot near the wall. I was so tired that, in spite of the light being left on all night and the constant stream of refugees arriving, I fell dead asleep. Usually I don't remember my dreams, but until the end of my life I shall remember the dream—or rather the nightmare—I had that night. I dreamed that the Soviets had returned and were searching for refugees from Hungary, refugees like us. The soldiers entered our room, lined us men up, and marched us out into the freezing night. They put us on big lorries and took us to a labour camp in Siberia. We protested in vain, but they didn't even allow us to say goodbye to our wives and children. I had this exact same dream many times in the coming months, long after we were safely in the West. Waking up was always so sweet.

So I was back in Austria, the country I had left more than ten years before, but under unimaginably different circumstances. Yes, I was again poor, hungry, and badly dressed,

Freedom

but I was a free man. I didn't have to wear the yellow Star of David, had no need to fear either Nazis or Russians, and there were no air raids. Austria too had changed: until the end of the war it had been part of the Reich, and scarcely a year had now passed since the last of the occupying Allied forces had withdrawn under an agreement that left this a neutral nation surrounded by Cold War enemies.

After a night spent under a blanket in the transit camp in Nickelsdorf, I got up, brushed the straw from my coat, and was given a simple breakfast by the Red Cross—a sandwich and some coffee. Not knowing exactly where Vera and István might be found amongst the other refugees, and with a full day on my hands before four o'clock when the buses would come for us, I decided to explore the village, the first I saw in the free world. I was joined in my exploration by the railwayman who had shared his plan with me on the train just the previous morning, and who had crossed the border with us by night. Looking each other up and down, we realised we had to rid ourselves of the dirt we had accumulated during our walk to freedom. While we were busy doing this, the village's Roman Catholic priest walked by and struck up a conversation with us. I had a reasonable command of German, from school and from the labour camp, and after a few polite exchanges the priest invited both of us for lunch.

'I'm not Catholic,' I warned him, but it didn't matter. Every day, he said, he would invite a couple of refugees to eat with him and his housekeeper, and today it was our turn. Ignoring our dishevelled appearance, he led us to his home where we met the Danish student who had taken our details at the reception centre during the night. The lunch—I can still smell it—consisted of meatballs and spinach, and for pudding *mákos beigli*, our traditional Hungarian Christmas cake—a baked Swiss roll filled with rich, sweet poppy seed paste. It reminded me of those fat noodles, smothered in ground poppy seeds and sugar, given to me by the kind old couple in Vienna during the war.

I had grown up a secular Jew and become an agnostic. This was the first time I had set foot in a Catholic rectory, and I was surprised that apart from saying grace there was no discussion of religion. The conversation, so far as I could understand and participate in it, was all about politics.

'Will the West intervene?'

'Unlikely, the British and French have burned their fingers in Suez.'

'When will the flow of refugees stop?'

'When they manage to put up the barbed wires and mines again.'

'What will happen in Hungary after the dust settles? Will the system be better or worse?'

'Probably worse. The Soviet Union must've learned its lesson. It'll stop any popular movement before it gets out of hand.'

The people of Nickelsdorf appreciated our plight: the Soviet Union had occupied Lower Austria and the Burgenland for a decade after the war, and the people had suffered. Besides, the Burgenland, in which Nickelsdorf lay, had been part of Hungary until the Treaty of Trianon in 1920. People understood well how the tides of history flowed back and forth so destructively across this landscape.

There was still time before the promised buses arrived to take us further west. I changed the last of my *forint* to Austrian *schilling* at the village pub. The exchange rate was atrocious, but I reasoned that the further I got from the frontier the lower the rate I would get: there would be little call elsewhere for the currency of a restive Communist state. As it happened, the inhabitants of the Burgenland were doing a roaring trade using refugees' surplus *forint* to buy pigs in Hungary before smuggling them into Austria to sell at a great profit.

There were other vultures circling, too, and refugees fell easy prey to them. There will always be somebody who will find a way to benefit from the misery of others. One, a young Hungarian man, approached people with a story about returning the next day to Hungary to fetch his wife and being willing to pass on messages and post letters.

'I have a letter, would you post it for me?' I asked him. 'And here's the telephone number of my mother-in-law. Tell her we're safe.' I handed over the letter and a piece of paper with the number, but he was not satisfied: 'I'll need money for the postage, and for the telephone, and also for a guide, and because my wife is pregnant, we'll need some transport.' He looked unsophisticated and honest, so I gave him some money. The letter never arrived, and Vera's mother never received the call. Only after about two weeks, when she and my mother received postcards from us, did they learn the good news. I was surprised that the authorities hadn't intercepted those cards, clearly legible, telling stories of escapes to freedom. Perhaps there were too many of them.

With my first Austrian money I bought a small toy for István—a helicopter on wheels—and a bottle of Coca Cola for myself. Coke, a symbol even then of Western freedoms, would not be available in Hungary until the late 1960s, but those privileged Hungarian sportsmen and artists who had travelled abroad and tasted it described it as not very pleasant. This, of course, had only made me want it even more. Who would believe such a story? Surely they said it just to please the authorities. I poured the cool, bubbly liquid slowly into a glass, full of expectation, and took a sip. I was disappointed to discover that they'd been right.

At the bus stop and I was reunited with my wife and son. Somewhere along the way he had lost his cap, but

Vera had obtained another for him from the Red Cross, who were always ready to help. The journey was not long, and we arrived at another Red Cross camp at Mödling, just outside Vienna, less than twenty kilometres from my old labour camp at Hafenzufahrtsstrasse. The camp this time had been some kind of military establishment, with several huge rooms all fitted with rows of double bunks, and around one hundred people to each room. There was hardly any space between our beds and those of our neighbours, but beggars could not—indeed should not under those circumstances—be choosers.

Fortunately Mödling too turned out to be for us just a transit camp, as families with children were quickly transferred to another camp that had been established in the nearby castle of Schloss Liechtenstein. Here we had only thirty-two people to one dormitory, each family separated by a little more space. There was a large family of peasants in our room, three generations, and all they could talk about was the pig they had slaughtered only to leave behind. Who would end up eating their sausages seemed to be their main concern. They could not explain precisely why they had left, nor where they wanted to go, and I suspect that in time they returned to Hungary. At least Vera, remembering the fat goose she had left behind, did have some sympathy for them.

We were warm and well fed in Schloss Liechtenstein, and received a little pocket money from the Red Cross. Occasionally people would come to the camp asking for volunteers to do some manual labour—sweeping snow off the roads of Vienna, unloading a wagon full of coal, and such like. There were always plenty of volunteers happy to break the monotony of life and earn a few *schilling*. Because they needed someone to interpret as well as to work I was appointed their team leader and had more than my fair share of these excursions. Here I was, yet again, in Vienna, with a shovel in my hand, but this time after a single shift I received as much money as I did in a month from the Red Cross. On the way home from work I would go shopping and return to Schloss Liechtenstein like Father Christmas, laden with fruit and chocolate.

During my frequent trips into the city I would visit the place where an American charity had established a soup kitchen. There was always a queue, but the food was worth waiting for. Their chicken noodle soup came in a paper cup, and their sandwiches were small, with butter and a thin slice of cheese or corned beef, nothing like the huge sandwiches Americans eat at home, but to a refugee they were delicious. After eating them I would go straight back outside and queue up again for a second helping. Nobody ever stopped me: we refugees must all have looked the same to the Americans. Or perhaps they knew but didn't mind.

While in the city one day, I tried to look up the old couple at number thirty-two who had fed me *mákos nudli* during the war. My parents had sent some parcels to the address from Orosháza as an expression of our gratitude, but the Hungarian authorities had never allowed us to send anything of value. I went to the house, only to learn that they had since died. I found Spiller und Sohn, our employer repairing railway lines, still in existence, so I made an appointment and visited them. I went with Bandi Szirt, whom I had bumped into unexpectedly in Vienna. It was Bandi who as a seven-year-old child had got his leg burned during the air raid on our camp. We both wanted a certificate from Spiller und Sohn confirming that we had worked there during the war, which might have been of use in claiming reparation from Germany. Two Spiller und Sohn officials received us in a warm but not particularly well-furnished office, but though I searched my memory hard I couldn't recognise either one. Maybe this was why they were delegated to talk to us. They acknowledged that during the war Jewish Hungarians had worked there, but they refused to certify that I was one of them: 'All our records were destroyed at the end of the war,' they insisted. 'We have no documentation.'

I didn't find the argument credible. I had been in the camp almost until the day Vienna was liberated, and their offices had survived undamaged up until then. Of course, it was possible, likely even, that they had destroyed the records themselves to avoid any such accusations of using forced labour. Bandi showed them his leg, badly scarred by the hot oven, as proof of his claim that he had been there, but they were not impressed. They remained polite, as Austrians do, but not in the least helpful, probably worried at the prospect of legal claims after so much time had passed.

From Schloss Liechtenstein people began to depart for destinations around the globe, many of them to places they knew little or nothing about. The now-neutral Austria was ready to offer asylum to anyone applying for it, but I didn't want to stay in a German-speaking country. A few dubious South American nations were busy recruiting strong, healthy young men. Other countries wanted certain professions only. The United States was taking in people who, like me, had relatives already living in the country, but I had never really had a longing to live in the US. Jews were being unconditionally accepted by Israel, but by this time I had no wish to go there. I felt European, and I wanted to go to England.

There were several reasons for this otherwise inexplicable choice. Firstly, Vera had relatives living in London. One, Feri, had stayed in Budapest during the war where he had been engaged in forging documents, including the ones which had saved the lives of Vera, Bertalan and their mother. Feri had managed to leave Hungary a few years after the war and now worked as a chemist in London. The other, Gyuri, had left Hungary before the war, married an English girl, and opened a small restaurant in London. Our second reason for choosing England was the Eastwood family, a congregational minister and his wife who during the years before the war had supported Vera as a child with food parcels sent through the Save The Children Fund. The Eastwoods had been the first people we had contacted after reaching Austria, and they had sent us a letter of guarantee, undertaking to look after us and promising that we would never become a burden on the state. Thirdly, though I didn't know much about England, I had heard a lot about Oxford University. Somehow I had got it into my head that it would be nice if István were eventually able to study there (as fate has it, in time I myself studied there for my doctorate but István wanted nothing to do with Oxford and chose Edinburgh instead). And lastly, I had always had a very high regard for the BBC. I had listened to the BBC's Hungarian Service broadcasts during the war, and after that under Communism. I especially enjoyed the contributions of one Professor McCartney, who spoke Hungarian and who with his charming accent and relaxed voice kept our spirits up in the most difficult of times.

While waiting for our British visas to arrive we had several visitors, who came bearing presents. One of them, a local man, came to the camp with sweets for the children. He told us that he was a simple worker in a bakery, and that this was all he could afford. He wished he could have done more and was quite apologetic. There were others too, men and women, who knew that this was a camp for children and who brought mainly sweets. Such visits started to restore our faith in the human race.

Another welcome face was Vera's brother, Bertalan, and his heavily pregnant wife. The two had followed us out of Hungary a week later, having paid a guide and travelled most of the way on a lorry. Then, at the most critical point, they had been made to get off the lorry, which drove off. They had had to cross the border on foot by wading through the swampy reed flats of the shallow Lake Fertő, the Austrians' Neusiedler See, and had got thoroughly wet in the process, no joke in midwinter. A Jewish charity now gave them enough money to stay in a small hotel. Eventually, they emigrated to Canada.

I too went to register my family with the same Jewish charity. The lady in charge wanted to make sure that all applicants were truly Jewish, and asked me to say a few words of prayer in Hebrew. From the back of my mind I dredged up what as the youngest child I had been taught to say at the feast of *Pészah*: *Ma nishtana halayla hazeh?* How does this night differ from all other nights? She was satisfied with my answer. To people born outside the Jewish tradition this might appear strange on my part, a little hypocritical even: after all, I had never been a practising religious Jew. Yet it had been my very Jewishness that had marked me out for persecution. I had been born Jewish and, though the course of my life from Orosháza to Schloss Liechtenstein had led me from secular observance to an agnosticism that bordered on atheism, I remained Jewish. I had not then, nor have I in the years since, fully cast off the traditions that I was heir to, or taken on another religion, and I could certainly not change my ethnicity. The political agenda of the fervently Zionist *Sómér* youth movement I had once been a part of was Marxist, but no less Jewish for its atheism. I had never turned my back on being Jewish, and now, in Schloss Liechtenstein, never for a moment thought that I was being hypocritical in accepting aid sent by American Jews, some of them no doubt also secular or even atheist, to fellow Jews in need.

So we got some extra pocket money, but for the meantime we stayed in the camp. I used the money to buy two suitcases for the clothing, the toys, and the toiletries we had accumulated from various charities. For the first time in my life, and purely out of the generosity of others, I felt as though I were almost rich.

In January of 1957, with the West faced with many times more Hungarian refugees than had been anticipated, quotas were revised and the British agreed to take another five thousand. All transport to Britain was processed through Traiskirchen, a huge camp a short distance away housing some four thousand.

The Traiskirchen camp had been hastily set up in the unused buildings of a former artillery school dating back to the late nineteenth century. In recent years it had been used as a military hospital and, until just a year earlier, as a barracks for the occupying Soviet Army. It was a forbidding, four-storey edifice with row upon row of windows beneath a mighty, red-tiled roof. The facilities, including the kitchen, were totally swamped by the numbers suddenly arriving, and a meal often consisted of a hunk of bread and a tin of sardines between two. Sometimes we got corned beef, still in the tin, and a few unpeeled boiled potatoes which we had to collect in our hands for want of bowls. One tin of sardines was not much for two hungry adults, but I would manage to get more. Hungarian peasants had never seen sardines, and did not eat them. On the other hand, they all smoked like chimneys and I always found someone ready to exchange their fish for Red Cross cigarettes.

The number of refugees wanting to go to Britain steadily increased, but there was no sign of any registration process being set in train. My biggest worry was that if an infectious disease were to arise among the refugees the whole camp would be quarantined for months. In that case even the letter of guarantee from the Eastwoods would be of scant help.

I became a German-to-Hungarian interpreter for the Red Cross representative at Traiskirchen, a tall, middle-aged lady of great intelligence, charm, and above all patience. While I was in her office one day, I was introduced to the representative of the British legation in Vienna, who had finally come to issue travel documents. From him I learned that registration for our transfer was due to start the following morning. As soon as this became widely known, in order to be sure of an early ticket out of Austria people started queuing in front of his office fully intending to stay there all night. It was clear to me, that when the guards arrived to enforce the nightly curfew there would be anarchy. Taking a piece of paper, and starting at the head of the queue, I wrote down names and handed out numbered slips bearing my signature, promising that come the morning each person would be admitted in turn. There was very little argument when registration started. The British representative remembered the chaos the last time he had been there and was most impressed with my scheme. He asked me to continue with it, as his unofficial aide and interpreter, until he had dealt with all five thousand refugees. His office, though, could process only two hundred and fifty people a day, and simple maths said the task would take almost three weeks. With my family's turn due to come up on the third day, I declined the offer and took my place in the queue. When our turn came, we were photographed, received our travel documents, and were told to be ready for departure on the following morning.

Freedom

Traiskirchen was perhaps the lowest point on our road to freedom. We were not in danger, not really hungry, and we didn't have to work; but somehow Traiskirchen took away our dignity. When we had settled down in England I wrote on a piece of paper '*Emlékezz Traiskirchenre*'—'Remember Traiskirchen'—and placed it in a prominent position on the mantelpiece, where it stayed for years. It was meant to remind us of past hardships and stop us complaining about unimportant things. I still have it.

How do you prepare yourself for a trip abroad, when you know nothing about the country you are going to? This was my problem. I knew that England was further north than Austria, and so I reasoned that it must be colder. From the Red Cross I managed to collect some really warm long johns and a hat. I had my well-worn but very warm winter coat, and felt fully prepared. But what was I to do when we got there? I had never assumed for a moment that my chemistry diploma from Pázmány Péter University would be acceptable in the West, and so I hadn't brought it with me in case we'd been caught trying to leave Hungary. I could always wash the glassware in a laboratory, I thought. In Traiskirchen, then again, some kind old English ladies doing charitable work had mentioned that in England anyone could get a job as a postman. I had spent countless days in Vienna heaving snow and coal, so I could always earn a living as a labourer. My biggest stumbling block was that, while I had learned some English in the *Gimnázium* in Orosháza, I couldn't yet carry on anything like a proper conversation. I had been desperately looking for a Hungarian–English dictionary, but nobody had had one. In the end I had managed only a German–English one, though this would come in useful when eventually I was interviewed for jobs.

WHEN EVEN THE POETS WERE SILENT

One morning, two hundred and fifty of us boarded a train under the leadership of an English guide and travelled first across Austria and then through Germany and Belgium. Our presence on the train had become a matter of public knowledge, and at almost every station where the train stopped we were met by local well-wishers and former Hungarian refugees, now resettled, waving the Hungarian flag, and handing out food, drinks, and basic necessities. Our English guide advised us to be polite and to accept everything, even if we were given too much, as we could always discreetly discard any surplus.

In the Belgian port of Ostend we boarded a ferry to Dover. This was the first time that we had seen the sea, and fortunately it was a calm day so no one got sick. The first Englishman I spoke to was taking photographs. I asked him if he would take one of us. He did, gladly, and wrote down his address for me, saying that after we had settled I could write to him and he would send me the picture. When I wrote to him, he did exactly as he said he would, and I still cherish not only the photograph, but also his warm accompanying letter wishing us well.

After docking in Dover we were taken by train to London, where we were met by Vera's relatives, Feri and Gyuri, who had found out about our arrival through the Red Cross. They congratulated us for choosing England, and treated us to coffee and fruitcake. But there was little time to reminisce, since from London we were taken directly north to a holding centre in Staffordshire. Legally we were free, but in practical terms we had to go wherever the rails took us. Where else could we go, and why?

RAF Hednesford was in the heart of the English midlands, but it was such a long journey that people thought we were being taken all the way to Scotland. The base, it turned out, had previously housed a Technical

Training School, where Air Force technicians had learned how to repair the airframes and engines that had carried the bombs that liberated Europe. The NCOs' quarters were allocated to families with small children. For the first time since closing our apartment door behind us we had one room all to ourselves. Exhausted from the journey, we went to sleep at once, and awoke late the next morning.

I washed myself in the communal shower, got dressed, and went outside to look around. It was early February, yet the weather was quite mild, and the sky above Brindley Heath was spotted with small white clouds. I stared and stared at them, for they were scudding along at a speed I had never seen in landlocked Hungary. It was that tiny observation that made me truly realise I was in a foreign country, one that I hoped would be my home for the rest of my life.

WHEN EVEN THE POETS WERE SILENT

Epilogue

IT WAS sixteen years before Vera and I summoned up the courage to revisit Hungary. By 1973 the Hungarian government had issued an amnesty to all those citizens who like us had fled illegally, and by this time we had our British passports, but still we didn't dare take twenty-year-old István with us in case he was recruited into the Hungarian Army. We received a visa from the Hungarian Embassy in The Hague, and people in the know assured us that this guaranteed safe exit as well as entry. People still wanted by the Hungarian police were simply denied a visa: to have arrested foreign nationals would have resulted in bad publicity for a country that, with its own brand of 'Goulash Communism', had been transformed from one of the most repressive to arguably the most liberal of the Eastern bloc.

We travelled across Europe by car. As we neared Hungary I began to search the dial for *Kossuth Rádió*, but Vera was much too nervous and asked me to switch it off. The same spot where in 1945 I had crossed the border with my parents, and where in 1956 Vera and I had escaped in the dead of a winter's night, was guarded now by a soldier in a watchtower with a submachine gun. He took a long, good look at us, as if judging if we were worthy of admission. After a while he opened the gate.

'I've changed my mind,' whispered Vera. 'I want to go back.'

We drove forward into Hungary, and found ourselves between two closed gates, as if in a trap, with no way backward or forward. We were both nervous as the border guard approached us and simply asked if we spoke Hungarian. He could see from our passports that we had been born in Hungary. But the main concern of the

Hungarians was not who came in, but who went out. He waved us on.

The only other time I had crossed that border *into* Hungary I had been penniless, a child looking for a lost childhood, bitter about what the Nazis had done to me and not knowing what to expect. Now we were termed by the new regime *távolba szakadt hazánk fia*, 'fellow patriots who had drifted away'. Was it us they were welcoming back with that apologetic euphemism for 'refugees', or the hard currency we brought with us, and which we had to exchange for *forint* on a daily basis? In 1945 I had thought I would stay in Hungary for ever; now I knew that after a fortnight we would be returning home.

This could only ever be a sentimental journey, and once in Budapest we tried to find the little window through which while I was a student we used to buy those fried, doughy *lángos*. It had gone. The only place we could still buy *lángos* was at the markets, so we went to the most famous, the Great Market Hall, which had become a thriving tourist attraction. They were cooking *lángos* there, and East German tourists were queuing to buy them. We bought one each, still hot, and held them in their small squares of greaseproof paper. They were greasy and, like many things nostalgic when at last you find them after so many years, a little disappointing. Perhaps we were searching not for *lángos* but for our youth.

In the early 1990s I revisited Orosháza, taking the train from Szeged, where I was teaching Hungarian managers about working in a market economy.

'Is Orosháza the next station?' I asked the young woman sitting next to me. She was well dressed, with subtle make-up and an alluring scent. Obviously, she belonged to the richer part of post-revolution Hungarian society. 'I

Epilogue

wonder,' I added, just to make conversation, 'are there any taxis at the station?'

'Usually there are a few. Why, where do you want to go?'

'Nowhere special, just to the centre of the town. I used to live there, but I haven't been there for some thirty years.'

'You know what? My husband will be waiting for me in our car, we'd be glad to give you a lift.'

When I had last lived in Orosháza we had travelled from the station in a horse-drawn *fiáker*. It wasn't far, about a mile and a half, but we were not used to walking in those days: physical exercise was considered unhealthy. Her husband was indeed waiting in his Skoda.

'Where exactly do you want to go?' he asked.

'Near to the Catholic Church. I want to see my old family house in Ond *utca*.'

'You'll find there's been a lot of changes,' he said. 'But I'll take you there, it's no problem.'

The journey was shorter than I remembered, barely a couple of minutes by car. Indeed there had been changes. My family home had disappeared along with all the rest of the houses bar one, and with them the beautiful acacia trees. They had been replaced by three ugly blocks of flats. Turning my back, I started walking towards my old school, but that too was no longer there.

The gates of the synagogue were closed, and the building was half derelict. The whole town bore a dreary air. The pavements were full of potholes. There was no war damage, no bullet or shrapnel holes in the walls of the houses like in Budapest, but the plaster was falling off and everywhere the paint was peeling.

I took lunch in the famous Hotel Alföld, the first time I had ever eaten a meal in its upmarket restaurant. I ordered the most expensive dish on the menu, venison with dumplings and game gravy, with wine, and coffee to finish.

The food was good, yet the atmosphere was depressing and inelegant. The wooden tables lacked tablecloths, the chairs were austere and uncomfortable. Instead of the Gypsy band of old there was a radio playing pop tunes. I was sure it had been different in the days when my parents had enjoyed steak there.

I asked for the telephone directory and went through all the names, searching for ones I knew. I found only two. One was Ravasz Karcsi, the butcher's son who had lived next door to us, and who was now a vet. Should I look him up? What could I say? He would surely have retired, and it was unlikely we would have anything in common. The other name was Zelenka. Doctor Zelenka and his wife had been friends of my parents. She had played rummy with my mother and their circle. They surely couldn't still be alive, but they had had two daughters, and a son, Lajcsi, a gynaecologist who must have been the same age as my elder brother István. I knew the Zelenka family well, and walked to their house to see them.

I rang the bell, but there was no answer. Eventually a window next door opened and a woman leaned out to see who was calling.

'I used to live in Orosháza,' I explained. 'My family was friendly with the Zelenkas. When can I find them at home?'

'They're all dead,' she answered. 'The parents and all three children.' Only a granddaughter was left.

I went to the Jewish cemetery and found my father's grave in a neglected state. I don't believe in life after death, but still I talked to him.

'I'm sorry, father, that I haven't visited you before, but I live far away. A lot has happened since you went. Your wife outlived you by eleven years and died in Manchester, in England. You'd be proud of me. I have a doctorate from the University of Oxford. Your grandson is a professor in

Epilogue

England. I live in the Netherlands now, I'm still married to the same girl I wed in Budapest, I've travelled the world, and enjoyed a luxurious life you never even dreamed of.'

Then I left Orosháza for the last time.

WHEN EVEN THE POETS WERE SILENT

Afterword

The Jews of Hungary: From Emancipation to Genocide

PROF. ISTVÁN POGÁNY, UNIVERSITY OF WARWICK

For Jews, the history of modern Hungary is, at once, a source of enormous pride and profound despair. During the nineteenth century, Jews began to migrate to Hungary in large numbers from neighbouring territories, attracted by the economic opportunities that Hungary offered and by its comparatively liberal social and political climate. From a community numbering a few tens of thousands in the mid-eighteenth century, Hungary's Jewish population soared to more than half a million by 1869 and exceeded 900,000 by 1910.

The overwhelming majority of Jews who settled in Hungary chose to integrate with the host community. By the late 1800s, most of the Jews living in Hungary defined themselves as Hungarian by nationality, i.e. in terms of their ethno-cultural and linguistic identity, and as 'Israelite', or Jewish, by religion. In the national census of 1900, 72 per cent of Hungary's Jews affirmed their sense of belonging to the Hungarian nation, while 63.8 per cent gave their mother tongue as Hungarian. By 1910, the proportion of Jews whose mother tongue was Hungarian had risen to 71.5 per cent in the country as a whole and to 85.6 per cent in the capital, Budapest.

Like my father and his family, living in Orosháza in eastern Hungary, most of the country's Jews regarded themselves as Jewish Hungarians rather than as Hungarian Jews. Their attachment to—and identification with—Hungary was unqualified. Not infrequently, the assimilation of Hungary's Jews was so thorough that they ate pork without compunction. In some instances, Jewish families—including my own—living in villages and in small country towns raised pigs for domestic consumption. Such dietary aberrations went hand in hand with occasional synagogue attendance.

In the latter decades of the nineteenth century, the desire of most of the Jews of Hungary to assimilate was reciprocated by the Hungarian elite. Hungary's political leaders had become concerned that Hungarians, or 'Magyars', were being reduced to a minority within the territories traditionally claimed by Hungary. Jews, who adopted Hungarian as their mother tongue and who embraced Hungarian culture, were welcomed as new recruits to the Hungarian 'nation', even though comparatively few chose to take the final step of converting to Christianity. Hungary's Jews were instrumental in helping to swell the Magyar demographic in a heterogeneous region where Romanians, Slovaks, Croats, Serbs, Ruthenes and others were clamouring for cultural and political recognition.

The growing convergence of Jews and Hungarians was already apparent in 1848, a time of revolutionary ferment across the continent. In that year, many thousands of Jews joined Hungarians in a rebellion against Austrian Habsburg rule. The Habsburg Empire had annexed Hungary in the late seventeenth century, following a century and a half of Ottoman Turkish occupation that had ended several centuries of Hungarian independence. Strikingly, the proportion of Hungary's Jews who served in the *Honvéd*, or Hungarian defence forces, in 1848-49, was much larger than the proportion of the country's Gentiles who joined up. According to Lajos Kossuth, Hungary's charismatic leader during the uprising, there were as many as 20,000 Jewish troops in the *Honvéd*, which comprised between 170,000 and 180,000 men.

The Jews of Hungary

Although the Hungarian revolt was crushed the following year with the military assistance of the Russian Tsar, many of Hungary's political claims were recognised by the Habsburgs in 1867. The Habsburg Empire was duly renamed Austria-Hungary.

Later that year, Hungary's parliament passed an emancipation law, formally ending centuries of discrimination against Jews. As recently as 1830, Jews in Hungary had been denied many basic civil rights, including the opportunity to seek employment in the state administration, the right to live and work anywhere within the country, freedom to choose a career other than in medicine or in certain sectors of commerce, or the right to rent or purchase property from Hungary's nobles. Jews had also been subject to a unique and invidious 'toleration tax'—they were taxed simply for being Jews.

In the latter decades of the nineteenth century, with the support and encouragement of Hungary's ruling elite, mostly landowners with a patrician disdain for commerce, Jews began to play an increasingly important role in the development of the country's economy. Although Hungary's political leaders had no desire to engage in finance, commerce or industry themselves, they understood the necessity for wide-ranging economic reforms.

In retrospect, it seems all too clear that the unprecedented freedoms and opportunities granted to Hungary's Jews in the latter half of the nineteenth century also posed significant dangers. Emancipation, which meant that Jews could select occupations that had formerly been denied to them, resulted in growing competition with non-Jewish Hungarians, particularly in the liberal professions, in engineering, in journalism and in the arts. Within a few decades, Jews became extraordinarily successful in all these fields. In 1910, according to figures cited by Raphael Patai in his book *The Jews of Hungary*, 42.4 per cent of Hungarian journalists were Jewish, as were 48.5 per cent of Hungarian doctors, 14.5 per cent of pharmacists, 40 per cent of veterinary surgeons, 26.2 per cent of writers and artists and 37.6 per cent of engineers, including chemical engineers. The heightened visibility and success of Jews in these sectors inevitably fuelled resentment and jealousy.

The high-profile activities of Jewish businessmen, bankers and industrialists, though contributing massively to the modernisation of the Hungarian economy, also provoked bitterness, particularly amongst the lower gentry and the peasants. Jews came to be seen as the agents of an unwelcome modernity in which profit and materialism had supposedly taken the place of 'traditional Hungarian values'. In reality, though, the great majority of Hungary's Jews were neither wealthy bankers nor successful lawyers. Instead, most earned a modest living as tailors and cobblers, as carters and peddlers, as schoolmasters, nurses and midwives, as shopkeepers and innkeepers or even as household cooks and maids. Registers of births and other documents from the turn of the twentieth century reveal that significant numbers of Hungary's Jews, particularly in outlying areas such as Máramaros, in the north east of the Empire, worked as *napszámos* or day labourers. Of these, many were completely illiterate, unable to write their own names.

The defeat of Austria-Hungary in World War One and the subsequent peace settlement imposed on Hungary, in the 1920 Treaty of Trianon, precipitated an existential crisis in Hungarian society from which it has never fully recovered. In accordance with the treaty, Hungary was forced to relinquish almost three quarters of its territory and one third of its pre-war population of ethnic Hungarians. The latter became sullen citizens of Czechoslovakia, Romania or the Kingdom of the Serbs, Croats and Slovenes.

In addition to the devastating effect on Hungarian morale and self-esteem, the territorial losses imposed by Trianon severely disrupted the economy, aggravating Hungary's post-war economic crisis. As Joseph Rothschild points out in his book, *East Central Europe Between The Two World Wars*:

> The loss in economic resources imposed on Hungary by the Trianon frontiers was staggering: 58 percent of her railroad and 60 percent of her road mileage; 84 percent of her timber resources and 43 percent of her arable land; 83 percent of her iron ore, 29 percent of her lignite, and 27 percent of her bituminous coal.

In an atmosphere of shock and recrimination, Jews became convenient scapegoats. Jews were widely blamed for Hungary's political, economic, social and other ills, particularly after the crushing of a short-lived Soviet regime established in Budapest in 1919. This Hungarian Soviet, which lasted from late March until the beginning of August, followed the collapse of a coalition government led by the liberal and reformist aristocrat, Count Mihály Károlyi.

Hungary's Soviet, which was increasingly resented because of its extremist, anti-clerical and dictatorial policies, was also widely detested because it was seen as Jewish. A Transylvanian-Hungarian Communist of Jewish descent, Béla Kun, headed the Soviet, while no less than thirty-two of the regime's forty-five commissars were of Jewish extraction. However, the prominence of Jews in the Hungarian Soviet should not obscure the fact that the overwhelming majority of the country's Jews were either apolitical, retained a lingering fondness for the old, multinational Austro-Hungarian monarchy, or supported conservative, liberal or social democratic parties. Marxist-Leninists like Béla Kun represented a tiny and wholly unrepresentative minority amongst Hungary's Jews.

The collapse of the Soviet precipitated a period that is known in Hungarian history as the 'white terror'. Jews, together with other presumed supporters of the Soviet, were abused, tortured and killed on a random basis. Up to six thousand people, a large proportion of whom were Jews, lost their lives in this indiscriminate, ideologically-fuelled bloodletting. In the following decades, when Hungary was governed by a succession of right-wing, authoritarian governments, Jews were often portrayed both as the harbingers of a Godless, communist revolution and as self-serving instruments of a soulless capitalism.

In the interwar period Hungarian politics was overshadowed by the international economic crisis, by the spectre of Trianon, by the growing power of Nazi Germany and by memories of the short-lived Hungarian Soviet. Power gradually shifted from the patrician, conservative figure of Count István Bethlen to the populist, virulently anti-Semitic Gyula Gömbös. Gömbös was appointed prime minister in 1932, remaining in office until his death in 1936. He revealed his political sympathies by becoming the first head of a foreign government to pay a courtesy call on Hitler after the latter's appointment as Germany's Chancellor.

Under Gömbös' successors, Kálmán Darányi, Béla Imrédy, Pál Teleki and László Bárdossy, Hungary inclined more and more towards the Axis powers, as much from opportunism as ideological conviction. With the diplomatic intercession of Germany and Italy, in 1938 Hungary recovered 20 per cent of the territory it had lost to Czechoslovakia as a result of Trianon. With the support of the same Axis powers, in 1940 Hungary regained northern and eastern Transylvania, amounting to two-fifths of the territory lost to Romania.

However, Hungary's eagerness to secure Axis support for its irredentist ambitions—as well as the steady growth of anti-Semitism within Hungary itself—led to the passage of a series of draconian anti-Jewish laws, beginning in 1938. The cumulative effect of the legislation was to exclude Jews from professional, public and cultural life, to strip them of their assets and to reduce them to a state of insecurity and abject poverty.

Strikingly, the Christian churches in Hungary, both Catholic and Protestant, were enthusiastic supporters of the first and second anti-Jewish laws, passed in 1938 and 1939, although some clerics vehemently objected to the application of discriminatory measures to Jewish converts to Christianity. However, the principle of discriminating against Jews, of restricting their right to vote in national or local elections, of excluding them from employment in the civil service and in local government, of drastically reducing their numbers in the professions and of banning them from serving as newspaper editors or as theatre directors raised no theological (or moral) objections from the influential Churches. On the contrary, senior clerics strongly supported the passage of the Jewish Laws. Bishop László Ravasz of the Hungarian Reformed Church, for example, endorsed the passage of the Second Jewish Law, or 'Law on the Restriction of the Expansion of the Jews in Public Life and Economic Affairs'. Speaking in the Upper House of the Hungarian Parliament on April 17th 1939, Bishop Ravasz lamented the fact that, 'it is not the Jews who have assimilated to the Hungarian spirit, but rather the Hungarian spirit which has assimilated to the Jews'. In the same chamber, Cardinal Serédi of the Catholic Church accused Hungary's Jews of destroying 'Christian values' in the economic life of the country—a charge that blithely ignored the feudal character of traditional Hungarian society, in which a small minority enjoyed wealth, power and privilege while several million—mostly landless peasants and smallholders subsisting on tiny plots of land—were condemned to lives of dire poverty and ignorance.

As Hungary found itself gradually drawn into World War Two on the side of the Axis powers, the Hungarian authorities were faced with the problem of what to do with Jews already serving in the armed forces as well as with tens of thousands of Hungarian Jewish males who would become eligible for conscription. The government created a system of *Munkaszolgálat*, or 'auxiliary labour battalions', for Jews and other 'undesirables'. Members of these battalions accompanied regular Hungarian military units, including on the Russian front. However, members of these battalions were not allowed to bear arms and were generally employed to dig ditches, to unload freight trains and to perform other arduous physical tasks, often without proper food, clothing or shelter.

According to the historian Raul Hilberg, approximately 80,000 Jewish men served in the *Munkaszolgálat*, of whom up to 40,000 died, many while serving on the Russian front or as victims of brutal and sadistic treatment at the hands of their Hungarian NCOs and officers. For example, fourteen men had died in Labour Battalion 101/5 by the beginning of October 1942 as a result of chronic weakness resulting from poor food, lack of shelter and constant beatings. The work of the Hungarian historian László Karsai has shown how the men of the battalion were mostly fed on black tea, without sugar, and on flour infested with weevils. Despite this meagre diet, the battalion was forced to work from dawn until dusk. Karsai notes that German army officers repeatedly warned their Hungarian counterparts, who were in charge of the auxiliary labour battalions, that they had to choose between beating the Jews and working them.

Several of Hungary's leading writers and artists served in the auxiliary labour battalions. These included the painter Imre Ámos, who later died in a German concentration camp, as well as the poet Miklós Radnóti. The title of this book, *When Even the Poets were Silent*, is taken from Radnóti's plaintive *Sixth Eclogue*, written in May 1944 just a few months before his untimely death. A devout convert to the Catholic faith and one of Hungary's foremost poets of the twentieth century, Radnóti was called up several times for compulsory labour service. On November 4th 1944, exhausted and no longer able to walk, Radnóti was shot dead by his Hungarian guards along with twenty-one of his fellow labourers. They were buried in a mass grave near the western-Hungarian town of Győr.

Ironically, though, service in one of Hungary's auxiliary labour battalions actually offered a degree of protection from the worst excesses of Germany's Jewish policy, particularly after German forces occupied Hungary in March 1944. The sudden entry of German troops into Hungary, which followed fumbling efforts by Hungary's leaders to extricate the country from the war, brought the 'Final Solution' to Hungary. Up to this point, Hungary's Jews, although subject to mounting persecution and poverty, had escaped genocide. They had not been handed over to the Germans for extermination in Auschwitz-Birkenau and in other camps, or systematically murdered by Hungarian gendarmes and soldiers.

Adolf Eichmann and a small contingent of *Sondereinsatzkommando* accompanied the German forces that occupied Hungary. By 1941, there had been an estimated 825,000 Jews in territories controlled by Hungary. Eichmann's brief was to organise and execute the orderly deportation of this Jewish population to the death camps.

Eichmann and his subordinates, assisted by Hungarian civil servants and gendarmes, began with the rounding up and deportation of Jews from territories that had been recently occupied and annexed by Hungary, including northern Transylvania. The victims of these measures included the future Nobel Peace Prize recipient Elie Wiesel and his family, who lived in the town of Sighet, near the Carpathian mountains. Wiesel, who unlike his mother, father and younger sister survived the camps, describes his final hours in Sighet in his best-known book, *Night*:

> [W]e marched to the station, where a convoy of cattle wagons was waiting. The Hungarian police made us get in—eighty people in each car. We were left a few loaves of bread and some buckets of water. The bars at the window were checked, to see that they were not loose. Then the cars were sealed. In each car one person was placed in charge. If anyone escaped he would be shot. Two Gestapo officers strolled about on the platform, smiling: all things considered, everything had gone off very well.

The second phase of Eichmann's meticulously planned and carefully executed destruction of Hungary's Jews targeted Jews living in the provinces. As noted by the historian David Cesarani: 'between 15 May and 7 July [1944], 437,000 Jews were rounded up and sent to the concentration and extermination camp complex at Auschwitz-Birkenau in Upper Silesia. Only a fraction were selected for work, and of them but a few thousand survived.'

Luck, a worsening shortage of German manpower, and the intervention of the Budapest Aid and Rescue Committee saved my father and his parents, as well as several thousand other Jewish Hungarians, from being included in the transports to Auschwitz. By this point in the war, my father's elder brother István had been conscripted into an auxiliary labour battalion.

The Aid and Rescue Committee, which was composed of Zionist elements drawn from Budapest and northern Transylvania, included a journalist and lawyer named Rezső Kasztner who was later assassinated in Israel by right-wing extremists. The best-known, if controversial, achievement of Kasztner and the Aid and Rescue Committee was to persuade Adolf Eichmann to allow 1,685 Transylvanian and Hungarian Jews to leave for Switzerland by train in the summer of 1944 in exchange for a ransom amounting to $1,000 per person.

In separate negotiations, Kasztner and the Aid and Rescue Committee persuaded the Germans to allow 30,000 Jewish Hungarians to be sent as forced labourers to Vienna and the surrounding area, half of whom would come from the Alföld, the flat heartlands of Hungary. Eichmann and his associates allowed the Committee to choose which Jews would be sent to Vienna rather than Auschwitz, although luck and even the 'black humour' of an SS officer may have played a part. In volume two of his *Destruction of the European Jews*, Raul Hilberg describes the process of selection:

> The Committee now had the awful task of selecting the Jews to be saved. Lists were made in Budapest and in the provinces. The lists were altered, enlarged, cut down. There were original lists and replacement lists. In the end, accident also played a part. An SS man, whether by mistake or as a 'little joke', switched two trains. A transport from Győr, and with it the rabbi of the Győr community, Dr Emil Roth, was delivered to Auschwitz. Instead of the Győr train, another that had been scheduled to go to Auschwitz arrived in Vienna.

The Jews of Orosháza, including my father and grandparents, had the extraordinary good fortune to be included in the tiny contingent of 15,000 provincial Jewish Hungarians who were despatched in sealed goods wagons to Vienna, rather than to Auschwitz. An estimated 75 per cent of the Jewish Hungarians sent to Austria for compulsory labour service survived the war.

As the Hungarian historian Szabolcs Szita points out, German agreement to sending up to 30,000 Jews to labour camps in and around Vienna, rather than directly to Auschwitz-Birkenau, was not an act of compassion. As Eichmann chillingly remarked, these Jews had merely been put 'on ice'. They could prove useful bargaining chips in any future negotiations with the Allies. In addition, the Nazis were to be paid $100 by the Rescue Committee for each Jew sent to the labour camps, while the Nazis would also receive the wages of the slave labourers from the German companies that employed them. Finally, the Nazis were mindful of the fact that conscription had resulted in severe shortages of manpower in Greater Vienna. There was a desperate need for construction workers, road builders and general labourers; even Jews were deemed acceptable.

Unlike most of the Jews of provincial Hungary, the bulk of Budapest's Jewish population escaped deportation to death camps. The growing shortage of trains and the rapidly approaching front, as the Soviet Red Army pressed forward, meant that the systematic extermination of Budapest's Jews was no longer an option by November 1944. However, in the previous month, a German-backed coup had installed the extremist Hungarian Arrow Cross movement in power in Budapest. Fanatically anti-Semitic, the Arrow Cross were responsible for the deaths of thousands of Budapest's Jews who were shot on the shores of the River Danube before their bodies were dumped in the freezing waters. Tens of thousands of the city's Jews, including my mother, maternal grandfather and a great uncle, were rounded up and led on foot towards the German border, a journey of almost 140 miles. The number of fatalities during these death marches was enormous; the marchers were not provided with adequate food, water or shelter, let alone medical attention. Most of the Jews who actually made it to Germany were either killed or died of maltreatment.

Amongst the members of my immediate family who were sent on these death marches, only my mother survived. Together with another young Jewish woman they lagged behind in the gathering dusk, pretending to tie their shoelaces. They were fortunate not to be spotted by the mounted Hungarian gendarmes who escorted the column of women. My mother made her way back to Budapest where she went into hiding for the rest of the war.

For the vast majority of Hungary's remaining Jews, the rout of German and Hungarian forces by the Soviet Red Army signified not just liberation but rescue from imminent death. If Soviet troops had not occupied Hungary, every Hungarian Jew would have been murdered by the Arrow Cross and its German allies. Unsurprisingly, many Jews, including my parents, joined the Communist Party after the war out of gratitude and from a naïve belief that Communist propaganda, which emphasised social justice and the ending of racist oppression and tyranny, would be faithfully reflected in the policies adopted by the Communists once they assumed power.

For the bulk of Gentile Hungarians, by contrast, Soviet rule represented an alien, Godless tyranny that was far more hateful and oppressive than the earlier German occupation. After all, the Germans had left many Hungarian political, cultural and economic institutions intact. The evident enthusiasm of many Jewish Hungarians for the Soviets and for the introduction of Communism merely confirmed the view of a sizeable proportion of Gentile Hungarians that Jews were unpatriotic and that they could never become 'real' Hungarians. These mutual suspicions and resentments, fuelled by very different historical memories of World War Two and of the subsequent Communist period, continue to overshadow Jewish-Gentile relations in Hungary.

However, for several thousand Jewish Hungarians including my father's elder brother, István, Soviet occupation did not signify liberation. Having survived the war serving in an auxiliary labour battalion, István was returning home on foot when he was seized by a Soviet military unit and transported to the USSR as a slave labourer where he died of starvation. Several hundred thousand more Hungarian citizens, civilians as well as prisoners of war, were held as slave labourers in the Soviet Union.

Despite the bitterness that many Jewish Hungarians felt at the complicity of Hungary in the Holocaust, a large proportion of the country's surviving Jews opted to remain in Hungary after the war, suggesting an abiding identification with Hungary, its language and culture. The novelist and essayist György Konrád, a Holocaust survivor who became a political dissident in Communist Hungary in the 70s and 80s, has asserted the continuing possibility—or even necessity—for Jews like himself of being both Jewish and Hungarian, despite the long, mournful shadows cast by twentieth-century Jewish-Hungarian history.

Professor István Pogány, Warwick, 2011

Acknowledgments

I am indebted to Rob Groot and Emeritus Professor Dudley Jackson for their encouragement and to Peter Bowing for not only correcting my English but also giving countless pieces of useful advice. Peter, I couldn't have done it without you. I also owe my gratitude to my publisher and editor Liam D'Arcy-Brown for his patience in dealing with my stubbornness and refusal to accept his advice. Of course, I am responsible for any mistakes remaining. I also received much useful advice and correction from my son Prof. Dr. István Pogány and I am grateful for the patience of Vera, my wife, who let me sit at my computer day after day without helping her.

www.ingramcontent.com/pod-product-compliance
Lightning Source LLC
LaVergne TN
LVHW041540070426
835507LV00011B/836